Flaunting Our Finest

From Historic Franklin

Published by
Junior Auxiliary of Franklin
Franklin, Tennessee

Purpose of Junior Auxiliary

The Junior Auxiliary is a nonprofit organization that encourages young women to render charitable services which are beneficial to the general public, with particular emphasis on children. Junior Auxiliary endeavors to promote leadership of its members by assuming responsibility in meeting problems of their community.

All profits realized from the sale of this cookbook will be returned to the community through the service projects of the Junior Auxiliary of Franklin.

Copyright 1982
by Junior Auxiliary of Franklin
Franklin, Tennessee

International Standard Book Number 0-939114-76-3

Printed by Favorite Recipes® Press
an imprint of

FRP.

P.O. Box 305142
Nashville, Tennessee 37230
1-800-358-0560

Manufactured in the United States of America

First Printing	1982	5,000 copies
Second Printing	1985	5,000 copies
Third Printing	1988	2,000 copies
Fourth Printing	1992	3,000 copies
Fifth Printing	1995	3,000 copies
Sixth Printing	2001	6,000 copies

TABLE OF CONTENTS

Acknowledgements

Cover by Vic Hollingsworth
Illustrations throughout this cookbook were done by Ben Johnson.
Magnolia blossom sketches by Mrs. Jim Darnell.

Swallowbarn Farm

This section includes recipes submitted by residents and former residents of the Franklin homes illustrating our cookbook. Many are original family recipes, and all are *specialties of the house.*

Specialties of the House

BEATEN BISCUITS
Very old recipe and is delicious!!

1 heaping quart sifted flour
¾ cup lard
1 cup cream
¼ cup water

1 teaspoon salt
1 Tablespoon sugar
¼ scant teaspoon soda

Use 1 cup of flour to flour rolling board. Mix all ingredients and roll or beat until as smooth as satin. Roll out about ½ inch thick and cut in desired shapes. Bake at 400 degrees for 10 minutes then 350 degrees for 15 minutes (until very light beige color). Delicious served hot with melted butter or country baked ham. *Yield:* 50.

Mrs. W. H. Wyatt (Margaret)

This recipe is submitted by the present owner of Wyatt Hall, a home featured in our cookbook.

REFRIGERATOR BRAN MUFFINS

2 cups boiling water
2 cups all bran cereal
3 cups sugar
1 heaping cup margarine
5 teaspoons baking soda

1 teaspoon salt
5 cups flour
1 quart buttermilk
4 eggs, beaten
1 large box raisins

Pour 2 cups boiling water over bran and let stand 10 minutes. Mix remaining ingredients except raisins. Add bran and raisins. Nuts and dates may be added, if desired. Dough keeps 5 weeks in refrigerator in sealed container. Bake at 400 degrees for 20 minutes. May be baked and frozen. *Yield:* 6 dozen.

Mrs. W. C. Keyes (Harriet)

This recipe is submitted by the present owners of Swallowbarn Farm, the home featured on the cover of our cookbook.

MEXICAN STYLE CORNBREAD

1 (8 ounce) carton sour cream
1½ cups self-rising corn meal
½ cup oil
2 eggs
1 (12 ounce) can Mexican
  style corn
1 small onion, chopped

1 cup shredded Cheddar
  cheese
1 teaspoon black pepper
1 teaspoon red pepper
2 Tablespoons Jalapeno
  peppers, chopped

Mix sour cream, corn meal, oil, eggs, corn, and onion in large mixing bowl. Pour ½ batter into 9 inch square cake pan. Over this sprinkle cheese, red pepper, black pepper, and Jalapeno peppers. Do not stir. Pour remaining batter over this. Bake at 450 degrees for 25 to 30 minutes. This is quite spicy. You may want to use less pepper and/or Jalapeno pepper. *Yield:* 9 servings.

Mrs. Chug Morton (Dottie)

This recipe is submitted by the present owners of the Harrison House, a home featured in our cookbook.

CONFEDERATE COFFEE CAKE

½ cup butter
1 cup sugar
½ cup milk
3 eggs
1½ cups flour
Pinch of salt

2 teaspoons baking powder
2 teaspoons nutmeg
2 teaspoons cinnamon
2 teaspoons sugar
½ cup chopped pecans

Cream sugar and butter. Add milk and unbeaten eggs, mix well. Sift flour, salt, and baking powder. Blend with sugar and butter, adding a dash of nutmeg. Pour into well greased 9⅝x5½x2¾ loaf cake pan. Sprinkle top with nutmeg, cinnamon, sugar, and nuts. Dot well with butter and bake at 350 degrees for 20 minutes. *Yield:* 1 cake.

Mrs. John Henderson (Margaret)

This recipe is submitted by Mrs. John Henderson, wife of Judge Henderson whose childhood home, the Courtney House, is featured in our cookbook.

MOTHER'S MAYONNAISE

1 egg, beaten very little
1 cup salad oil (enough until thick)
2 Tablespoons lemon juice
1 teaspoon salt
1/8 teaspoon paprika or to taste

Beat egg very little; on high speed on your mixer, pour in salad oil very slowly until thick; add lemon juice, salt, and paprika. If the first lot doesn't seem to want to thicken, start again with another egg, adding first lot slowly to this egg. *Yield:* 1½ cups.

Mrs. Sam Jamison (Lucinda)

This recipe is submitted by Mrs. Sam Jamison whose childhood home, the Trabue-Brown House, is featured in our cookbook.

SWEET MARGARET SALAD DRESSING

1 cup salad oil
½ cup vinegar
½ cup sugar
2 teaspoons salt
½ teaspoon black pepper
2 heaping teaspoons paprika
2 heaping teaspoons tomato ketchup
1 small onion, minced
2 garlic buttons, minced
½ teaspoon chili powder

Combine all ingredients and blend. The flavor is increased with age. *Yield:* 1½ pints.

Frances Haynes

This recipe is submitted by the present owner of the Crouch-Haynes House, a home featured in our cookbook.

RICE CASSEROLE

2 cups chicken broth
¼ cup butter
1 (4 ounce) can mushrooms

1 cup raw rice
1 onion, grated
½ cup celery, chopped

Mix above ingredients and put in 2 quart pyrex dish, cover and bake at 325 to 350 degrees for 1 hour. *Yield:* 6 servings.

Mrs. William Ewin (Mildred)

This recipe is submitted by the former owners of the Ewin House, a home featured in our cookbook.

CREOLE GREEN BEANS

2 (#2) cans green beans,
   drained
1 (12 ounce) bottle chili sauce
1 large onion, minced

1 Tablespoon vegetable oil
½ teaspoon sugar
Pinch of salt

Simmer for several hours until liquid has cooked away. *Yield:* 10 servings.

Mrs. Tom Ridley (Alma)

This recipe is submitted by the present owners of The Walker-Ridley House, a home featured in our cookbook.

CRANBERRY RECIPE
Quick, simple, and good.

3 cups cranberries
1½ cups sugar

¾ cup water

Wash and remove stems and soft berries. Combine and bring all ingredients to a boil and continue boiling for 10 minutes. Good condiment for many things besides turkey. TRY IT. *Yield:* 3 cups.

Mrs. James H. Campbell (Gordy)

This recipe is submitted by the present owner of the Otey-Campbell House, a home featured in our cookbook.

FRIED APPLES
Old fashioned recipe.

6 large firm cooking apples,   ½ to ¾ cup sugar
   quartered and cored   ¼ teaspoon salt
4 Tablespoons bacon fat   ¼ cup water

Wash apples. Slice fairly thick. Heat bacon fat in heavy skillet. Pour in apples and cover. Cook at a heat hot enough to brown underside. Turn and brown again. Add sugar, salt, and water. Simmer apples until tender and crusty. Cooking apple skins add to flavor and vitamins. Take care not to burn apples, but be sure they are well browned for best flavor. *Yield:* 4 to 6 servings.

Mrs. Livingfield More (Agnes)

This recipe is submitted by the present owners of River Grange, a home featured in our cookbook.

BAKED TOMATOES

4 medium or 6 small tomatoes   2 slices white bread, torn into
4 Tablespoons butter   coarse crumbs
¼ cup finely chopped onion   2 teaspoons chopped parsley
1 teaspoon prepared mustard
½ teaspoon Worcestershire
   sauce

Wash tomatoes, slice off top, and remove core. Place in shallow baking pan. In 2 tablespoons butter, sauté onion. Stir in mustard and Worcestershire sauce. Fill hollows in tomatoes. Melt remaining butter in same skillet. Stir in bread crumbs and parsley. Sprinkle over top of tomatoes. Bake, uncovered, 20 minutes at 350 degrees or until tomatoes are heated through and crumbs are golden brown. *Yield:* 4 to 6 servings.

Mrs. James M. Ferrell (Lola)

This recipe is submitted by the present owners of The Marshall House, a home featured in our cookbook.

ZUCCHINI BAKE

4 medium zucchini	Salt to taste
4 Tablespoons butter	Black and red pepper to taste
4 Tablespoons Romano cheese, finely grated	1 Tablespoon fresh bread crumbs
¾ cup sour cream	

Bring water to boil with salt. Add zucchini and return to boil. Remove from heat *immediately* and drain. Butter 12x8x2 inch baking dish and add zucchini. Heat butter with 3 tablespoons cheese. Add salt, sour cream, and pepper. Spread over zucchini. Sprinkle with bread crumbs and remaining cheese. Bake at 425 degrees for 10 minutes. *Yield:* 4 servings.

Mary Frances Ligon

This recipe is submitted by the present owner of the Long-Babbitt House, a home featured in our cookbook.

SKILLET BEEF AND NOODLE— FAMILY FARE

2 Tablespoons salad oil	½ teaspoon salt
1 pound ground beef	½ teaspoon sugar
3 Tablespoons dehydrated onion soup mix	¼ teaspoon oregano
1 (16 ounce) can tomatoes	1 Tablespoon prepared mustard
5 ounces uncooked thin noodles	1 (16½ ounce) can whole kernel corn
⅛ teaspoon black pepper	

Brown beef in salad oil for about 10 minutes, leaving meat in fairly large chunks. Add remaining ingredients, except corn, and simmer, covered, 15 to 20 minutes. Stir occasionally. About 5 minutes before done, add corn. *Yield:* 4 to 5 servings.

Frances Haynes

This recipe is submitted by the present owner of the Crouch-Haynes House, a home featured in our cookbook.

KING CRAB SALAD PIE

Pastry Shell:

1¼ cups flour
2 teaspoons baking powder
½ teaspoon salt
½ cup butter, softened

¼ cup milk
1 Tablespoon freezer dried
  or frozen chopped chives

Sift flour, baking powder, and salt. Cut in butter. Add milk and chives, stirring until ball forms. Pat into bottom and on sides of a deep 9-inch pie pan.

Crab Filling:

1 (7½ ounce) can Alaskan king
  crab or ½ pound frozen
  Alaskan king crab, thawed,
  drained and sliced
3 hard-boiled eggs, diced
½ cup chopped celery
2 Tablespoons minced
  green onion

1 cup shredded Cheddar
  cheese
1 cup mayonnaise or salad
  dressing
1 (10 ounce) package frozen
  broccoli or asparagus, salted,
  cooked and drained

Fold crab, eggs, celery, onion, and cheese into mayonnaise. Place broccoli or asparagus evenly in bottom of pastry shell. Spoon crab mixture evenly over top. Bake at 375 degrees for 30 minutes or until golden. Serve warm or chilled. Cut into wedges. *Yield:* 6 servings.

Mary Frances Ligon

This recipe is submitted by the present owner of the Long-Babbitt House, a home featured in our cookbook.

SPECIALTIES OF THE HOUSE

GINGERBREAD
An antebellum recipe

½ cup butter or margarine
1 cup sugar
1 cup molasses
2 eggs, separated
3 cups cake flour

1 teaspoon salt
1 teaspoon soda
2 teaspoons ginger
2 teaspoons cinnamon
1 cup buttermilk

Cream butter and sugar until light and smooth. Add molasses and beaten egg yolks. Mix thoroughly. Sift flour with salt, soda, and spices. Add flour mixture alternately with buttermilk. Fold in stiffly beaten egg whites. Pour into well oiled and floured 13x9x2 inch pan. Bake at 350 degrees for 30 to 40 minutes. Serve hot with hard sauce or lemon frosting. *Yield:* 24 servings.

Hard Sauce:
½ cup butter or margarine
1½ cups sifted powdered sugar

1 egg, separated
2 teaspoons grated lemon rind

Cream butter and sugar. Add egg yolk, beating constantly. Blend in lemon rind. Fold into stiffly beaten egg white. Chill. *Yield:* 2 cups.

Lemon Fluff Frosting:
½ cup margarine
Dash of salt
4 cups powdered sugar

3 Tablespoons lemon juice
2 Tablespoons lemon rind

Cream margarine, add salt, and part of sugar. Cream well. Add remaining sugar alternately with lemon juice. Cream until light and fluffy. Add lemon rind and mix thoroughly. If mixture is too stiff to spread well, add lemon juice to get good spreading consistency.

Mrs. J. E. Ragan (Edna)

This recipe is submitted by the former owners of the Kirkpatrick-Powell House, a home featured in our cookbook.

MOM'S BUTTERMILK PIE

1¾ cups sugar
1 heaping teaspoon flour
3 whole eggs
½ cup butter, melted

1 teaspoon vanilla
1½ cups buttermilk
1 (9 inch) pie shell, unbaked

Mix sugar and flour. Add eggs and butter and mix. Add vanilla and buttermilk. Stir well. Pour into pie shell and bake in moderate oven (300 to 350 degrees) for 45 minutes. *Yield:* 6 to 8 servings.

Bunn Gray

This recipe is submitted by the present owner of Clouston Hall, a home featured in our cookbook.

GRANDMOTHER'S TEA CAKES

1½ cups sugar
1½ cups butter
3 eggs
3½ cups sifted flour

2 teaspoons baking powder
2 Tablespoons milk
Vanilla or grated orange
  rind to taste

Cream sugar and butter. Add eggs. Add flour and baking powder, sifted. Add milk and flavoring. Roll thinly and cut with round cutter. Bake at 375 degrees for 12 minutes. *Yield:* 4 to 5 dozen.

Bunn Gray

This recipe is submitted by the present owner of Clouston Hall, a home featured in our cookbook.

INCREDIBLE COCONUT PIE

½ cup self rising flour
1⅓ cups sugar
4 eggs, beaten
2 cups milk

¼ cup melted margarine
1 teaspoon vanilla
1 (7 ounce) can flaked coconut
1 deep 9 inch pie plate

Combine flour and sugar. Add eggs, milk, margarine, and vanilla. Mix well and stir in coconut. Pour into pie plate. Bake at 375 degrees for 40 to 50 minutes. Done when knife comes clean in middle of pie. This makes its own pie crust. *Yield:* 6 to 8 servings.

Mrs. W. C. Keyes (Harriet)

This recipe is submitted by the present owners of Swallowbarn Farm, the home featured on the cover of our cookbook.

CALIFORNIA LEMON DESSERT

1 (3 ounce) package lemon
  flavored gelatin
½ cup hot water
½ cup sugar
½ cup lemon juice

1 (13 ounce) can evaporated
  milk, refrigerated
  overnight
3 Tablespoons butter, melted
2 cups graham cracker crumbs

Dissolve gelatin in hot water. Add sugar and lemon juice. Cool. Whip evaporated milk until peaks stand and mix well with gelatin mixture. Mix butter and 1¾ cups cracker crumbs. Press into a 12x8x2 inch pan. Pour milk and gelatin mixture into pan and top with remaining ¼ cup cracker crumbs. Refrigerate. *Yield:* 12 servings.

Dr. Rosalie Carter

This recipe is submitted by the descendant of the original owners of the Carter House.

FROZEN GINGER PUDDING

Custard:
2 heaping Tablespoons flour
1 cup sugar
2 eggs
1 quart milk
Pinch of salt
2 teaspoons vanilla
6 macaroons, well crumbled
   and soaked in ⅓ cup sherry
   or more

2 Tablespoons preserved
   ginger, cut in tiny pieces,
   soaked in maple syrup
1 pint whipping cream

Mix flour, sugar, and eggs. Stir in hot milk, cook until thick. Cool. Add a pinch of salt and vanilla. Put in a tray and freeze. The next day mash well. Add macaroons that have been soaked in sherry and preserved ginger that has been soaked in maple syrup. Add whipping cream. Put in trays to freeze and stir 2 or 3 times while freezing. *Yield:* 6 servings.

Mrs. Livingfield More (Agnes) via Miss Kate Wemyss

This recipe is submitted by the present owners of River Grange, a home featured in our cookbook.

PEACH ICE CREAM

1 quart fresh peaches, chopped
3 cups sugar
6 eggs
1 pint whipping cream
1 (14 ounce) can sweetened
   condensed milk

½ teaspoon almond flavoring
Pinch of salt
Milk

Chop peeled peaches in blender and sweeten with 1 cup sugar. Combine eggs and cream. Place in a 4 quart ice cream freezer with remaining ingredients and stir. Add milk to fill line. Pack in ice and freeze. *Yield:* 1 gallon.

Mary Frances Ligon

This recipe is submitted by the present owner of the Long-Babbitt House, a home featured in our cookbook.

FRESH PEACH CREAM PIE

2 cups ripe peaches   ½ cup sugar

Peel and slice peaches, sprinkle with sugar, cover and chill for later use.

1½ cups milk   1 teaspoon vanilla
⅔ cup sugar   1 Tablespoon butter
2½ Tablespoons flour   1 10 inch pastry shell, fully
2 eggs   baked
¼ teaspoon salt   ½ pint whipping cream,
¼ teaspoon cream of tartar   whipped

Note: This sauce is a blend of milk, sugar, and eggs stirred over heat until it thickens into a cream. If it comes near the simmer, the eggs will scramble. (Maximum temperature is 165 degrees on the candy thermometer.) Scald milk in top of double boiler over simmering water. Mix sugar with flour and add to milk. Beat eggs and combine with salt, cream of tartar, and vanilla. Slowly add ½ cup of hot milk mixture to beaten eggs mixture, then return all to double boiler. Add butter. Stir over simmering heat until thick and smooth. Cover and chill sauce about 4 hours or longer. Drain fruit and fold into custard. Spoon into cooked pastry shell. Chill. Before serving add whipped cream topping. *Yield:* 8 servings.

Frances Haynes

This recipe is submitted by the present owner of the Crouch-Haynes House, a home featured in our cookbook.

CHICKEN TETRAZINNI
Very rich and DIVINE!

8 chicken breasts

Boil until tender in salted water with celery leaves. Cool and remove all skin and bones. Leave chicken in medium pieces.

¾ pound margarine	**2 cups half-and-half**
½ cup flour	**2 cups milk**

Melt margarine, add flour, mix well. Add half-and-half and milk. Stir over medium heat until thick. Set aside.

⅔ pounds sharp Cheddar cheese, cubed	**1 (10¾ ounce) can tomato soup**

Melt cheese and soup in a sauce pan, stirring often.

1 teaspoon salt	**½ teaspoon garlic powder**
¼ teaspoon pepper	**½ cup dry sherry**

Combine the 2 sauces, add salt, pepper, garlic powder, and sherry.

1 pound fresh mushrooms	**¼ cup margarine**

Sauté mushrooms in margarine and add to sauce with chicken. Heat in large casserole and serve over thin spaghetti. *Yield:* 8 servings.

Mrs. James T. Ogelsby (Pam)

This recipe is submitted by the present owners of the Mordecai Puryear House, a home featured in our cookbook.

BLOODY MARY MIX

1 (46 ounce) can tomato juice
1 (10½ ounce) can beef consomme
1 teaspoon salt
1 Tablespoon celery salt
3 Tablespoons hot sauce

1 (5 ounce) bottle Worcestershire sauce
1 Tablespoon black pepper
Juice of 3 lemons
4 Tablespoons sugar

Combine all ingredients in large pan. Heat over low heat, stirring often, just until ingredients are combined. Allow to cool and refrigerate until needed. *Yield:* About 8 cups.

Mrs. Chug Morton (Dottie)

This recipe is submitted by the present owners of the Harrison House, a home featured in our cookbook.

Cliffe-Jordan House

This 1½ story Federal-style frame home was thought to have been built in 1798 in Franklin's historic central district. It was the family home of Mr. and Mrs. Joe Cliffe. The home had been restored by its present owners, Mr. and Mrs. Peter Jordan.

Appetizers

SWEDISH NUTS

2 egg whites
1 cup sugar
½ teaspoon vanilla extract

Dash of salt
¼ cup butter
6 cups nuts, any type

Beat egg whites until stiff. Slowly add sugar, vanilla, and salt. Beat until firm and peaks form. Melt butter on cookie sheet with sides. Fold 6 cups nuts into egg white mixture and spread over butter on cookie sheet. Bake slowly at 325 degrees stirring often for 30 to 40 mintues. Remove from oven and stir frequently until cool.

Mrs. Richard Marshall (Cindy)

PEPPERMINT CLOUD
Unusual, Refreshing, MMM!

½ cup whipping cream,
   whipped
1 Tablespoon powdered sugar

2 peppermint sticks or candy
   canes, crushed

Beat chilled whipping cream and sugar in bowl until stiff. Add crushed peppermint candy. Use as a dip with sliced red delicious apples (dipped in fruit fresh or lemon juice) or fill small cream puffs with peppermint cloud filling.

Mrs. Donald Westfall (Nancy)

CHEESE BALL

2 (8 ounce) packages cream
cheese, softened
2 cups shredded sharp
Cheddar cheese
1 teaspoon lemon juice
1 Tablespoon finely chopped
onion
1 Tablespoon chopped
pimento

1 Tablespoon chopped green
pepper
1 Tablespoon Worcestershire
¼ teaspoon garlic salt
Dash of salt
Dash red pepper
1 cup chopped pecans

Mix all ingredients well except pecans. Shape into a ball. Roll in
chopped pecans. *Yield:* 1 cheese ball.

Mrs. Don Snow (Anne)

CHEESE MOLD

8 ounces shredded Cheddar
cheese
1 (8 ounce) carton sour cream
3 Tablespoons mayonnaise
2 Tablespoons grated onion
2 Tablespoons minced celery

2 Tablespoons minced green
pepper
1 (2 ounce) jar diced pimento
½ teaspoon garlic salt
1 envelope unflavored gelatin
¼ cup water

Combine all ingredients except gelatin and water. Soften gelatin in
water, heat in a small saucepan; when hot, pour into cheese mixture.
Mix thoroughly. Pour into slightly oiled 4 cup mold. Chill overnight.
Unmold and serve with assorted crackers. *Yield:* 4 cups.

Mrs. T. W. Perkinson (Martha)
Brentwood, Tennessee

CHEESE ROLL CRESCENT PUFFS

1 (8 ounce) package crescent
rolls
8 (1 inch) cubes mozzarella
or Cheddar cheese

¼ cup Italian dressing
3 Tablespoons sesame seeds
3 Tablespoons grated
Parmesan cheese

Separate rolls into triangles. Place cheese mound in each triangle.
Pinch together and seal well into ball. Dip ball into salad dressing.
Roll in sesame seeds and Parmesan cheese. Place in muffin tins
sprayed with cooking oil. Bake 15 to 20 minutes at 375 degrees.
Yield: 8.

Mrs. Edmond Reed (Pam)

HOLIDAY CHEESE BALL

2 (8 ounce) packages cream
cheese, softened
1 (8½ ounce) can crushed
pineapple, drained

2 cups chopped pecans
¼ cup chopped green pepper
2 Tablespoons chopped onion
1 Tablespoon seasoned salt

Mix all ingredients well. Shape into ball. Chill and serve with
crackers. *Yield:* 1 cheese ball.

Mrs. Phil Ryan (Gail)
Waco, Texas

OLD ENGLISH CHEESE SPREAD

½ pound Old English Cheese,
shredded
4 Tablespoons finely chopped
onion
6 stuffed olives, chopped
6 Tablespoons sweet pickle
relish

4 hard-cooked eggs, grated
1 cup cracker crumbs
8 Tablespoons salad dressing
(enough to make spreadable)

Mix all ingredients well. Refrigerate for several hours. Spread on
crackers or bread. Great for lunches and snacks.

Miss Anne Westfall

HOT CHEESE PUFFS

2 cups (8 ounces) shredded
   sharp cheese
½ cup butter or margarine

1 cup self-rising flour
1 cup chopped dates
½ cup chopped walnuts

Mix cheese and butter; stir in flour until blended. Add dates and nuts. Shape into balls, place on ungreased baking sheet. Bake at 375 degrees for 15 to 20 minutes. *Yield:* 5 dozen.

Mrs. Tom Robinson (Mary)

BEER CHEESE

6 ounces of beer
1 pound sharp cheese
2 cloves garlic, finely chopped
¼ medium onion, finely
   chopped

1 teaspoon Worcestershire
¼ teaspoon red pepper
¼ teaspoon Tabasco

Boil beer and let cool. Soften cheese, preferably overnight. Blend all ingredients. Serve soft with crackers.

Mrs. J. W. Cross, III (Caroline)

SPECIAL OCCASION CHEESE BALL

1 (8 ounce) package cream
   cheese
1 (4 ounce) package bleu cheese

½ (9 ounce) bottle chutney
Crushed walnuts

Mix cheeses and chutney and form into a ball. Roll in crushed walnuts. Serve with wheat crackers. This is really better to make ahead and freeze, thawing before time to serve. *Note:* I use Crosse and Blackwell Major Grey's chutney. *Yield:* 1 cheese ball.

Mrs. Fred Durham (Paula)

HOT ARTICHOKE DIP

1 (14 ounce) can artichoke
  hearts
1 cup mayonnaise
1 cup grated Parmesan cheese

Dash garlic powder
Dash salt
Lemon juice (optional)

Drain artichokes well. Squeeze out all juice with your hands. Break artichokes into small pieces. Add mayonnaise and cheese. Mix well. Add seasonings and mix lightly. Place mixture in a shallow baking dish that can be used for serving. Bake at 350 degrees until brown on top, about 20 minutes. Blot excess grease from top with paper towel. Serve hot with melba toast, king size corn chips, or crackers. *Yield:* 12 to 15 servings.

Mrs. Harry Chapman (Angela)

TEX-MEX MIX

3 medium ripe avocados
½ teaspoon salt
¼ teaspoon pepper
2 Tablespoons lemon juice
1 cup sour cream
½ cup mayonnaise
1 package taco seasoning mix

2 cans jalapeño bean dip
1 bunch green onions, chopped
3 medium tomatoes, chopped
2 cans pitted ripe olives, sliced
8 ounces shredded Cheddar
  cheese
Taco chips

Mash avocados. Add salt, pepper, and lemon juice. Combine sour cream, mayonnaise, and taco seasoning mix. Set both these mixtures aside. Layer all ingredients in a 13x9x2 inch dish as follows: bean dip, avocado mixture, sour cream mixture, onion, tomato, olives, and top with the cheese. Serve with large taco chips. Better served cold! *Yield:* 12.

Mrs. Donald Hillenmeyer (Chris)

MEXI-CHILE DIP

1 (3 ounce) can pitted black
  olives, chopped
1 (4 ounce) can green chilies
1 medium onion, chopped

1 large tomato, chopped
1½ Tablespoons vinegar
3 Tablespoons olive oil
1 teaspoon garlic salt

Combine olives, chilies, onion, and tomato. Combine vinegar, olive oil, and garlic salt; add to vegetable mixture, stirring well. Chill at least 2 hours before serving. Serve with tortilla chips. *Yield:* 2½ cups.

Mrs. Ron Seltz (Mary Anne)

HOT CRAB DIP

1 (8 ounce) package cream
  cheese
1 (6 ounce) can crabmeat
2 Tablespoons chopped onions

1 Tablespoon milk
½ teaspoon horseradish
¼ teaspoon salt
½ cup toasted sliced almonds

Combine all ingredients except almonds (food processor with plastic blade does well). Spoon mixture into 8 inch pie pan. Sprinkle almonds on top. Bake at 375 degrees for 15 minutes. Serve hot with small wheat crackers. *Yield:* 6.

Mrs. George L. Caldwell (Nancy)
Sun City, California

HOT BEEF CASSEROLE

2 packages smoked chipped
  beef
1 medium onion, chopped
1 small green pepper, chopped
1 (8 ounce) package cream
  cheese, softened

½ cup sour cream
1 Tablespoon mayonnaise
½ teaspoon horseradish
½ cup chopped pecans
1 large package dip size
  corn chips

Combine all ingredients, top with chopped pecans. Bake at 350 degrees for 20 to 25 minutes. Serve hot with corn chips. *Yield:* 10 servings.

Mrs. Chuck Armour (Peggy)

NANCY'S BROCCOLI DIP

1 onion, chopped fine
½ cup margarine
5 (10 ounce) boxes chopped
　frozen broccoli
3 (6 ounce) rolls garlic
　cheese

2 (8 ounce) cans mushrooms,
　drained
3 (10¾ ounce) cans cream
　of mushroom soup
2 teaspoons MSG (optional)
Salt and pepper to taste

Over low heat, sauté onion in margarine. Add all ingredients except broccoli. Cook broccoli and drain well. Add to melted mixture and cook slowly until all blends well. Serve hot in chafing dish. Best with dip sized corn chips. *Yield:* 20 servings.

Mrs. Robert Hutcheson (Nancy)

LAKE CHARLES DIP

8 ounces sour cream
2 packages Italian dressing
　mix
2 Tablespoons mayonnaise
Juice of 1 lemon

2 ripe avocados, chopped
1 tomato, chopped
Dash of Tabasco
Tortilla chips

Mix all ingredients, except chips, well. Chill and serve with chips.

Mrs. Larry Pendley (Paulette)
Waco, Texas

SURPRISE ASPARAGUS DIP

1 (14½ ounce) can asparagus
　spears, drained
½ cup sour cream

¼ teaspoon hot sauce
1 teaspoon dried dill weed
1 teaspoon seasoned salt

Place all ingredients in blender, whip until smooth. Add more seasoning to taste, if desired. Serve with corn chips.

Mrs. George E. Bivins, Jr. (Maxine)

SHRIMP DIP

1 cup shrimp, drained, rinsed, and chopped
1 (8 ounce) carton sour cream
¼ cup chili sauce

2 Tablespoons lemon juice
1 teaspoon horseradish
Salt and pepper to taste

Combine ingredients in order given, mixing well. Refrigerate for at least 1 hour to blend flavors.

Mrs. Henry Sparkman (Monta)

Variation: Omit sour cream, chili sauce, and horseradish. Add 1 (8 ounce) package cream cheese, dash garlic juice, dash Worcestershire sauce, and dash Tabasco.

Mrs. S.S. King (Marguerite)
Albany, Georgia

ASPARAGUS ROLLS

4 ounces bleu cheese
8 ounces cream cheese

1 egg

Mix the above ingredients. Set aside.

2 loaves very thinly sliced whole wheat bread
2 (14½ ounce) cans asparagus spears

1 cup butter, melted

Cut crusts off bread. Roll each piece flat with rolling pin. Spread cheese mixture on each slice. Place 1 asparagus spear on each slice and roll. Melted butter is then brushed on outside of each roll. Cut each roll into 3 pieces. Freeze. Bake at 350 degrees for 20 minutes. *Yield:* 100.

Mrs. Fred Durham (Paula)

ARTICHOKE CAKES

2 jars marinated artichoke
  hearts
1 bunch green onions, minced
1 clove garlic, crushed
1 cup Cheddar cheese,
  shredded
½ teaspoon Worcestershire
  sauce
¼ teaspoon hot sauce
4 well beaten eggs
4 Tablespoons melted
  margarine
½ cup cracker crumbs
3 Tablespoons minced parsley

Drain artichoke hearts, reserving oil. Sauté onions and garlic in 3 tablespoons of oil. Chop artichokes and add onions, garlic, cheese, Worcestershire, hot sauce, and eggs. Pour into greased 8 inch square cake pan and sprinkle with buttered cracker crumbs and parsley. Bake at 325 degrees for 35 to 40 minutes. *Yield:* 36 to 48 servings.

Mrs. Rich McDavitt (Linda)

FRENCH FRIED MUSHROOMS

1 egg
½ cup milk
⅓ cup flour
½ teaspoon salt
20 medium sized fresh
  mushrooms
1 cup cornflake crumbs
Vegetable oil
Seasoned salt

Combine egg and milk, beating well. Stir together flour and salt. Dredge mushrooms in flour and dip into egg mixture. Roll in cornflake crumbs. Deep fry in hot oil (375 degrees) until golden brown. Drain on paper towels. Sprinkle with salt. Serve immediately. *Yield:* 20 servings.

Christy Wilz
Dayton, Ohio

MUSHROOMS IN PATTY SHELLS

10 small frozen patty shells
2 Tablespoons butter or
  margarine
1 pound fresh mushrooms,
  sliced

1½ cups sour cream
¾ cup Parmesan cheese
3 Tablespoons cooking sherry
Dash of garlic powder

Bake shells according to directions on package. In a large skillet, over medium heat, melt butter or margarine. Add mushrooms to the melted margarine and sauté, stirring constantly. Drain off butter and add sour cream, cheese, sherry, and garlic powder. Cook over low heat until mixture is thoroughly heated. Spoon mushroom mixture into patty shells. Serve immediately. *Note:* Mushroom mixture may be made a day ahead and reheated. *Yield:* 8 to 10.

Mrs. Ray Tucker (Susan)

STUFFED MUSHROOM CAPS

1 pound large fresh mushroom
  caps
1 pound Italian sausage

1 (8 ounce) package cream
  cheese, softened

Wash mushrooms, set aside. Brown sausage and drain. Mix sausage with cream cheese. Stuff this mixture into mushroom caps. Broil 3 to 4 minutes until brown. Serve hot. *Yield:* 10.

Mrs. Charles Bayless (Janie)
Atlanta, Georgia

ZUCCHINI FANS

6 small zucchini

3 to 4 ounces grated Parmesan

Steam small whole zucchini 3 to 4 minutes just to slightly soften. Permit to cool. Slice thinly lengthwise, but not all the way to the end. Spread zucchini out like fans on cookie sheet, sprinkle with grated Parmesan and broil until golden brown.

Dr. Jim Manson

APPETIZERS

SPINACH BALLS

2 (10 ounce) boxes frozen, chopped spinach
2 cups herb bread stuffing mix
1 medium onion, chopped fine
2 eggs, beaten
¾ cup melted butter or margarine

½ cup Parmesan cheese
1 Tablespoon garlic salt
½ Tablespoon black pepper
1 teaspoon accent seasoning

Cook and drain spinach according to directions. Mix in remaining ingredients. Make into marble size balls. Bake at 350 degrees about 20 minutes. Can be frozen before or after baking. I prefer to freeze on a cookie sheet then store frozen in a plastic bag. Bake any quantity as needed. *Yield:* 5 dozen.

Mrs. Nancy J. Massey
Nashville, Tennessee

BACON BOW TIES

1 (1 pound) box club crackers   1 pound bacon or more

Wrap ½ slice bacon tightly around rectangle of cracker. Put on broiler pan on rack. Bake at 275 degrees for 1½ hours. Serve on silver platter. *Yield:* 40 to 50.

Mrs. William Elstun (Margi)
Philadelphia, Pennsylvania

PARMESAN CHICKEN WINGS

1 cup grated Parmesan cheese
2 Tablespoons chopped parsley
1 Tablespoon oregano
2 teaspoons paprika
½ teaspoon salt

½ teaspoon pepper
20 chicken "drumettes" (meaty portion of wing)
½ cup butter, melted

Mix cheese, spices, and parsley. Dip each "drumette" in melted butter and then in cheese mixture. Arrange in shallow baking dish on foil. Bake at 350 degrees for about 1 hour. *Yield:* 20 pieces.

Mrs. Tom Cagle (Glenda)

32

MEATBALL APPETIZERS

2 pounds ground chuck   2 pounds hot sausage

Mix and roll into small balls, brown, and drain.

Sauce:

1 (28 ounce) bottle barbecue   1 (32 ounce) jar grape jelly
  sauce with onions
1 (16 ounce) bottle barbecue
  sauce with onions

Mix both jars of barbecue sauce with grape jelly. Pour over meatballs in large pan. Heat slowly on low until hot. Serve in chafing dish. *Yield:* 5 to 6 dozen.

Mrs. Hugh Sloan (Pam)

WEINERS IN PUFF PASTRY

Puff pastry:
½ pound butter   2 cups flour
½ pound cream cheese

Mix all ingredients with hands thoroughly. Form into a ball. Wrap in plastic wrap and refrigerate overnight. Next day, take a portion at a time, roll thinly and use for wrap around weiners.

Weiners:
1 pound skinless franks   Prepared mustard

Cut franks into quarters lengthwise. Cut each quarter into equal thirds. Apply a bit of mustard on each and roll in wrap. Depending on your oven, bake at 400 or 425 degrees approximately 15 minutes or until brown. These may be made ahead and frozen unbaked. Do not defrost before baking. This pastry is also delicious for wraps for chicken livers, jams, or jelly as long as you pinch closed to hold contents. *Yield:* 60.

Mrs. H. W. Lane (Evelyn)
Hillside, New Jersey

AUNT LEE'S PIZZA SNACKS

1 pound sausage	2 teaspoons oregano
1 pound ground beef	Garlic powder to taste
1 Tablespoon Worcestershire sauce	½ pound box processed cheese
	1 to 2 loaves small party rye

Cook and drain meat. Add Worcestershire sauce, oregano and garlic. Add cheese, stir over heat until cheese is melted. Spread on small party rye. Place on cookie sheet and freeze. When frozen put in plastic bags and keep frozen until ready to serve. To serve, place needed amount on cookie sheet. Bake in 350 degree, preheated oven, for 10 minutes. An extra pound of ground beef can be substituted for sausage. *Yield:* 35 to 40 servings.

Mrs. John Bernard (Lee)

SAUSAGE BALLS IN CLAM SAUCE

1 pound mild pork sausage	1 (7½ ounce) can clams, minced

Form sausage into 1 inch balls. Arrange in a shallow baking pan. Bake at 400 degrees for 7 minutes. Turn and bake 7 minutes more. Drain on paper towels. Drain clams and reserve liquid.

Sauce:

3 Tablespoons butter	½ to 1 teaspoon dried dillweed
3 Tablespoons flour	or 1 Tablespoon fresh dill
½ cup reserved clam liquid	1 to 2 Tablespoons dry sherry
1⅓ cups half and half	Salt and pepper to taste

Melt butter and add flour. Cook and stir about 3 minutes. Gradually add clam liquid and half and half. Cook until smooth and thickened. Season with dill, sherry, salt, and pepper. Add clams and sausage balls and heat through. Serve hot. May be served in chafing dish. Sausage can be prepared ahead and frozen. *Yield:* 40 balls.

Mrs. Tom Cagle (Glenda)

CRAB PUFFS

½ pound king crabmeat
4 green onions, chopped, include tops
½ cup Cheddar cheese, shredded
½ cup Monterey Jack cheese, shredded
½ cup mayonnaise

1 teaspoon lemon juice
¼ teaspoon curry powder
1 (5 ounce) can water chestnuts, drained and chopped
1 (10 ounce) package flaky style refrigerator biscuits

In a bowl, combine all ingredients except biscuits. Separate each biscuit into 3 layers. Place on baking sheet and put a mound of crabmeat mixture on each biscuit. Bake about 10 minutes, or until golden brown, at 400 degrees. *Yield:* 30.

Helen Ingold
Brentwood, Tennessee

BROILED CRAB MELT-A-WAYS

⅓ cup margarine
2 Tablespoons mayonnaise
½ teaspoon seasoned salt
½ teaspoon garlic salt
1 (7 ounce) jar sharp Cheddar spread

1 (6 ounce) package frozen crabmeat, thawed and drained or 1 (7 ounce) can, rinsed and drained
6 English muffins

Mix all ingredients, except English muffins. Split muffins and spread with mixture. Cut into fourths. Put on cookie sheet (may be frozen at this point). Broil until golden brown when ready to serve. *Yield:* 12 to 16 servings.

Mrs. John Bell (Wanda)
Nashville, Tennessee

CRAB CHEESE DIP

1 (8 ounce) package cream
   cheese, softened
¼ cup light cream
2 teaspoons lemon juice
1½ teaspoons Worcestershire
   sauce

1 clove garlic, minced
Dash salt
Dash pepper
1 (6½ to 7½ ounce can) or
   (1 cup) crabmeat

Beat softened cream cheese, gradually adding light cream, beat until smooth. Add lemon juice, Worcestershire sauce, minced garlic, salt, and pepper. Remove bony bits from crabmeat, drain. Snip meat in fine pieces and stir into cream-cheese mixture. Chill. *Yield:* 1½ cups.

Hellen Garrett
Monroe, Louisiana

SMOKED OYSTER DIP

1 (3 ounce) package cream
   cheese, softened
2 Tablespoons mayonnaise
2 Tablespoons milk
1 Tablespoon nuts, chopped
   fine

2 teaspoons pimento, chopped
1 (3 ounce) can smoked
   oysters, drained and
   chopped

Combine all ingredients. Chill. Serve with crackers or chips. *Yield:* 6 to 8 servings.

Mrs. Floyd Reynolds (Margie)

SHRIMP BUTTER

1 (8 ounce) package cream
   cheese, softened
2 (5 ounce) cans wet pac
   shrimp, drained well

¾ cup butter, softened
1 Tablespoon minced onion
Juice of 1 lemon
Salt to taste

Blend all ingredients well in mixer. Serve on crackers.

Mrs. Joe Mac Lipscomb, Jr. (Frances)
Springfield, Tennessee

SHRIMP MOLD
Pretty in a fish mold with a green olive eye.

1 (10¾ ounce) can tomato soup
3 (3 ounce) packages cream
  cheese
2 Tablespoons gelatin
¼ cup cool water
1 cup mayonnaise
12 ounces cooked, cleaned,
  and chopped shrimp
  (fresh or canned)

1 small onion, grated
½ cup green pepper, chopped
  fine
½ cup celery, chopped fine
Juice of 1 lemon
¼ teaspoon garlic salt
Dash Worcestershire sauce

Heat soup and cream cheese over low heat. Beat until well blended. Dissolve gelatin in water, add to soup mixture; remove from heat and let cool. Add mayonnaise, shrimp, onion, green pepper, celery, lemon juice, garlic salt, and Worcestershire. Pour mixture into a 3 quart greased mold. Chill 12 hours minimum. Remove from mold and decorate with parsley. Serve with crackers. *Note:* May be made 2 to 3 days in advance. *Yield:* 1 mold.

Kay Becker
El Paso, Texas

SHRIMP SPREAD

2 (3 ounce) packages cream
  cheese
4 Tablespoons mayonnaise
3 Tablespoons catsup
½ teaspoon mustard

¼ teaspoon garlic powder
1 (4½ ounce) can shrimp, finely
  chopped
½ cup celery, finely chopped
3 teaspoons onion, grated

Mash cream cheese well. Blend mayonnaise, catsup, mustard, garlic powder, and shrimp. Add celery and onion. Combine with cream cheese and mix well. Spread on crisp crackers.

Mrs. Grady DeVan (Ann)

SAGANAKI
Pretty served in a shell with toothpicks.

1 (9 ounce) package frozen
  artichoke hearts
½ pound boiled shrimp
1 (7 ounce) jar marinated
  mushrooms and liquid

1 clove garlic, pressed
½ cup chopped fresh parsley

Place artichokes in 1 cup salted water with 2 strips of lemon peel. Bring to a boil, cover and reduce heat, and cook 10 minutes. Drain well and combine with shrimp, mushrooms and liquid, and garlic. Cover and refrigerate overnight. Mix in parsley just before serving. *Yield:* 8 servings.

Mrs. Douglas C. York (Vicki)

PEPPER JELLY TURNOVERS

1 (5 ounce) jar sharp cheese
  spread
½ cup butter

1 cup flour
2 Tablespoons water
1 (4 ounce) jar pepper jelly

Cut cheese and butter into flour. Quickly stir in water and shape into a ball. Refrigerate overnight. Roll out dough thinly, about ⅛ inch, and cut into small circles, about 2 inches, with cutter. Place ¼ to ½ teaspoon of pepper jelly in the center of each circle. Fold over and crimp edges with a fork. Bake at 375 degrees for 10 minutes. Turnovers may be frozen before or after baking. If frozen after baking, reheat before serving. *Yield:* 3 to 4 dozen.

Mrs. Tom Cagle (Glenda)

Mordecai Puryear House

MORDECAI PURYEAR HOUSE

Mordecai Puryear built this home around 1830. This house is 1½ stories high with a four-columned, one-story portico porch. A new addition was made around 1900 to give it a T shape. The home is owned today by Mr. and Mrs. James Oglesby.

Beverages

FRESH MINT TEA
So refreshing!

4 Tablespoons loose tea
(9 ripped open tea bags)
2 to 3 cups sugar
1 quart boiling water
1 large handful of mint, the
more the better

1¼ cups lemon juice
6 Tablespoons orange juice
(frozen concentrate,
undiluted)

Pour water over tea, sugar, and mint. Let steep 15 to 30 minutes. Strain tea mixture into container. Add lemon and orange juice. Add enough water to make 1 gallon. *Yield:* 1 gallon.

Mrs. Russell Sullivan (Lyn)

SPICED TEA

¾ cup instant tea
2 cups sugar
1 (1 pound 2 ounce) jar instant
orange drink

2 teaspoons ground cinnamon
1 teaspoon ground cloves
1 package lemonade mix
(unsweetened)

Combine all ingredients. Mix well. Store dry mixture in covered container. To serve, use 2 teaspoons per cup of water (hot or cold). Mix well.

Nancy Conway

TEA PUNCH

6 regular tea bags
1 quart boiling water
1½ cups sugar
1 (6 ounce) can limeade
concentrate

1 (6 ounce) can lemonade
concentrate

Steep tea bags in boiling water for 15 minutes. Remove bags. Add sugar, concentrates, and enough water to make 1 gallon. Serve well chilled. *Yield:* 1 gallon.

Mrs. Richard Roselle (Mary Lea)

FOURTH GENERATION BOILED CUSTARD
A very old recipe that is delicate, delicious, and velvet in texture.

2 quarts milk
8 eggs
2 cups sugar

3 Tablespoons vanilla extract or any special flavoring desired

In double boiler put milk to get hot, but not boil. Beat the eggs until light; add sugar and mix well. Pour small portion of hot milk into the eggs and sugar to warm and to thin this portion. Pour slowly into hot milk. Cook, stirring constantly with wooden spoon until it coats the spoon. Add flavoring. After mixture cools, strain through large strainer and place in refrigerator. Serve very cold. *Yield:* ½ gallon.

Mrs. Lenox D. Rawlings (Libby)

HOMEMADE KAHLUA

3 cups white sugar
1 cup instant coffee
4 teaspoons vanilla

1 cup water
1 fifth vodka
2 jiggers brandy

Mix white sugar, instant coffee, vanilla, and water. Warm over low heat until sugar is melted, about 15 minutes. DO NOT BOIL. Cool completely. Add liquor. Store in airtight bottle 10 days to 2 weeks. Always shake before using. *Yield:* About 6 cups.

Mrs. David S. Myers (Carla)

CRÈME de MENTHE

4 cups water
4 cups sugar
Few drops green food coloring
2 teaspoons peppermint
flavoring

½ teaspoon vanilla
2 teaspoons glycerine
3 cups grain alcohol (185 proof)

Boil water and sugar 10 minutes. Cool. Add coloring, peppermint, vanilla, glycerine, and alcohol. *Yield:* 8 cups.

Anonymous

GALIANO

4 cups water
4 cups sugar
Yellow food coloring
(few drops)

2 teaspoons anise flavoring
½ teaspoon vanilla
2 teaspoons glycerine
3 cups grain alcohol (185 proof)

Boil water and sugar 10 minutes. Cool. Add food coloring, anise, vanilla, glycerine, and alcohol. Bottle and let stand 4 weeks for best flavor. *Yield: 8 cups.*

Anonymous

ORANGE REFRESHER

1 (0.28 ounce) envelope
    unsweetened orange punch
    mix
½ cup sugar

1 quart cold water
⅓ cup grenadine syrup
⅓ cup lemon juice
1 pint orange sherbet

Combine drink mix and sugar. Add water and stir until sugar is dissolved. Add grenadine syrup and lemon juice. Mix well. Chill. Just before serving, add sherbet and stir until partially melted. *Yield:* 12 (4 ounce) servings. *Note:* I use Hawaiian Punch.

Mrs. Joseph Schellaci (Jeanette)
Irvine, California

SANGRIA

1 bottle dry red wine
Juice of ½ lemon
Juice of 1 orange
Orange peel spiral (cut spiral
    from orange peel before
    squeezing)

8 to 10 ice cubes
⅓ cup sugar
Salad fruit, drained (this is the
    canned fruit which comes in
    whole pieces)
1 liter club soda

Combine wine, juices of lemon and orange, orange peel spiral, ice cubes, sugar, and salad fruit. Add club soda just before serving for sparkly, bubbly effect. Also make sure you have a spoon when you pour it so that each serving gets one piece of whole fruit. *Yield:* 5 cups.

Mrs. William W. Wells (Joan)

SPICED CRANBERRY PUNCH

4 quarts cranapple juice
¼ cup brown sugar
4 cinnamon sticks

1½ teaspoons whole cloves
1 lemon, thinly sliced

Mix all ingredients in a 5 quart Dutch oven or similar pan. Heat to boiling. Simmer 15 to 20 minutes and it is ready to serve. *Yield:* 25 servings.

Mrs. E. Fred Durham (Paula)

RASPBERRY-LEMON COOLERS

1 (0.28 ounce) envelope raspberry punch drink mix
1 cup sugar
1 (6 ounce) can lemonade concentrate, partially thawed

1 (28 ounce) bottle club soda, chilled
Ice cubes
Lemon slices (optional)

Mix the first 3 ingredients well. Just before serving, gradually add club soda, stirring slowly. Add ice cubes and use lemon slices for garnish, if desired. *Yield:* 18 (4 ounce) servings. *Note:* I use Hawaiian Punch.

Mrs. Joe Schillaci (Jeanette)
Irvine, California

BANANA DAFFODILS

1½ quarts water
3 cups sugar
1 (12 ounce) can orange juice, thawed, undiluted

1 (46 ounce) can pineapple-grapefruit juice drink
4 ripe bananas, mashed
3 bottles club soda

Mix water and sugar until sugar dissolves. Add juices and mashed bananas. Pour into freezer containers and freeze. *Note:* I use large Tupperware cake container. About 2 hours before serving, remove from freezer. Add 1 quart club soda per 2 quarts frozen mixture or add ½ club soda and ½ champagne. *Note:* May use rum or vodka instead. *Yield:* 1¼ to 1½ gallons.

Mrs. Thomas Patterson (Becky)

BANANA PUNCH

6 cups water
3 cups sugar
3 cups pineapple juice
2 cups orange juice

Juice of 2 lemons
3 large bananas, blended
   in mixer
2 bottles ginger ale

Mix first 6 ingredients and freeze in large container or divide into 2 smaller containers. Remove from freezer 3 hours before ready to serve. Transfer to punch bowl and add 2 bottles ginger ale at time of serving. Should be icy. *Yield:* 12 to 14 servings.

Mrs. Walter Stewart (Dorothy)

JELLO PUNCH

1 (3 ounce) package lemon
   flavored gelatin
1½ cups sugar
2 cups hot water
4 cups cold water
8 Tablespoons reconstituted
   lemon juice or juice from
   4 lemons

1 (46 ounce) can pineapple juice
2 (33.8 ounce) bottles ginger
   ale
Ice ring

Dissolve jello and sugar in hot water. Add cold water and lemon juice. Just before serving add pineapple juice and ginger ale. Use ice ring to keep cool. *Yield:* 30 cups.

Mrs. James G. Harris (Barbara)

PUNCH

1 (46 ounce) can cranapple juice
1½ cups orange drink mix,
   undiluted, or 12 ounces
   canned orange juice

⅓ cup lemon juice
1 quart uncola carbonated
   drink

Mix all ingredients and serve chilled. If using the drink mix, some water may be added to dilute before adding to remaining ingredients. *Yield:* 22 cups. *Note:* I use Tang and Sprite.

Mrs. J. W. Cross, III (Caroline)

MARGARITA PUNCH

6 (6 ounce) cans limeade,
  thawed
3 (6 ounce) cans lemonade,
  thawed
½ gallon white wine

1 container margarita salt
1 lime, sliced into quarter
  sections
12 to 16 long-stemmed glasses
Ice ring or ice cubes

Prepare limeade and lemonade as per directions on can. Pour into large punch bowl and add white wine to taste. Add ice ring or ice-cubes. Place lime slices and margarita salt in 2 decorative dishes next to punch bowl along with glasses. Rub a lime slice around edge of glass and dip into margarita salt before pouring punch.

Mrs. Richard Marshall (Cindy)

MARGARET'S EGGNOG

1 dozen eggs, separated
1 cup sugar
2 cups whipping cream,
  whipped

1 cup brandy
Nutmeg

Beat egg yolks, adding sugar gradually, until lemon color. Beat whites as for meringue. Beat cream until very stiff. Blend meringue into yolks, then add cream and brandy. Sprinkle with nutmeg. May need a little sugar added to egg whites so they will stiffen properly. This almost has to be eaten with a spoon. If you want to serve it to a large crowd at a stand-up party, thin with milk and brandy. Makes a medium punch bowl full.

Mrs. J. R. Smith (Margaret Rawlings)
Wilson, North Carolina

HOT CHOCOLATE MIX

6 quarts dry milk
8 ounces instant chocolate
  drink mix

3½ ounces non-dairy creamer
½ box powdered sugar

Mix all ingredients together. Store in airtight container. Use ¼ cup mix per cup of hot water. Mix well.

Julie Westfall (12 yrs.)

Myles Manor

Breads

YEAST BREAD

Warm water	8 cups sifted flour
1 (14 ounce) can sweetened condensed milk	1 Tablespoon sugar
	1 Tablespoon salt
⅓ cup shortening	1½ packages dry yeast

Add enough warm water to milk and shortening to make 1 quart liquid. Mix 6 cups flour with sugar, salt, and yeast. Into this stir the liquid and mix well. Add remaining flour. Let rise until double in bulk (1½ to 2 hours). Put on board and knead well, adding flour as needed. Divide into 4 equal parts and place each in greased 7x3x2 inch pan and let rise about 40 minutes. Bake at 350 degrees for 40 minutes. *Yield:* 4 loaves.

Mrs. Jake Russell (Pat)
Beaver Dam, Kentucky

HONEY WHEAT BREAD

2 cups whole wheat flour	2 Tablespoons honey
½ teaspoon salt	1 cup buttermilk
1 teaspoon baking soda	1 egg, slightly beaten

In large bowl, mix flour, salt, and soda. Make a well in the center. Add honey, buttermilk, and egg. Stir just until moistened (batter will be soft). Place in greased 1 quart casserole and bake at 375 degrees for 20 to 25 minutes. Cool before serving. *Yield:* 8 to 10 servings.

Mrs. Marvin Wallace (Alice)

ROADSIDE POTATO BREAD

3½ cups milk
6 Tablespoons sugar
6 Tablespoons lard or butter
2 teaspoons salt
¼ cup instant mashed
   potatoes, dry

2 packages dry yeast
½ cup warm water
10 to 11 cups sifted flour
3 Tablespoons corn meal

Scald milk, pour into large bowl and stir in sugar, lard or butter, salt, and instant potatoes. Cool to lukewarm. Sprinkle yeast in warm water, stir to dissolve. Add yeast and 4 cups flour to milk mixture. Beat 2 minutes with electric mixer at medium speed or until batter is smooth. Or beat by hand. Mix in just enough of remaining flour, a little at a time, first with spoon, and then with hands, to make a dough that leaves the sides of the bowl. Turn onto lightly floured board, cover, and let stand 10 to 15 minutes. Knead until smooth, about 10 minutes. Place in greased bowl, turn dough over to grease top. Cover and let rise in warm place until double, 1½ to 2 hours. Punch down dough, cover, and let rise again until double, about 45 minutes. Turn onto board and divide into 3 equal parts, form into balls, cover and let stand 10 minutes. Meanwhile, grease three 9⅝x5½ inch loaf pans. Sprinkle bottoms and sides of pans with corn meal and let rise until double, 50 to 60 minutes. Bake in moderate oven at 375 degrees for 45 minutes or until loaves are rich brown and have a hollow sound when tapped with fingers. Remove from pans, cool on wire racks. *Yield:* 3 loaves.

Mrs. Harvey Crawford (Eunice)

BEER BREAD

3 cups self-rising flour
3 Tablespoons sugar

1 (12 ounce) can beer

Mix flour and sugar. Add beer and stir gently. Mixture will be lumpy. Pour into greased loaf pan. Bake at 350 degrees for 45 to 60 minutes. Remove from pan immediately and brush with butter. *Yield:* 1 loaf.

Judy Zwemke via Mrs. Bernard Leshner (Sharon)

SWEDISH RYE BREAD

2 packages dry yeast
1½ cups warm water
¼ cup molasses
⅓ cup sugar

1 Tablespoon salt
2 Tablespoons shortening
2½ cups rye flour
2¼ to 2¾ cups white flour

Dissolve yeast in warm water. Stir in molasses, sugar, salt, shortening, and rye flour. Beat until smooth. Mix in enough white flour to handle dough easily. Turn out onto lightly floured board. Cover and let stand 15 minutes. Knead until smooth. Place in greased bowl. Turn greased side up. Cover and let rise until doubled, about 1 hour. Punch down, round up, and let rise again until double. Sprinkle greased baking sheet with corn meal. Punch down dough and divide in half. Shape each half into a round slightly flat loaf. Cover and let rise 1 hour. Bake in a preheated oven 30 to 35 minutes at 375 degrees. *Yield:* 2 loaves.

Betty Washington

CORN LIGHT BREAD

1½ cups buttermilk
4 Tablespoons oil
⅓ cup sugar

⅔ cup self-rising flour
1½ cups self-rising meal

Mix buttermilk, oil, and sugar together, thoroughly. Add flour and meal and let stand 5 minutes. Beat down and pour into loaf pan. Bake 50 minutes at 400 degrees or until brown. *Yield:* 1 loaf.

Mrs. James Lanier, Jr. (Marie)

EASY OLD FASHIONED CORN LIGHT BREAD
Delicious and very moist

3 cups self-rising meal
¾ cup flour
1 cup sugar

3 cups buttermilk
¼ cup oil

Grease a tube pan. Mix all ingredients until smooth. Bake at 250 degrees on top shelf of oven for 1 to 2 hours or until light brown. Remove from oven and wrap immediately in tea towel. *Yield:* 1 loaf.

Mell Isaacs

MILLIE'S CORN LIGHT BREAD

3 cups self-rising white meal
⅔ cup sugar
⅔ cup flour

½ teaspoon salt
3 cups buttermilk
⅓ cup oil

Heat oil in tube pan in 325 degree oven. Using a large metal or glass tempered mixing bowl, combine all dry ingredients and add buttermilk. When thoroughly mixed, add hot oil. Sprinkle bottom of the pan with meal and return to oven. When meal has browned, add bread mixture and cook 1 hour at 325 degrees. When bread is done, loosen from sides of pan with a spatula, and turn out onto wood tray. Place the pan over bread and leave until cool. This will give the bread a wax consistency. This bread is better prepared a day ahead. *Yield:* 10 servings.

Mrs. Bobby Stanfield (Mildred)
College Grove, Tennessee

YEAST CORN LIGHT BREAD
Different, new and delicious

1 cake yeast
¼ cup lukewarm water
½ cup corn meal
1¾ cups boiling water

1½ teaspoons salt
2 Tablespoons sugar
3 Tablespoons shortening
2¾ to 3 cups sifted flour

Soften yeast in lukewarm water. Cook corn meal in boiling water 10 minutes; add salt, sugar, and shortening. Cool until lukewarm, stirring occasionally to prevent a film. When cool, add softened yeast mixture and beat well. Add flour and mix well. Knead, using as little flour on board as possible. Put into a greased bowl and let rise until almost doubled in bulk. Punch down and let rise again. Shape into 2 loaves, place each in loaf pan and let rise until it has almost doubled in bulk. Bake at 400 degrees for 30 to 35 minutes until done. *Yield:* 2 loaves.

Mrs. H. L. Malone (Lib)
Nashville, Tennessee

KENTUCKY CORN BREAD

1½ cups self-rising meal
2 eggs
⅔ cup oil
1 cup sour cream

1 cup cream style corn
3 Tablespoons chopped onion
1 (8 ounce) package sharp
Cheddar cheese, shredded

Mix all ingredients except cheese. Pour ½ of batter into greased square pan, sprinkle with ½ of the cheese. Pour remaining batter and top with remaining cheese. Bake at 350 degrees for 35 to 45 minutes. *Yield:* 10 servings.

Mrs. A. C. Frensley (Betty)

MEXICAN BREAD

1 egg
1 (8 ounce) can cream style
corn
½ cup cooking oil
¼ cup buttermilk
2 to 3 Tablespoons sweet green
pepper, chopped

2 to 3 Tablespoons hot pepper,
chopped
2 to 3 Tablespoons onion,
chopped
1½ cups self-rising meal
1 cup sharp cheese, shredded

Mix all ingredients except cheese. Pour ½ mixture into hot greased black iron skillet then spread ½ cheese over mixture. Pour remaining mixture on top of cheese then spread remaining cheese on top and bake at 350 degrees for 45 minutes or until done. *Yield:* 10 servings.

Mrs. James Culberson (Frances)

CORN MEAL DUMPLINGS
Great with turnip greens and sweet potatoes!

Country ham hock broth
3 cups self-rising meal
1 egg

1 Tablespoon onion, chopped
   fine
Pepper to taste

Mix above ingredients. Pour boiling ham broth over mixture until consistency easy to handle in making round balls that hold together well. Drop balls into boiling broth. Cook for 10 minutes. *Yield:* 6 to 8 servings.

Mrs. Walter Berg (Ruth)
Nashville, Tennessee

MISS VIRGINIA'S RIZ BISCUIT

4 cups self-rising white flour
2 cups whole wheat flour
¾ cup sugar
2 packages dry yeast

1½ cups lard or shortening
4 cups warm water (may need
   a little more or less)
Melted butter or oil

Sift together flours, sugar, and yeast. Cut in lard or shortening. Gradually add warm water. Knead until smooth. Make into a large ball and sprinkle with hot water. Place in deep bowl and let rise until double. Punch down dough and roll ⅓ dough at a time. Cut into biscuits. Place on greased pans in warm place and let rise until double. Brush with melted butter or oil. Bake at 375 degrees about 15 minutes until brown. Cool and package. *Yield:* 72 biscuits.

Virginia C. Jefferson

ALABAMA BISCUITS

1 package dry yeast	4 Tablespoons sugar
1 cup warm buttermilk	½ teaspoon soda
2½ cups flour	6 Tablespoons shortening
½ teaspoon salt	Melted butter

Dissolve yeast in buttermilk. Combine dry ingredients and mix in shortening. Add milk mixture to flour mixture and mix slightly. Pour this onto floured board and knead about 30 times. Roll thin (¼ inch). Cut out. Dip each biscuit into melted butter and stack two. Let rise in warm place for 2 hours. Bake 15 minutes at 375 degrees. *Yield:* 1 dozen (large).

Mrs. Baxter Fisher, Jr. (Julia)
Martin, Tennessee

SOUR CREAM BISCUITS

4 cups flour	½ teaspoon soda
2 Tablespoons baking powder	1 (16 ounce) container sour
2 teaspoons salt	cream
2 teaspoons sugar	½ cup shortening

Preheat oven to 425 degrees. In large bowl with fork, mix flour, baking powder, salt, sugar, and soda. With pastry blender or two knives used scissor-fashion, cut in sour cream and shortening until mixture resembles coarse crumbs. With hands, knead dough 6 to 8 strokes to mix thoroughly. (If dough is dry, add a little water, a teaspoon at a time, while kneading.) On lightly floured surface, with floured rolling pin, roll dough ½ inch thick. Cut biscuits with floured 2½ inch round cookie cutter. Place biscuits on ungreased cookie sheet, 1 inch apart. Bake 10 to 15 minutes until golden brown. *Yield:* 20 biscuits.

Ann E. Lynch
Nashville, Tennessee

ANGEL BISCUITS
Bake without rising - can be kept in refrigerator.

5 cups flour	1 package dry yeast
1 teaspoon soda	2 Tablespoons warm water
1¼ teaspoons salt	2 cups buttermilk
3 teaspoons baking powder	1 cup shortening
¼ cup sugar	Melted butter

Sift dry ingredients together. Dissolve yeast in warm water; add to buttermilk. Cut shortening into dry ingredients. Stir yeast mixture into flour mixture and mix well. Turn out onto lightly floured board and add flour if needed to make soft dough. Roll to ¼ inch thickness. Cut and dip into melted butter and fold over. Bake 15 minutes at 400 degrees. May half recipe for 2½ dozen biscuits. Will stay in refrigerator up to 1 week. Pinch off as much as you need for biscuits each serving, leaving remainder in tightly covered container. *Yield:* 5 dozen.

Mrs. Richard K. Hill (Blanche)

MRS. HERBERT'S YEAST ROLLS

2 cups milk	2 eggs, well beaten
2 teaspoons salt	2 packages dry yeast
½ cup sugar	4 Tablespoons warm water
½ cup shortening	6 cups flour

Place milk, salt, sugar, and shortening in microwave to melt or on stove to scald. Let cool. When mixture has cooled, add well beaten eggs. In small bowl, mix yeast with warm water and add to milk mixture. Measure flour into mixing bowl. Pour milk mixture slowly into flour and beat until smooth. Place in greased bowl and refrigerate several hours or overnight. Roll out using very little flour. Cut into ¼ inch rolls. Dip in melted butter and fold over. Let rise 2 to 3 hours. Bake at 375 degrees for 15 to 20 minutes until brown. *Note:* I use bread flour. *Yield:* 4 to 5 dozen.

Mrs. Wilson Herbert (Ann)

THELMA'S YEAST ROLLS

1 package dry yeast
¼ cup lukewarm water
1 teaspoon salt
⅓ cup sugar
2 eggs, beaten

½ cup oil or margarine
1 cup milk
4 cups sifted flour
Margarine, melted

Dissolve yeast in lukewarm water. Combine salt, sugar, eggs, oil and mix. Add warm milk. Beat until well mixed. Add yeast and mix well. Add 2 cups flour; beat 3 minutes. Add remaining flour or more as needed to make smooth dough. Cover. Let rise approximately 2 to 3 hours or until double in size. Roll on floured board. Cut in circles of desired size. Melt margarine over low heat (enough to dip each roll in). Dip each roll in melted margarine, fold over, and place in greased pan. Bake at 350 degrees for 30 minutes. *Yield:* 3 dozen.

Thelma Alexander (deceased)

Thelma K. Alexander was the cook for the Franklin Special School District and for several prominent Franklin families for many years. Her prized recipes for yeast rolls and "Halloween Carnival" Spaghetti (see Index) are special additions to this collection.

POCKETBOOK ROLLS

½ cup warm water
1 yeast cake
1 egg, beaten
½ cup shortening

½ cup hot water, boiling
¼ cup sugar
3 cups self-rising flour

Dissolve yeast cake in ½ cup warm water. Mix yeast and egg together. Dissolve shortening in ½ cup boiling water and add sugar. Combine with yeast mixture and add flour (1 cup at a time) until all is mixed. Cover with tea towel and refrigerate overnight. Next day, roll out and cut, then fold over to make pocketbook. Let rise in warm place for at least 1 hour. Bake in 450 degree oven for 8 to 10 minutes. *Yield:* 2 dozen.

Carol R. Bond

REFRIGERATOR ROLLS
Delicious and Versatile

3½ cups milk
1 cup sugar
1 cup shortening
8 cups flour (about)
1 Tablespoon salt

2 teaspoons soda
2 yeast cakes or packages
½ cup lukewarm water
1 Tablespoon sugar

Heat 1 cup milk with sugar and shortening until they are dissolved. Pour into large mixing bowl and add remaining milk. Mix 3 cups flour, salt, baking powder, and soda. Add to milk mixture. Dissolve yeast in lukewarm water to which 1 tablespoon sugar has been added. Add dissolved yeast mixture to milk mixture (make sure the milk mixture is lukewarm so that it does not kill yeast). Add enough flour to the mixture to make consistency of cake batter. Cover and let rise until doubled in bulk. Add enough flour to make soft dough. Knead 5 minutes. Place in greased container. Cover dough with oil or shortening so that it is not dry. Cover and refrigerate. When needed take required amount and knead well. Work as little flour as possible into dough. Roll to ½ inch thickness. Cut into circles. Butter ½ of each circle and fold. Seal half circle with the edge of a spoon. Place on greased sheet and let rise 1½ hours. Bake at 425 degrees for 10 to 15 minutes. Will keep 8 to 15 days in refrigerator. May also be used for cinnamon rolls, hamburger, and hot dog buns. I use a coffee can to cut hamburger buns. *Yield:* 100 rolls.

Mrs. Ronald Crutcher (Joyce)

SPOON ROLLS

2 packages dry yeast
2 cups lukewarm water
¾ cup melted margarine

¼ cup sugar
1 egg, slightly beaten
4 cups self-rising flour

Dissolve yeast in lukewarm water. Add melted margarine, sugar, and egg. Gradually add flour. Spoon into greased muffin tins. Bake at 325 degrees for 15 to 20 minutes. *Note:* This batter may be stored in refrigerator until needed (4 to 5 days). *Yield:* 36 rolls.

Mrs. Gary Neill (Debbie)
Brentwood, Tennessee

PARKER HOUSE CORN ROLLS
Unusual, a pleasing surprise.

1¼ cups flour
½ cup milk
¾ cup corn meal (plain)
2 eggs

4 teaspoons baking powder
½ teaspoon salt
2 Tablespoons shortening

Mix flour, milk, corn meal, eggs, baking powder, and salt. Turn onto floured board. Roll ½ inch thick and cut with biscuit cutter. Spread ½ of each roll with shortening; fold over remaining half. Bake in quick oven at 450 degrees for 15 minutes. *Yield:* 10 servings.

Mrs. Robert E. Wells (Cooper)

SOUR CREAM MUFFINS

1 Tablespoon sugar
¾ cup self-rising flour

1 whole egg
1 (8 ounce) carton sour cream

Preheat oven to 400 degrees. Mix all ingredients. Pour into greased muffin tins and bake for 20 minutes. Serve hot. *Yield:* 8 servings.

Mrs. Jesse Jones

POPPY SEED MUFFINS

1½ cups baking mix
¾ cup sour cream
⅓ cup sugar

1 egg
1 Tablespoon poppy seeds
1 teaspoon vanilla

Preheat oven to 400 degrees. Grease bottoms only of 12 muffin cups, 2½x1¼ inches, or line with paper baking cups. Mix all ingredients until moistened. Fill muffin cups about ½ full. Bake until golden brown, 15 to 18 minutes. Immediately remove from pan. *Note:* I use Bisquick. *Yield:* 1 dozen.

Joyce Smithson
College Grove, Tennessee

BANANA NUT MUFFINS

1 cup flour
½ cup sugar
2½ teaspoons baking powder
½ teaspoon salt
¼ teaspoon baking soda
¾ cup uncooked oatmeal
1 egg, beaten

3 Tablespoons melted or
  liquid shortening
½ cup milk
½ cup ripe bananas, mashed
⅓ cup chopped pecans or
  walnuts

In large bowl, stir dry ingredients together. Add remaining ingredients; stir only until all are moistened. Fill medium sized greased muffin tins ⅔ full. Bake in preheated oven at 400 degrees for 15 minutes. *Yield:* 1 dozen.

Mrs. Harv Gerecke (Mary)
Pekin, Illinois

WOODLAND SWEET POTATO MUFFINS

½ cup butter
1¼ cups sugar
2 eggs
1½ cups canned sweet
  potatoes, mashed
1½ cups flour
2 teaspoons baking powder
¼ teaspoon salt

1 teaspoon cinnamon
½ teaspoon nutmeg
1 cup milk
½ cup pecans or walnuts,
  chopped
¼ cup raisins, chopped
  (optional)

Preheat oven to 400 degrees. Grease small muffin tins. Cream butter and sugar. Add eggs and mix well. Blend in sweet potatoes. Sift flour with baking powder, salt, cinnamon, and nutmeg. Add alternately with milk. Do not over mix. Add nuts and raisins. Fill muffin tins ⅔ full. Bake for 25 minutes. *Note:* These freeze well. *Yield:* 5 to 6 dozen small muffins.

Mrs. Cecil Crowson (Evelyn)

SPICED APRICOT BREAD

1½ cups dried apricots, diced
1 cup sugar
½ teaspoon cloves, ground
¼ teaspoon nutmeg, ground
½ teaspoon cinnamon, ground
½ teaspoon salt

6 Tablespoons butter
1 cup water
1 egg, beaten
2 cups flour, sifted
1 teaspoon soda
1 cup chopped nuts

Cook apricots, sugar, cloves, nutmeg, cinnamon, salt, butter, and water for 5 minutes. Cool thoroughly. Add egg, flour, soda, and nuts; mix and turn into well greased loaf pan. Bake 1 hour at 350 degrees. *Yield:* 1 loaf.

Mrs. Nelson Sweeney (Beth)

SPICY PEACH NUT BREAD

2 cups flour
⅔ cup sugar
2 teaspoons baking powder
½ teaspoon salt
½ teaspoon soda
¼ teaspoon ground cloves
2 Tablespoons butter or
  margarine, softened

1 (16 ounce) can (2 cups) sliced
  peaches or apricot halves,
  drained, reserve syrup
½ cup reserved syrup
2 eggs
¾ cup chopped nuts
1 cup raisins (optional)

Lightly spoon flour into measuring cup; level off. In large bowl, blend ingredients at low speed, until moistened. Beat 2 minutes at medium speed, scraping bowl occasionally. Stir nuts and raisins into batter. Pour into greased and floured 9x5 inch or 8x4 inch loaf pan. Bake for 60 to 70 minutes at 350 degrees or until toothpick inserted in center comes out clean. Immediately remove from pan and cool completely. If desired, drizzle with powdered sugar glaze. *Yield:* 1 loaf.

Mrs. Steven Roussel (Janie)

ORANGE NUT BREAD

3 cups baking mix
⅔ cup sugar
¾ cup orange juice
3 eggs

1 Tablespoon grated orange rind
1 cup chopped pecans

Combine first 5 ingredients in mixing bowl. Beat on low speed of electric mixer for 30 seconds. Beat on high speed 3 minutes. Stir in pecans. Spoon batter into 9x5x3 inch loaf pan. Bake at 350 degrees for 55 minutes. Cool in pan 10 minutes. Turn out onto a wire rack. Cool.

Orange Glaze:
2 Tablespoons butter or margarine, melted
½ cup sifted powdered sugar

½ teaspoon orange juice
½ teaspoon grated orange rind

Combine all ingredients; mix well. Drizzle bread with orange glaze. *Yield:* 1 loaf.

Mrs. Steve Roussel (Janie)

PUMPKIN TEA BREAD

2 cups sugar
1 cup oil
3 eggs
2 cups pumpkin, canned or cooked and mashed
3 cups flour
½ teaspoon salt

1 teaspoon baking powder
1½ teaspoons cinnamon
1 teaspoon nutmeg
1 teaspoon cloves
¾ teaspoon soda
1 cup nuts (optional)

Combine sugar and oil, blending well. Add eggs and beat until light and creamy; stir in pumpkin. Combine remaining ingredients; add to creamed mixture and beat until well blended. Pour into 3 greased and floured 8½x4½x2⅝ inch loaf pans or two 9 inch loaf pans. Bake at 325 degrees for 1 hour or until lightly browned. Cool 15 minutes in pans. Remove from pans and cool completely on rack. Bread freezes very well. *Yield:* 2 or 3 loaves.

Mrs. Connie Turvy

DUTCH BROWN BREAD

1½ cups raisins
1½ cups water
1 egg, well beaten
1 cup sugar
2 Tablespoons oil

1 teaspoon vanilla
2 cups flour
2 teaspoons soda
½ teaspoon salt
1 cup nuts

Boil raisins in water for 1 minute and cool. Add egg, sugar, oil, and vanilla and mix well. Add flour, soda, and salt and mix well. Fold in nuts. Pour into 3 number 303 cans which have been rubbed with oil. Fill cans ½ full. Bake 1 hour at 300 degrees or a little longer if necessary. Turn cans upside down for 10 minutes (loaves should come out clean). *Note:* Recipe may be doubled and baked in 7 cans. *Yield:* 3 loaves.

Mrs. James Maupin (Sara)

SOPAIPILLAS
Serve this bread with chili or other spicy foods.

2 cups salad oil in medium
   skillet
1¾ cups sifted flour
2 teaspoons baking powder

1 teaspoon salt
2 Tablespoons shortening
⅔ cup cold water

Start heating salad oil. Combine flour, baking powder, and salt. Sift into mixing bowl. Cut in shortening with pastry blender. Add enough water to make a stiff dough. Turn dough onto lightly floured board and knead lightly until smooth. Cover with tea towel and let rest 10 minutes. Roll dough very thin (about ⅛ inch) into a rectangle about 15x12 inches. Cut into 3 inch squares, or use a biscuit cutter. When oil is very hot (385 to 400 degrees on thermometer) drop a few squares of dough into it at a time. Turn frequently so that sopaipillas will puff up evenly. Remove with a slotted spoon and drain on paper towels. Serve hot with honey. *Yield:* 18 to 20.

Mrs. Gary Quick (Joan)

CUSTARDY POPOVERS

4 eggs
1 cup milk
1 cup unbleached white flour

½ teaspoon salt
4 Tablespoons melted butter

Beat eggs and milk together. Add flour and salt. Beat with a fork until mixture is uniform. Preheat a muffin tin in 375 degree oven for 5 minutes. Brush the cups and the top surface generously with melted butter. Fill each muffin cup ⅔ full with batter. Work quickly so the tin stays hot. Place in oven and bake for 35 minutes without opening oven. Prick each popover with a fork to let steam escape. (This will help them hold their shape.) Serve immediately with butter and jam. *Yield:* 1 dozen.

Mrs. Robert Pilling (Nancy)

APPLE PUFFED PANCAKES

6 eggs
1½ cups milk
1 cup flour
3 Tablespoons sugar
1 teaspoon salt

¼ teaspoon cinnamon
½ cup butter
2 apples, peeled and thinly sliced
2 to 3 Tablespoons brown sugar

Preheat oven to 425 degrees. In a blender or large bowl, mix eggs, milk, flour, sugar, vanilla, salt, and cinnamon until blended. If using a mixer, batter will remain slightly lumpy. Melt butter in a 12 inch fluted quiche dish in oven. Add apple slices to baking dish. Return to oven until butter sizzles. *Do not let brown.* Remove dish from oven and immediately pour batter over apples. Sprinkle with brown sugar. Bake in middle of oven 20 minutes or until puffed and brown. Serve immediately. *Yield:* 6 to 8 servings.

Mrs. Richard Marshall (Cindy)

BUTTERMILK PANCAKES

1 cup flour
½ teaspoon soda
¾ teaspoon baking powder
1 to 2 teaspoons sugar

½ teaspoon salt
1 egg
1 cup buttermilk
2 Tablespoons melted butter

Sift flour, soda, baking powder, sugar, and salt. Beat egg with buttermilk and add to dry ingredients. (Do not beat too much.) Add melted butter. Pour batter onto hot griddle. Bake on both sides until golden brown.

Mrs. Ira V. Miller (Mary K.)
Dayton, Ohio

BLUEBERRY COFFEE CAKE

1 cup sugar
½ cup shortening
2 eggs
1 cup sour cream
1 teaspoon vanilla

2 cups flour
½ teaspoon baking soda
Pinch salt
1½ teaspoons baking powder

Filling:
½ cup sugar
2 teaspoons cinnamon
1 cup nuts

1 cup blueberries, canned,
frozen or fresh

Cream sugar and shortening. Add eggs, sour cream, vanilla, and sifted dry ingredients. Beat until smooth. Mix sugar, cinnamon, and nuts. Grease a 10 inch tube pan and pour ½ the batter into it. Add ½ filling, then add blueberries. Add remaining batter and top with remaining filling. Bake at 350 degrees for 1 hour. *Yield:* 12 servings.

Mrs. Reuben Smith (Jane)

DANISH COFFEE TWIST

1 package dry yeast
¼ cup warm water
1 teaspoon sugar
½ cup butter
6 Tablespoons sugar
½ teaspoon salt
Flavoring (may use ½ teaspoon
  cardamon or 1 teaspoon
  grated orange peel or
  2 teaspoons vanilla)

3 eggs
4 cups flour
¾ cup warm milk
Nut streusel filling
1 egg white beaten
Sugar
Chopped nuts

Dissolve yeast in warm water and add 1 teaspoon sugar. Set aside. Cream butter. Add sugar, salt, flavoring, and eggs. Add 1 cup flour and beat well. Add warm milk and yeast mixture. Beat until smooth. Gradually add remaining flour. Beat until smooth with mixer or wooden spoon. Turn onto floured board and knead lightly. Cut dough in half. Roll ½ dough into a 10x14 inch rectangle. Spread with ½ of filling. Roll up longways and place seam side down on buttered baking sheet. Repeat with remaining dough and filling. Cut through rolls to within ½ inch of the bottom at ¾ inch intervals. Pull and twist each dice to lie flat. First twist one side and then the other. Cover with a towel and let rise until double, about 45 minutes. Brush with egg white and sprinkle with sugar and nuts. Bake at 325 degrees for 30 to 35 minutes until golden brown. *Yield:* 2 rings.

Nut Streusel Filling:
1 (8 ounce) can almond paste
¼ cup soft butter
2 Tablespoons sugar

⅓ cup finely chopped filberts,
  almonds or pecans
1 egg

Mix all ingredients together and beat until smooth.

Mrs. Steven G. Hall
Nashville, Tennessee

CHOCOLATE CINNAMON BUNS

1 package dry yeast
¾ cup warm water
¼ cup shortening
1 teaspoon salt
¼ cup sugar
1 egg

⅓ cup cocoa
2¼ cups flour
1 Tablespoon softened butter
3 Tablespoons sugar
1½ teaspoons cinnamon

In mixing bowl, dissolve yeast in warm water. Add shortening, salt, sugar, egg, cocoa, and 1 cup flour. Beat 2 minutes with electric mixer at medium speed. Scrape sides and bottom of bowl. Stir in remaining flour; blend well. Scrape sides of bowl. Cover with cloth; let rise until double. Punch down. Turn out onto well floured board. Roll into rectangle, 12x9 inches. Spread with butter and sprinkle with sugar and cinnamon mixture. Roll up and cut into 12 pieces. Place in greased 9 inch square pan. Let rise in warm place. Bake at 375 degrees for 25 minutes. Glaze and serve warm.

Glaze:
¾ cup powdered sugar   Pecans
2 Tablespoons milk (enough
   to moisten)

Combine sugar and milk. Glaze tops of rolls and sprinkle with nuts. *Yield:* 12 buns.

Linda Magness
Monticello, Arkansas

CINNAMON ROLLS

1 cup water
1 cup shortening

1 teaspoon salt
1 cup sugar

Melt these ingredients together in a saucepan. Cool to lukewarm.

2 packages yeast
1 cup lukewarm water

2 eggs, beaten
7 cups flour, sifted

Dissolve yeast in lukewarm water. When first mixture has cooled to lukewarm, add eggs and yeast mixture. Add flour and mix well with spoon. Let stand in bowl covered with a wet towel in refrigerator overnight. Remove dough mixture. On floured surface, roll dough out like pizza dough. Melt butter and spread in bottom of baking pans. (Use 4 round cake pans.)

½ cup butter, melted
Brown sugar

Granulated sugar
Cinnamon

Spread butter evenly over dough, followed with brown sugar, granulated sugar, and cinnamon. (I cover the dough mixture with these ingredients until I barely see any dough.) Roll dough mixture evenly into jelly roll style. Slice to ½ inch thickness and place bottom side down in baking pans. Let sit in lukewarm oven to rise, approximately 30 to 45 minutes. Bake at 350 degrees 15 to 20 minutes. *Yield:* 3 to 3½ dozen.

Mrs. John Lowney (Beth)
Hendersonville, Tennessee

CARAMEL PECAN ROLLS

1 package dry yeast
1 cup warm water
¼ cup sugar
1 teaspoon salt

2 Tablespoons margarine,
  softened
1 egg
3¼ to 3½ cups flour

In large bowl, dissolve yeast in warm water (105 to 115 degrees). Stir in sugar, salt, margarine, egg, and 2 cups of flour. Beat until smooth. With spoon or hand, work in enough remaining flour until dough is easy to handle. Place greased side up in greased bowl; cover tightly. Refrigerate overnight or up to 4 or 5 days.

Topping:
⅓ cup margarine, melted
½ cup brown sugar, packed
1 Tablespoon corn syrup
⅔ cup pecan pieces

½ cup sugar
2 teaspoons cinnamon
Melted margarine

Combine margarine, brown sugar, corn syrup, and pecans. Pour into greased 9x13x2 inch pan. Combine sugar and cinnamon. On floured board, roll dough into 15x9 inch oblong. Spread with melted margarine and sprinkle with sugar-cinnamon mixture. Roll up tightly, beginning at wide side. Seal edge well. Cut into 1 inch slices and place in prepared pan. Cover; let rise in warm place until double, about 1½ hours. Heat oven to 375 degrees. Bake 25 to 30 minutes. *Yield:* 15 rolls.

Mrs. Harry Gramann (Marilyn)

GENIE'S CHEESE BISCUITS

½ pound margarine
½ pound (8 ounces) sharp
  Cheddar cheese, shredded
4 dashes red pepper

1 egg
1 long thinly sliced loaf
  commercial bread, (will cut
  easier if frozen first)

Place first 4 ingredients in small bowl and beat with electric mixer until fluffy. Stack bread with 3 slices per stack. Remove crusts. Cut stacks into quarters. Spread cheese mixture generously between slices, then on top and sides very thinly. Bake at 350 degrees for 12 to 15 minutes. Serve warm. *Note:* These freeze beautifully and require no thawing before baking. (To freeze, place biscuits on flat tray, and place uncovered in freezer until firm, then store in plastic bag.) *Yield:* 2½ dozen.

Mrs. Hampton Pitts (Debbie)
Nashville, Tennessee

FRENCH BREAD SUPREME

1 (8 ounce) package Monterey
  Jack cheese, shredded
1 cup mayonnaise
1 (4 ounce) can green chilies,
  chopped and drained

½ cup margarine, softened
Dash garlic
1 package 4 small loaves
  French bread or 1 large loaf
  French bread

Mix cheese with mayonnaise; set aside. Combine chilies with margarine and garlic, add to cheese and mayonnaise mixture. Slice French bread lengthwise. Spread mixture on bread and broil until bubbly and slightly brown. *Note:* Cut small as appetizers or larger to accompany salad or soup. *Yield:* 10 to 20 servings.

Mrs. Dennis Mackin (Susan)

BACON-SWISS FRENCH BREAD

1 cup butter or margarine	2 medium onions, chopped
2 to 3 garlic cloves	2 loaves French bread
1 pound bacon	1 pound Swiss cheese, sliced

Cream butter and insert whole garlic cloves. Refrigerate overnight. Remove cloves. Cook bacon (drain and crumble). In 3 tablespoons bacon grease, sauté chopped onions. Mix onions and bacon into butter. Slice loaves diagonally in 1½ inch slices trying not to slice through bottom of loaf. Spread each slice with butter mixture. Place small slice of cheese in each slit made in bread. Wrap loaves separately in foil and bake at 350 degrees for 1½ hours. *Yield:* 16 to 20 servings.

Mrs. Richard Erickson (Priss)

FRENCH TOAST GRAND MARNIER

8 slices French bread, ¾ to 1 inch thick	¼ teaspoon salt
4 eggs	2 Tablespoons orange cognac brandy
1 cup milk	2 Tablespoons butter
1 Tablespoon sugar	Powdered sugar
½ teaspoon vanilla	

Arrange bread in flat, oblong baking dish. In mixing bowl, beat eggs, milk, sugar, vanilla, salt, and orange cognac brandy. When blended, pour over bread and refrigerate 4 hours or overnight. Fry as French toast in 2 tablespoons butter until golden brown. Sprinkle powdered sugar on top. *Note:* I use Grand Marnier Liqueur.. *Yield:* 4 servings.

Mrs. Cliff Mortensen (Dorothy)
Seattle, Washington

Wyatt Hall

WYATT HALL

Wyatt Hall was built sometime in the early 1800's. It is a classic Georgian style of architecture. Wyatt Hall is owned by Mrs. W. H. Wyatt.

Cheese, Eggs, Rice, and Pasta

CHEESE SOUFFLE

8 slices of white bread,
  buttered
1 pound shredded American
  cheese
6 eggs, beaten

3 cups milk
¾ teaspoon dry mustard
¾ teaspoon salt
¼ teaspoon red pepper

Cut bread into ½ inch cubes. Alternate layers of bread and cheese in buttered baking dish. Mix eggs with milk, mustard, salt, and pepper. Pour over bread and cheese mixture. Let stand overnight in refrigerator or for several hours. Remove 1 hour before baking. Bake 1 hour uncovered at 350 degrees. Serve at once. *Yield:* 6 servings.

Mrs. Hill Paschall (Evelyn)

FARMER'S OMELET

1 (5.5 ounce) package hash
  brown potatoes with onion
3 cups boiling water
3½ Tablespoons butter or
  margarine
½ cup chopped green pepper
½ cup chopped onion

½ teaspoon salt
⅛ teaspoon pepper
6 eggs, slightly beaten
3 Tablespoons sour cream
½ cup shredded Cheddar
  cheese
Dash red pepper sauce

Place potatoes in bowl. Add boiling water and let stand 15 minutes. Drain well. In a heavy skillet, melt butter. Add potatoes and cook until lightly brown. Add green pepper and onion. Continue to cook until onion and pepper are tender. Season with salt and pepper. In a small bowl, combine eggs, sour cream, cheese, and pepper sauce. Mix lightly. Pour egg mixture over hash browns. Reduce heat and continue cooking until eggs are set. Cover with lid or foil to cook top. Garnish with green pepper slices. About 335 calories per serving. *Yield:* 4 servings.

Mrs. H. L. Malone (Lib)
Nashville, Tennessee

CONTINENTAL CHEESE BAKE

1 cup sliced onions
1 Tablespoon margarine,
  melted
8 hard-boiled eggs, sliced
2 cups Swiss cheese,
  shredded
1 (10¾ ounce) can cream of
  mushroom soup

¾ cup milk
1 teaspoon prepared mustard
½ teaspoon seasoned salt
¼ teaspoon dill weed
¼ teaspoon pepper
6 slices caraway rye bread,
  buttered and cut into
  4 triangles each

Cook onions in margarine until tender but not brown. Place in 2 quart dish. Top with egg slices; sprinkle with cheese. Combine soup, milk, mustard, salt, dill weed, and pepper; pour over eggs and cheese. Overlap bread slices on top around edges. Bake at 350 degrees for 30 to 35 minutes. Broil until bread is toasted. Good with Canadian bacon. *Yield:* 6 servings.

Mrs. T. W. Perkinson (Martha)
Brentwood, Tennessee

HOT DEVILED EGGS WITH SOUR CREAM
Great for brunch!

18 eggs, hard-boiled
12 Tablespoons butter, softened
3 teaspoons grated onion
8 teaspoons minced parsley
2½ teaspoons prepared
  mustard
1 teaspoon salt

½ teaspoon pepper
Worcestershire sauce to taste
Mayonnaise
2 cups sour cream
1 cup dry bread crumbs
Parmesan cheese

Cut eggs in half, lengthwise. Remove yolks and mix with 6 tablespoons butter, onion, parsley, mustard, salt, pepper, Worcestershire and enough mayonnaise to bind ingredients. Fill egg whites and place cut side down in a shallow baking dish. Cover with sour cream and sprinkle with crumbs. Dot with remaining butter and sprinkle with Parmesan cheese. Bake at 350 degrees for 25 minutes. *Yield:* 6 servings.

Sarina Sherwin
Irvine, California

RICED EGGS
"Very good for Christmas morning brunch".

15 hard-boiled eggs	½ teaspoon dry mustard
2 Tablespoons Worcestershire sauce	Salt and pepper to taste
2 Tablespoons soy sauce	2 cups thick white sauce

Press hard-boiled eggs through a potato ricer or grater. Add Worcestershire sauce, soy sauce, and dry mustard. Add salt and pepper. Mix well.

White sauce:

4 Tablespoons butter	⅛ teaspoon white pepper
4 Tablespoons flour	1 cup hot milk
½ teaspoon salt	

Melt butter and add flour; blend well. Add salt and pepper. Cook over medium heat for 2 minutes. Pour hot milk slowly in butter and flour mixture. Cook until thick, about 2 minutes. Mix white sauce with egg mixture. Butter a 2 quart casserole well. Pour in egg mixture and bake at 350 degrees for 35 minutes. *Yield:* 10 to 12 servings.

Mrs. Van Spaulding (Alice)

BREAKFAST SOUFFLE

1 pound sausage	3 slices bread cut into ¼ inch cubes
9 eggs, slightly beaten	1½ cups shredded Cheddar cheese
3 cups milk	
1½ teaspoons dry mustard	
1 teaspoon salt	

Brown and crumble sausage. Drain grease. Mix eggs, milk, mustard and salt. Stir in bread cubes, sausage, and cheese. Pour mixture into a greased 13x9x2 inch dish. Refrigerate overnight. Bake uncovered at 350 degrees for 1 hour. *Yield:* 6 servings.

Mrs. Richard Lane (Susan)

BRUNCH EGG CASSEROLE
Bacon, eggs, and "toast" - all in one delicious dish!

2 cups plain croutons
4 ounces shredded natural
　Cheddar cheese
4 slightly beaten eggs
2 cups milk

½ teaspoon salt
½ teaspoon prepared mustard
⅛ teaspoon onion powder
Dash of pepper
4 slices bacon (or more)

In bottom of greased 10x6x1¾ inch baking dish, combine croutons and cheese. Combine eggs, milk, salt, mustard, onion powder, and pepper. Mix until blended. Pour over crouton mixture. Cook bacon until crisp; drain and crumble. Sprinkle over top of mixture. Bake at 325 degrees for 55 to 60 minutes or until eggs are set. Garnish with bacon curls, if desired. Serve with baked apples or pears and/or cheese grits. *Yield:* 6 servings.

Mrs. B. R. Wilkerson (Lu)

SWISS EGG BAKE

2 (10½ ounce) cans cream of
　chicken soup
1 cup milk
4 teaspoons instant minced
　onion
1 teaspoon prepared mustard

2 cups (8 ounces) processed
　Swiss cheese, shredded
12 eggs
12 (½ inch thick) slices French
　bread, buttered and halved
Snipped parsley

Combine soup, milk, onion and mustard. Cook and stir until smooth and heated through. Remove from heat; stir in cheese until melted. Pour 1 cup sauce into each of two 10x6x1½ inch baking dishes. Break 6 eggs into sauce, gently, in each casserole. Carefully spoon remaining sauce around eggs. Stand French bread slices around edges of casserole with crusts up. Bake in 350 degree oven for 20 minutes until eggs are set. *Yield:* 12 servings. *Note:* Can be prepared ahead of time except for baking and kept in refrigerator.

Mrs. Jerry Holcomb (Tinker)

MINIATURE QUICHE

Crust:

½ cup margarine, softened
4 ounces cream cheese,
  softened

1 cup flour

Blend all 3 ingredients well. Refrigerate for 4 hours. Form into 36 balls. Press each ball into a miniature muffin pan cup and press up to the top.

Filling:

2 eggs, beaten
¼ cup mayonnaise
1 Tablespoon flour
¼ cup milk

¼ pound Swiss cheese,
  shredded
½ pound bacon, fried crisp
  and crumbled

Mix eggs, mayonnaise, flour, and milk. Add cheese and bacon. Fill cups ⅔ full. Place the muffin pan on a cookie sheet and bake at 350 degrees for 10 to 15 minutes until they bubble. Can be served immediately or frozen and reheated at 350 degrees until warm. *Yield:* 36 quiches.

Mrs. Paul F. Hayes, Jr. (Dee)
Nashville, Tennessee

QUICHE MICHELE

1 cup fresh mushrooms,
  sliced
½ cup diced ham
2 Tablespoons butter
2 beaten eggs
1 cup whipping cream
½ cup (2 ounces) shredded
  Cheddar cheese

¼ teaspoon ground nutmeg
½ teaspoon salt
Dash pepper
1 (9 inch) baked quiche or
  pie shell

Cook mushrooms and ham in butter until mushrooms are tender (about 5 minutes). Set aside. Combine eggs, cream, cheese, nutmeg, salt, and pepper. Place ham and mushroom mixture in bottom of baked shell. Pour egg mixture on top. Bake at 350 degrees for 25 minutes. Let stand 10 minutes before serving. *Yield:* 6 servings.

Mrs. Joe Brent (Catherine)

QUICHE LORRAINE

1 Tablespoon butter
½ cup ham, chopped
2 frozen pie shells
1 cup Swiss cheese, shredded
2 small white onions, finely chopped

4 eggs
2 cups cream
¼ teaspoon nutmeg
½ teaspoon salt
½ teaspoon red pepper
½ teaspoon white pepper

Sauté onions in butter until transparent. Place ham on bottom of pie shells. Sprinkle cheese and onion over ham. Beat eggs, cream, and seasonings and pour over onion-cheese mixture. Bake at 350 degrees for 25 minutes. These may be frozen at this point, if desired. If frozen bake on lower oven shelf at 450 degrees for 15 minutes. Reduce heat to 350 degrees and bake for 45 minutes on upper shelf until custard is set. *Note:* Bacon can be substituted for ham and sautéed mushrooms can be added. *Yield:* 16 servings.

Mrs. Sandra Chesney
Knoxville, Tennessee

EAST OF THE RIVER QUICHE

6 to 8 slices bacon
1 small onion, diced
½ pound Gruyere cheese
½ pound Swiss cheese
5 or 6 eggs
1¼ cups half and half
¼ cup grated Parmesan cheese

¼ teaspoon nutmeg
Dash of salt
Dash of pepper
¼ cup parsley flakes
1 (9 inch) pie crust

Fry bacon, sauté onion in 1 tablespoon bacon drippings. Dice cheese into small cubes. Beat eggs and add half and half, Parmesan, nutmeg, salt, pepper, and parsley. Crumble bacon into bottom of pie shell. Add onion. Pour milk and egg mixture over all. Bake at 450 degrees for 15 to 20 minutes. Reduce heat to 350 degrees and bake 30 to 45 minutes longer. Sprinkle with Parmesan 15 minutes before done. *Yield:* 6 servings.

Mrs. Robert T. Embry (Bettye)

IMPOSSIBLE HAM PIE

2 cups cooked smoked ham, chopped
1 (4½ ounce) jar sliced mushrooms, drained
½ cup sliced green onions
½ teaspoon salt

1 cup shredded natural Swiss cheese (may also substitute Cheddar cheese)
1½ cups milk
¾ cup biscuit baking mix
3 eggs

Pre-heat oven to 400 degrees. Lightly grease pie plate, 10½x1½ inches. Sprinkle ham, mushrooms, onions, salt, and cheese into pie plate. Beat remaining ingredients until smooth. Pour into pie plate. Bake until golden brown until knife inserted comes out clean, 30 to 35 minutes. Let stand 5 minutes before cutting. Refrigerate any remaining pie. *Yield:* 6 to 8 servings.

Mrs. Floyd Soeder (Suzanne)

FIESTA MEXICAN RICE

1 cup long grain white rice
2 Tablespoons cooking oil
¾ cup chopped onion
2 cloves garlic
5 or 6 green chilies with seeds removed or 1 (4 ounce) can, chopped

1 whole tomato
2 cups water
¼ cup butter
Salt and white pepper to taste

Sauté rice in cooking oil until golden brown. Remove rice from oil. Add onion to oil and sauté until limp. Add garlic, and then green chilies and sauté a few minutes longer. Chop and add one whole tomato and sauté for 3 minutes longer. Add rice and water. Simmer for 25 to 30 minutes until rice is fluffy; then add butter and season with salt and white pepper. *Yield:* 4 servings.

Mrs. David Gaines (Donna)
Brentwood, Tennessee

CUMIN RICE

1 medium onion, chopped
¼ cup green pepper, diced fine
2 Tablespoons bacon grease
1 cup uncooked rice
1 (13¾ ounce) can chicken
  broth

1 (10½ ounce) can beef
  consommé
1 teaspoon Worcestershire
  sauce
½ teaspoon salt
½ teaspoon powdered cumin

Sauté onion and green pepper in large skillet with bacon grease and rice. Add chicken broth, consommé, Worcestershire, salt and cumin. Cover and cook on low heat for 30 minutes until all the juice is absorbed. *Yield:* 6 servings.

Mrs. David Pittman (Sydney)

DIRTY RICE

1 cup long grain rice, uncooked
½ cup margarine

1 (10¾ ounce) can onion soup
1 (10¾ ounce) can beef broth

Place all ingredients in uncovered baking dish; stir and bake at 350 degrees for 1 hour. *Yield:* 6 to 8 servings.

Mrs. Joel Bonnette (Nancy)
Pekin, Illinois

SOUBISC

½ cup rice
4 quarts boiling water
1½ Tablespoons salt
4 Tablespoons butter
6 to 7 cups thinly sliced
  yellow onions

½ teaspoon salt
½ teaspoon pepper
¼ cup shredded Swiss cheese
2 Tablespoons butter
1 Tablespoon parsley, chopped
¼ cup cream

Preheat oven to 300 degrees. Cook rice in boiling water with 1½ tablespoons salt for 5 minutes and drain. Melt 4 tablespoons butter in a 3 quart casserole dish. Add onions and stir well to coat. Cover and bake 15 minutes. Add rice, ½ teaspoon salt, and pepper. Cook covered for 1 hour. Remove and add Swiss cheese, 2 tablespoons butter, parsley and cream before serving. *Yield:* 6 servings.

Mrs. Robert Oldham (Cathie)

RICE CASSEROLE

½ cup margarine
1 cup chopped onions
1 (4 ounce) can drained
  mushrooms
1 cup uncooked rice
2 (10¾ ounce) cans beef
  consommé

1 soup can of water
Salt
Pepper
Garlic powder

In skillet, brown onions and mushrooms in margarine. Add rice and brown, stirring constantly. Pour into buttered 2 quart casserole. Add consommé and water. Season to taste with salt, pepper, and garlic powder. Bake covered at 350 degrees for 60 to 90 minutes. (When done, rice will be cooked and most all liquid will be gone). *Yield:* 6 to 8 servings.

Mrs. Robert Frazier (Jeanette)
Sikeston, Missouri

MACARONI ITALIANO

3 Tablespoons margarine
3 Tablespoons flour
1½ teaspoons sugar
1 envelope spaghetti sauce mix
1 medium onion, grated
2 Tablespoons chopped
  parsley

3 cups tomato juice
1 (8 ounce) package elbow
  macaroni, cooked and
  drained
1 (8 ounce) mozzarella cheese,
  sliced

Melt margarine in saucepan, remove from heat. Blend in flour, sugar, spaghetti sauce mix, onion, and parsley. Add slowly and stir in tomato juice. Cook, stirring constantly, until mixture thickens and boils 1 minute. Layer half of the cooked and drained macaroni into a buttered shallow 2 quart baking dish; pour half the tomato sauce over; top with half the cheese slices. Repeat to make another layer of each ending with cheese slices on top. Bake at 350 degrees for 40 minutes or until cheese is melted and sauce is bubbly. *Yield:* 6 servings.

Mrs. Harry Gramann (Marilyn)

MACARONI & CHEESE DELIGHT

¼ cup chopped onion
1 cup stuffed olives, sliced
4 eggs, slightly beaten
1½ cups cream
1 Tablespoon seasoned salt
½ teaspoon black pepper
4 cups cooked and drained
   macaroni

1 cup grated Parmesan cheese
3 cups American cheese,
   shredded
2 Tablespoons butter or
   margarine

Grease bundt pan with butter and sprinkle with flour. Combine onions, olives, eggs, cream, salt, and pepper. Add macaroni and cheese. Pour into bundt pan and bake at 350 degrees for 30 to 45 minutes. *Yield:* 12 servings.

Mrs. Spaulding Bell (Bertha)

GREEN CHILI PASTA

6 slices bacon, diced
8 ounces vermicelli or thin
   spaghetti
1 large onion, chopped
1 (14 ounce) can regular
   strength beef broth
1 (16 ounce) can Italian-style
   tomatoes

1 (4 ounce) can green chilies,
   seeded and chopped
2 Tablespoons red wine
   vinegar
Salt and pepper to taste
Freshly grated Parmesan
   cheese

In a Dutch oven, cook bacon over medium heat until crisp; with a slotted spoon remove bacon; set aside. Discard all but ¼ cup of the drippings. Break vermicelli into about 2 inch pieces (you should have about 2 cups); stir into the pan drippings. Add onion and sauté over medium heat, stirring until golden brown. Add broth, tomatoes (breaking them up with a spoon), chilies, and vinegar; stir well. Cover and simmer until vermicelli is tender and most of the liquid is absorbed (about 15 minutes). Season with salt and pepper. Turn into a serving dish; top with bacon. Pass cheese in a separate bowl. *Note:* Decrease the amount of chilies in this dish if you prefer a milder flavor. *Yield:* 6 servings.

Mrs. Gordon C. Anderson (Joy)

SPAGHETTI RING
A very colorful dish

1½ cups cooked spaghetti
1 cup shredded Cheddar
  cheese
1 (2 ounce) jar pimento
3 Tablespoons minced parsley
1 onion, minced

Salt and pepper to taste
1 cup crumbled white bread
1 egg, beaten
1 cup milk
3 Tablespoons butter

Preheat oven to 350 degrees. Mix spaghetti and cheese. Add pimento, parsley, onion, salt and pepper. Mix well. Add bread and egg. Heat milk until hot; add butter to melt. Pour into spaghetti mixture and mix well. Pour into a well greased ring mold. Set ring in a pan of water and bake at 350 degrees for 40 minutes. Invert spaghetti ring and fill center with peas, mushrooms or water chestnuts. *Yield:* 12 to 14 servings.

Mrs. Van Spaulding (Alice)

OLD FASHION EGG NOODLES IN CHICKEN BROTH

1 egg
Flour

Chicken broth

Break egg into a bowl. Fill each ½ egg shell with water and empty into bowl with egg. Beat until smooth. Mix enough flour to make a stiff dough. Roll out very thin on floured board. Cut into narrow strips and drop one at a time into boiling broth. Cook about 15 to 20 minutes or until done. *Yield:* 4 servings.

Mrs. B. H. Burt (Little Mama)

LASAGNA

6 strips lasagna noodles
6 quarts boiling water
Salt
Parsley sprigs
3 Tablespoons chopped onion
1 Tablespoon cooking oil
12 ounces cottage cheese
2 eggs, slightly beaten
2 Tablespoons chopped
parsley
5 Tablespoons Parmesan
cheese

Salt and pepper to taste
1 pound ground beef
½ green pepper, chopped
1 onion, chopped
1 (16 ounce) can tomatoes
2 (6 ounce) cans tomato paste
½ teaspoon garlic powder
1 Tablespoon oregano
1 teaspoon salt
1 teaspoon pepper
1 pound mozzarella
cheese, shredded

Place noodles in boiling water with salt, parsley sprigs, 3 table-spoons chopped onion, and cooking oil. Cook 15 minutes at full boil. Add cold water until noodles can be handled. Do not drain until ready to assemble. Place cottage cheese in bowl and add eggs, parsley, 1 tablespoon Parmesan cheese, salt and pepper to taste. Mix well and set aside. Brown meat, green pepper, and onion; add tomatoes, tomato paste, garlic powder, oregano, 1 teaspoon salt, and 1 teaspoon pepper, mixing well. Grease a 2 quart rectangular baking dish. Drain noodles. Lightly cover bottom of dish with meat sauce. Add a layer of noodles and cover with meat sauce. Dab several tablespoons of cottage cheese mixture over sauce, cover with a generous amount of mozzarella and sprinkle with Parmesan cheese. Repeat layers ending with mozzarella and Parmesan. Bake at 350 degrees for 45 minutes. *Yield:* 6 to 8 servings.

Mrs. C. D. Berry, IV (Kathy)

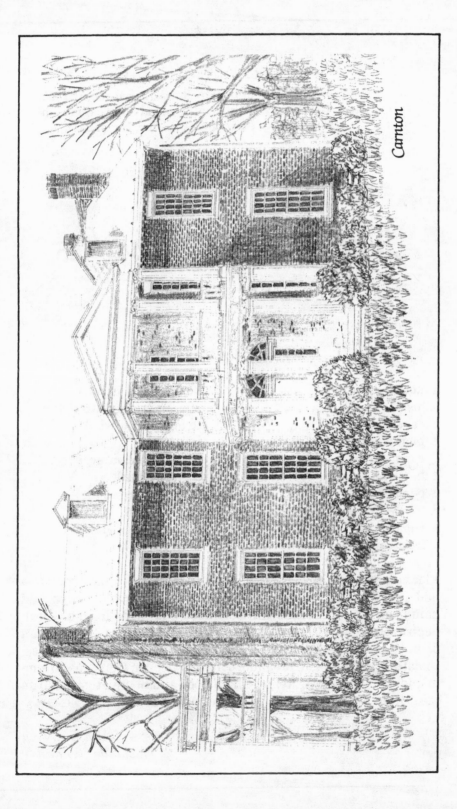

Carnton

CARNTON

This historical mansion was built by Randal McGavock in 1825. It is a Greek Revival style with some Federal and Georgian influences. It is owned by the Carnton Association, Inc. and is under restoration.

Soups and Sandwiches

NAVY BEAN SOUP

1 pound (2 cups) dry, navy
  beans
6 cups water
1 pound ham hocks
2 cups water
1 bay leaf
4 peppercorns
3 whole cloves
1 cup coarsely-chopped
  fresh spinach

½ cup chopped onion
½ cup mashed potato flakes
1 (28 ounce) can whole
  tomatoes
2 cloves garlic, minced
1 teaspoon basil
1 teaspoon oregano
1 teaspoon salt
½ teaspoon pepper

Place navy beans in a large soup pot with 6 cups water. Bring to a boil. Boil 2 minutes; remove from heat. Allow to stand 1 hour. Add ham hocks, 2 cups water, and bouquet garni made from bay leaf, peppercorns, and cloves. Simmer over medium heat 1 to 1½ hours or until beans are tender. Stir in spinach, onion, potato flakes, tomatoes, garlic, basil, oregano, salt, and pepper. Continue to simmer 20 to 30 minutes. Remove ham hock and bouquet garni. Trim meat from ham hocks, dice, and return to soup. *Yield:* 3½ quarts.

Ann E. Lynch
Nashville, Tennessee

GAZPACHO

1 cucumber
2 fresh tomatoes
1 large onion
2 bell peppers
5 stalks celery
1 teaspoon garlic salt
3 Tablespoons salad oil

3 Tablespoons vinegar, white
   apple cider
1 Tablespoon chili powder
1 Tablespoon Worcestershire
   sauce
1 (12 ounce) can tomato juice
1 (46 ounce) can vegetable juice

Grate vegetables removing all skins or peels by grating with peel side up on fine side of grater. Combine and add spices, oil, vinegar, and Worcestershire sauce to grated vegetables. Add vegetable juice and tomato juice. Stir well and chill covered for at least 2 hours before serving. Can be made the day before. For aspic: Omit oil and add 2 packages softened gelatin and shrimp (if desired). *Note:* I use V-8 juice for the vegetable juice. *Yield:* 12 servings.

Mrs. David Porter (Fay)

COLD TOMATO SOUP

2 (10¾ ounce) cans tomato
   soup
1 quart heavy cream

1 cucumber, peeled and grated
1 small onion, grated
Dash of Worcestershire sauce

Add cream to undiluted soup; add cucumber, onion, and Worcestershire sauce. Mix well with mixer or blender. Chill several hours before serving.

½ cup sour cream

2 teaspoons chives

To serve, top with teaspoon of sour cream and sprinkle with chives. *Yield:* 6 servings.

Mrs. Hampton Pitts (Debbie)
Nashville, Tennessee

CREAM OF CHEESE SOUP

2 teaspoons instant chicken bouillon
2 teaspoons instant vegetable flavor bouillon
2 cups boiling water
¼ cup grated carrot
½ cup finely chopped celery
2 Tablespoons minced onion
3 Tablespoons melted butter
4½ Tablespoons flour
⅛ teaspoon pepper
1 teaspoon salt
1 cup water
1 cup evaporated milk
2 cups shredded Cheddar cheese
Chopped parsley, optional

Dissolve instant bouillon in 2 cups boiling water. Add carrots and celery. Cover and simmer 8 minutes. Sauté onion in butter until tender; add flour, salt, pepper, blending until smooth. Add 1 cup water and 1 cup milk to onion mixture. Cook, stirring constantly, until smooth and thickened. Stir in bouillon mixture. Add cheese, stirring until melted. Spoon into bowls. Garnish with parsley, if desired. *Yield:* 6 servings.

Mrs. William F. Greenwood, Jr. (Sandra)

PRISON SOUP

Named by my friends' children because it was served so often they felt it must be prison fare.

1 pound ground beef
1 pound sliced Polish sausage
1 (2 ounce) envelope onion soup mix
1 (16 ounce) can tomatoes
6 cups water
¼ teaspoon oregano
½ teaspoon seasoned salt
¼ teaspoon basil
1 Tablespoon soy sauce
1 cup chopped celery
⅓ cup split beans
1 cup uncooked macaroni
Parmesan cheese

Brown beef and sausage and drain. Add remaining ingredients, except macaroni, and cook slowly 3 hours. (If using a slow cooker, 8 to 10 hours on low or 4 to 5 hours on high.) Add macaroni 20 minutes before serving (1 hour before serving if using a slow cooker). Sprinkle each serving with Parmesan cheese. *Yield:* 6 to 8 servings.

Betty Washington

SHRIMP SOUP

1 ham bone with ham
1 onion, chopped
¼ head cabbage, chopped
½ cup celery, chopped
1 (20 ounce) bag frozen soup
    vegetables
¼ cup barley

1 (16 ounce) can tomatoes
3 potatoes, diced
16 to 20 ounces frozen shrimp,
    peeled and deveined
1 teaspoon seafood seasoning
Salt and pepper to taste

In a Dutch oven cook ham bone, onion, cabbage, and celery in 4 cups water until tender. Add mixed vegetables and tomatoes and bring to a boil. Add barley and lower the temperature to a simmer. Season with seafood seasonings, salt, and pepper. Simmer 1 hour. Add potatoes; when cooked, add shrimp. If soup is to be frozen omit potatoes and increase barley. *Note:* I use Old Bay Seafood Seasoning. You may substitute seafood seasoning with ⅛ teaspoon each: celery salt, dry mustard, ground cloves, laurel leaves, cardamon, ginger, and paprika. Add any dabs of vegetables you may have in the refrigerator. *Yield:* 6 servings.

Mrs. Richard K. Hill (Blanche)

HEARTY VEGETABLE SOUP

1 (16 ounce) package mixed
    vegetables or gumbo mix
    (If using only vegetables,
    add 1 (10 ounce) package
    frozen okra)
1 (6 ounce) can tomato paste
3 medium potatoes, diced
½ cup regular white rice
4 ounces spaghetti, broken
    into small pieces

Worcestershire sauce, as
    desired
Salt and pepper, as desired
3 beef bouillon cubes
Meat cut into small chunks,
    optional
Cabbage, optional

Put all ingredients into a 5 quart pot and fill with water. Simmer for 2 hours after bringing to a boil. Stir frequently. *Yield:* 1 gallon.

Mrs. Pat Hagerty (Sharon)

EGG NOODLE BROCCOLI CHEESE SOUP

2 Tablespoons margarine	2 packages frozen chopped
¾ cup chopped onion	broccoli
6 cups water	⅛ teaspoon garlic powder
6 chicken bouillon cubes	6 cups milk
8 ounces very fine noodles	1 pound American cheese,
(about 4 cups)	shredded
1 teaspoon salt	¼ teaspoon pepper

In large saucepan heat margarine, add onion and sauté over medium heat 3 minutes. Add water and bouillon cubes. Heat to boiling, stirring occasionally, until cubes are dissolved. Gradually add noodles and salt so that mixture continues to boil. Cook 3 minutes, stirring occasionally. Stir in broccoli and garlic powder and cook 4 minutes. Add milk, cheese, and pepper. Do not let boil or milk will curdle, but continue cooking, stirring constantly, until cheese melts. To freeze, cool quickly and pack into containers. Freeze up to 1 month. To reheat, place in top of double boiler, stirring occasionally, over boiling water. One frozen quart will thaw and heat in about 30 minutes. This recipe can be halved.

Note: The small noodles are usually found in Kosher Department of super markets, or a delicatessen. *Yield:* 4 quarts or 12 servings.

Mrs. Syd Oliver, Sr. (Thelma)

GERMAN POTATO SOUP

4 leeks	5 pounds potatoes, cubed
1½ to 2 pounds salt pork or	2 Tablespoons chopped chives
country bacon	Maggi to taste
1 cup celery	1 large onion, chopped
White pepper to taste	2 Tablespoons margarine
Salt to taste	

Sauté onion in margarine. Cook salt pork, leek, and celery in 2 quarts of water until meat is half done. Add potatoes and onion. Cook until potatoes are done. Add maggi, salt, and pepper. Sprinkle with chives. Do Not Overcook. *Note:* Maggi may be purchased at specialty food stores.

Mrs. Fred Wurster (Elli)

SWEET AND SOUR CABBAGE SOUP

2 pounds cubed stew beef
2 small white onions, quartered
2 (16 ounce) cans tomato wedges
2 (16 ounce) cans water
1 large head cabbage, cut into strips
1 package onion soup mix
1 teaspoon salt
½ teaspoon black pepper
Juice of one lemon or 2 Tablespoons reconstituted lemon juice
2 Tablespoons white sugar
2 Tablespoons brown sugar

In a large Dutch oven, brown cubed stew beef, add quartered white onions, and cook until transparent; add tomato wedges and water (more water may be necessary, it is a personal preference). Bring to a boil for 5 minutes and lower heat to lowest point. Add cabbage strips slowly. At first only ½ will fit in Dutch oven, but after 5 minutes of simmering, cabbage will cook down. Add onion soup mix, salt, black pepper, lemon juice, white sugar, and brown sugar. Cook on low heat for 2 hours. Freezes very well. *Yield:* 6 servings.

Mrs. James Ramey (Betty)

SWISS ONION SOUP

2 pounds onion, sliced
½ cup butter or margarine
½ teaspoon paprika
¾ cup flour
½ cup vegetable oil
¾ teaspoon celery salt
6 cups beef stock (homemade, canned stock, or bouillon)
Salt and pepper to taste
8 ounces dark beer
French bread or croutons
Cheese slices, swiss or mozzarella

Sauté onions in butter until limp, not brown. Add paprika. Make roux by mixing flour with vegetable oil; brown until light brown. Add roux, celery salt, stock, salt, and pepper to onions, stir to boiling. Simmer 2 hours. Before serving add beer, bringing to serving temperature and place in bowls. Top with slice of French bread or croutons. Put cheese slice over bread and broil until bubbly. *Yield:* 10 servings.

Chris Wendzicki
Brentwood, Tennessee

ONION SOUP

6 large yellow onions,
  thinly sliced
2 Tablespoons butter
1 Tablespoon olive oil
6 cups beef stock
½ cup red port wine
½ cup diced Gruyere cheese
6 slices buttered dry-toasted
  French bread

1 cup mixed shredded Gruyere
  and Parmesan cheese
1 Tablespoon melted butter
6 slices of Monterey Jack or
  mozzarella cheese
Salt and pepper to taste

Use a heavy 3 quart covered pan with a heavy bottom. Sauté onions in butter and olive oil until limp. Cover and let simmer slowly for 15 minutes. Pour in beef stock and simmer for 30 minutes. Pour soup and port wine into an ovenproof, earthenware casserole, cover and heat in a 350 degree oven for 30 minutes. Remove from oven and sprinkle with diced Gruyere cheese. Cover with an even layer of toasted French bread and sprinkle with shredded cheeses. Dribble melted butter over it. Put back in 425 degree oven for 10 minutes and cover casserole with pieces of cheese. Turn on broiler and heat until the cheese browns lightly on top, forming a crusty layer. Serve at once. Instead of a large casserole, individual crocks can be used. *Yield:* 6 servings.

Mrs. Donald Hillenmeyer (Chris)

FRENCH ONION SOUP

¼ cup butter or margarine
1½ pounds onions, thinly sliced
½ teaspoon salt
¼ teaspoon sugar
7 cups beef broth (canned or beef bouillon)
½ cup dry white wine

8 slices French bread, toasted
½ cup grated Parmesan cheese
½ pound Swiss or mozzarella cheese

In Dutch oven melt butter and add onions. Sauté over low heat until onions are coated. Cover and continue cooking 15 minutes until onions are limp. Uncover, sprinkle with salt and sugar, and cook until onions are golden. Pour in beef broth and wine. Cover and simmer 20 minutes until onions are tender. (Can be refrigerated for two days or frozen if desired.) Preheat oven to 375 degrees. Put soup into oven proof bowls. To each add 1 slice of bread, then sprinkle with Parmesan cheese and top with Swiss or mozzarella cheese and bake 10 minutes. *Yield: 8.*

Mrs. William Milton (Lucy)

TOMATO AND MUSHROOM SANDWICHES

Topping:

1 cup mayonnaise
½ teaspoon lemon peel
1 Tablespoon lemon juice

1 Tablespoon chives
½ cup Parmesan cheese, grated

Combine all and blend well.

Butter
Thick sliced bread (not
sandwich thin slice)
Tomato slices

2 cups mushrooms, thinly
sliced

Spread butter on both sides of bread and toast. Overlap 4 tomato slices on each slice of bread. Divide ⅓ cup of mushrooms on each slice (rows of mushrooms overlapped). Spoon topping on mushrooms and broil. *Yield:* 6 servings.

Mrs. William Elston (Margie)
Philadelphia, Pennsylvania

QUICK CORNED BEEF BARBECUE SANDWICH

1 (12 ounce) can corned beef
1 Tablespoon shortening
1 medium onion

1 cup tomato catsup
3 Tablespoons vinegar
2 teaspoons chili powder

Heat shortening in skillet and add corned beef, crumbled. Put onion, catsup, vinegar, and chili powder in blender and blend until smooth. Pour over crumbled corned beef. Simmer on low heat for 6 to 10 minutes. Spoon over buns. *Yield:* 6 servings.

Mrs. Jeff Compton (Patricia)

CRUNCHY HAM SANDWICHES

8 slices white bread
Butter or margarine, softened
Prepared mustard
4 slices baked ham
4 slices American cheese

1 tomato, thinly sliced
2 slightly beaten eggs
2 Tablespoons milk
Dash of onion salt
1¼ cups crushed potato chips

Spread 4 slices of bread with butter on one side. Spread remaining 4 slices of bread with mustard. Top each mustard slice of bread with ham, cheese, tomato, and second slice of bread with buttered side down. Combine eggs, milk, and salt. Dip sandwich in egg mixture and crushed chips. Brown in medium high skillet (lightly greased) about 8 minutes. *Yield:* 4 sandwiches.

Mrs. Joel Bonnette (Nancy)

CUCUMBER SHRIMP SANDWICHES

2 cups minced, cooked shrimp
1 cup chopped cucumbers
1 Tablespoon minced onion
3 Tablespoons French dressing

Salt and cayenne pepper to taste
Mayonnaise to bind

Mix all ingredients and spread on whole wheat bread. *Yield:* 6 servings.

Sara Ann Crockett

PIMENTO CHEESE SPREAD
An old family recipe

1 pound American cheese,
  shredded
1 (13 ounce) can evaporated
  milk
1 (4 ounce) jar chopped
  pimento

1 egg, well beaten
¼ teaspoon salt (optional)
¼ teaspoon paprika

Add cheese to milk and heat in a double boiler. When cheese is melted, add pimento and egg. Cook 10 to 15 minutes and season with salt and paprika. The mixture will be very thin. Pour into jars. When cool it will be creamy and spread easily. You may use canning jars and seal for longer storage. Store in refrigerator. *Yield:* 3½ cups.

Mrs. Joseph L. Willoughby (Betty)

SPRINGTIME SANDWICHES

1 (8 ounce) package cream
  cheese
½ cup sour cream

2 cups watercress, chopped
¼ cup chives, chopped
Salt and white pepper to taste

Soften cheese; whip until fluffy. Add sour cream and remaining ingredients. Blend well and serve on whole wheat or rye bread. *Yield:* 6.

Sara Ann Crockett

MELTED CHEESE OLIVE SANDWICHES

2 cups shredded sharp cheese
1 can chopped ripe olives

½ cup mayonnaise
Grated or dried onions to taste

Mix all ingredients together. Spread on ½ English muffin. Bake at 350 degrees for 15 minutes or until melted. Freezes well before baking. *Yield:* 6.

Mrs. T. W. Perkinson (Martha)
Brentwood, Tennessee

Carter House

Salads, Salad Dressings, and Sauces

SEVEN LAYER SALAD

½ head iceburg lettuce, shredded or torn
1 cup finely chopped celery
1 medium red onion, cut into rings
1 cup Cheddar cheese, shredded (Parmesan cheese may be substituted)

½ (3¼ ounce) jar bacon bits
1 (10 ounce) package frozen English peas, cooked
3 hard-boiled eggs, finely chopped
1½ cups mayonnaise, not salad dressing

In large (2 quart) glass bowl, layer lettuce, celery, and onion. Salt to taste. Continue layering salad, with Cheddar cheese, bacon bits and peas. Salt to taste. Use chopped eggs for next layer and seal top of salad with mayonnaise. Cover with plastic wrap and refrigerate for several hours before serving. Stays fresh 2 to 3 days when prepared and sealed in an air-tight container. *Yield:* 6 servings.

Mrs. David S. Myers (Carla)

"OUT OF THIS WORLD" SALAD

1 head iceburg lettuce
1 to 2 packets Melba toast

¼ cup Romano cheese, grated
2 tomatoes, coarsely chopped

Tear lettuce into small pieces; break Melba toast into small pieces and sprinkle over lettuce. Sprinkle cheese over lettuce and add tomatoes.

Dressing:
1 cup mayonnaise
1 teaspoon steak sauce
1 teaspoon Worcestershire sauce

Dash hot pepper sauce
⅛ teaspoon black pepper
¼ teaspoon garlic salt

Combine ingredients and spread over lettuce, toss and serve. *Yield:* 4 to 6.

Mrs. Hugh O'Donnell, (Susie)

STUFFED LETTUCE

1 medium sized head iceburg
lettuce, cored

Stuffing:
1 (8 ounce) package cream
cheese, at room temperature
1 Tablespoon mayonnaise
1 teaspoon finely grated
yellow onion
¼ cup minced sweet red
or green pepper

¼ cup peeled, minced,
and drained tomato
Few drops liquid hot pepper
sauce
¼ teaspoon salt

Mix stuffing ingredients and pack firmly into hollow. Wrap lettuce
in foil or plastic wrap. Chill well. Slice crosswise about ¾ inch thick
and serve with French or Thousand Island dressing. *Note:* About
160 calories per serving. *Yield:* 6 servings.

Mrs. Mark Levy (Cheryl)

ASPARAGUS CONGEALED SALAD

2½ cups asparagus spears
2 envelopes unflavored gelatin
½ cup cold water
½ teaspoon salt
½ cup sugar
½ cup vinegar

1 Tablespoon lemon juice
½ cup water chestnuts, sliced
1 (4 ounce) jar pimentos,
chopped
½ cup pecans, chopped
¼ cup spring onions, sliced

Drain asparagus. Reserve liquid and add enough water to make 1
cup; bring to a boil. Soften gelatin in cold water, add to hot liquid,
stir until dissolved. Add salt, sugar, vinegar, and lemon juice; stir
until dissolved. Chill until thickened. Fold remaining ingredients into thickened mixture. Arrange asparagus in a 9 inch square mold
and pour gelatin mixture over asparagus. Chill until firm. *Yield:* 10
to 12.

Louise Long
Nashville, Tennessee

SPINACH SALAD

1 (10 to 16 ounce) package
fresh spinach, chopped,
stemmed, and washed
1 (8 ounce) can water
chestnuts, drained and
sliced
2 hard-boiled eggs, sliced

5 to 6 strips fried bacon,
crumbled
1 (14 ounce) can bean sprouts,
drained or the equivalent of
fresh sprouts, washed and
drained
3 to 4 green onions, chopped

Mix the spinach, water chestnuts, eggs, bacon, bean sprouts, and onions well in a large salad bowl. Chill until serving time..

Dressing:
¾ cup sugar
1 cup salad oil
⅓ cup catsup

¼ cup apple cider vinegar
3 Tablespoons Worcestershire
sauce

Mix dressing ingredients well and refrigerate until serving time. Should be very cold. Pour over salad just before serving. If all salad is not being eaten, pour dressing on individual salads and save remaining salad. *Yield:* 6 servings.

Mrs. Phil Ryan (Gail)
Waco, Texas

RAW VEGETABLE SALAD

1 bunch broccoli
1 head cauliflower
1 (16 ounce) package frozen
green peas

1 cup sour cream
1 package buttermilk salad
dressing mix
1 cup mayonnaise

Break broccoli and cauliflower into bite size pieces. Add thawed peas. Mix sour cream, dressing mix, and mayonnaise. Pour over vegetables and refrigerate. *Note:* I use Hidden Valley Ranch salad dressing mix.

Mrs. Tom Neal (Betty)
Arrington, Tennessee

CRISPY KRAUT SALAD

1 (16 ounce) can chopped
  sauerkraut
½ cup chopped onion
½ cup chopped celery

¼ cup chopped green pepper
½ cup cider vinegar
¼ cup salad oil
½ cup sugar

Drain kraut well. Mix vinegar, oil, and sugar. Blend all ingredients together and marinate for 1 hour or longer. *Yield:* 6 servings.

Mrs. Cecil Crowson, Sr. (Evelyn)

WILZ' WALDORF COLE SLAW

3 cups red cabbage
3 cups green cabbage
2 cups chopped red and
  golden apples, unpeeled,
  cored

½ cup raisins
¼ cup dry roasted peanuts
1 cup salad dressing or
  more to moisten

Combine and toss lightly. *Yield:* 8 to 10 servings.

Mrs. Thomas Wilz (Paty)
Dayton, Ohio

SOUTH PACIFIC SALAD

3 cups fresh or canned
  pineapple chunks, sweetened
½ cup celery, chopped
2 cups cold cooked rice
½ cup raisins

¼ cup sour cream
¼ cup salad dressing
½ teaspoon salt
½ teaspoon ginger

Combine pineapple, celery, rice, and raisins, toss lightly. Stir remaining ingredients together. Pour over rice mixture and toss. Cover and chill. Serve in a bowl lined with crisp salad greens. *Yield:* 6 servings.

Mrs. Gentry Akers (Louella)

GEORGE McCANDLESS' POTATO SALAD

1 pound boiled potatoes
1 small onion, chopped
¼ cup vinegar
1 (2 ounce) can cut pimentos

¾ cup mayonnaise
2 hard-cooked eggs, shredded
Salt and pepper to taste

Peel and cut potatoes before boiling. Cover onion in a small bowl with salt and water and let set until onion juice is extracted. Wash onions, drain, and add to chopped potatoes. Add vinegar while potatoes are hot. Add remaining ingredients and mix thoroughly. Season with salt and pepper. Serve cold. *Yield:* 6 servings.

Mrs. Robert H. Hutcheson, Sr. (Elisabeth)

STUFFED PEAR SALAD

Filling:
18 gingersnaps, crushed
½ cup drained, crushed
  pineapple
1 (8 ounce) package cream
  cheese

2 Tablespoons mayonnaise
1 (2 pound) can sliced pears

Mix together gingersnaps, pineapple, cheese, and mayonnaise. Stuff half of a pear and top with another half. Chill.

Sauce:
½ cup sugar
3 Tablespoons lemon juice
½ cup orange juice
1 egg, well beaten

¼ teaspoon salt
½ cup whipping cream,
  whipped

Mix sugar, lemon juice, orange juice, egg, and salt in top of double boiler. Cook over hot water until thickened, stirring constantly. When cool, mix in whipped cream. Pour over stuffed pears arranged on lettuce leaves. The sauce will hold up several days. *Yield:* 6 to 8.

Mrs. Mickey Curry (Thea)
Petal, Mississippi

FRESH FRUIT SALAD

½ watermelon
1 cantaloupe
1 honeydew melon

1 pint fresh strawberries
1 pint fresh blueberries
Seedless grapes

Make balls out of melons and toss with remaining fruit. This may be served in shelled out watermelon half. *Yield:* 2 gallons.

Fresh Fruit Salad Dressing:
1 teaspoon poppy seeds
½ cup salad oil
¼ cup fruit juice
1 teaspoon grated lemon rind

2½ Tablespoons light corn
   syrup
1 teaspoon salt

Mix all ingredients and pour over fruit before serving. *Yield:* ¾ cup.

Mrs. Mike Bond (Carol)

MANDARIN ORANGE AND ONION SALAD
WITH POPPY SEED DRESSING

Salad:
1 small head of lettuce, rinsed,
   drained, and chilled
1 small red onion

1 (11 ounce) can mandarin
   oranges, drained

Tear lettuce into bite sized pieces. Peel and slice onion into very thin rings. Combine lettuce, onion, and oranges. Toss with dressing in salad bowl.

Dressing:
2 Tablespoons wine vinegar
1 teaspoon Dijon mustard
½ teaspoon salt
⅛ teaspoon red pepper

1 Tablespoon honey
6 Tablespoons oil
1½ teaspoons poppy seeds

Combine ingredients in a jar and shake well. *Yield:* 6 servings.

Mrs. W. Collins Bond (Suzanne)
Milan, Tennessee

FROZEN CRANBERRY SALAD

1 (8 ounce) package of cream
  cheese, softened
½ cup mayonnaise
1 (14 ounce) jar cranberry-
  orange relish
1 (20 ounce) can crushed
  pineapple, drained

½ cup chopped pecans
½ cup powdered sugar
1 cup whipping cream,
  whipped

Blend cream cheese with mayonnaise. Set aside. Combine relish with pineapple and nuts. Mix pineapple mixture with cream cheese mixture. Fold powdered sugar into whipping cream. Mix all ingredients together. Line muffin tins with paper baking cups. Fill cups and freeze. When frozen well, remove from tins and store in plastic bags in freezer. To serve, remove paper cups and place on lettuce leaves. *Yield:* 16 to 18 servings.

Mrs. Van Spaulding (Alice)

CINNAMON APPLESAUCE SALAD

2 (3 ounce) packages lemon
  flavored gelatin
½ cup red cinnamon candies
2 cups boiling water
2 cups unsweetened
  applesauce
1 Tablespoon lemon juice

Dash salt
½ cup walnuts, broken
2 (3 ounce) packages cream
  cheese, softened
½ cup milk or light cream
2 Tablespoons salad dressing

Dissolve gelatin and candy in boiling water. Stir in applesauce, lemon juice, and salt. Chill until partially set. Add nuts. Pour into 8x8x2 inch pan. Blend remaining ingredients and spread through gelatin mixture for marble look. Chill firm. *Yield:* 9 servings.

Miss Lottie Lunn

LEMON SALAD

1 cup boiling water
1 (3 ounce) package lemon
  gelatin
½ cup sugar
1 (8 ounce) can crushed
  pineapple, drained

1 (8 ounce) jar pimento cheese
  spread
2 cups whipped topping

Dissolve gelatin and sugar in water. Add pineapple. Pour into a small mixing bowl and chill until thickened. Add cheese spread and whipped topping. Mix well. Pour into a 9x9 inch pan. Refrigerate. *Yield:* 8 to 10 servings.

Mrs. Robert Frazier (Jeanette)
Sikeston, Missouri

PISTACHIO SALAD

1 (3¾ ounce) box Pistachio
  instant pudding and pie
  filling
1 (15½ ounce) can crushed
  pineapple

1 (12 ounce) container of frozen
  non-dairy whipped topping

Empty package of pudding into bowl. Drain juice from pineapple over the pudding and mix well. Add pineapple and whipped topping. Mix well. Can be served frozen or unfrozen. *Yield:* 6 servings.

Mrs. Doyle Lee Neeley (E.J.)
Assistant Curator of Sales, Carter House
College Grove, Tennessee

ORIENTAL SALAD

4 cups diced cooked chicken
1 (15 ounce) can pineapple
chunks
1 cup celery, chopped
1 (11 ounce) can mandarin
oranges
½ cup pitted ripe olives
1 cup mayonnaise

1 Tablespoon prepared
mustard
½ cup chopped green pepper
(optional)
2 Tablespoons grated onion
(optional)
1 (5 ounce) can chow mein
noodles

Combine chicken, pineapple chunks, celery, orange slices, olives, mayonnaise, mustard, green pepper, and onion. Chill. Just before serving, mix well with noodles. Serve on lettuce leaf immediately. *Note:* If all of salad is not served at once, do not mix in noodles but place noodles on lettuce leaf and top with salad mixture. This prevents noodles from becoming soggy. Serve with buttered saltines for a cool meal. *Yield:* 4 to 8 servings.

Mrs. Fred Byrd (Frances)

SKILLET HAM SALAD

2 Tablespoons oil
½ cup chopped onion
½ cup chopped green pepper
½ cup chopped celery
3 cups cooked chopped ham

2 cups cooked potatoes, diced
¾ cup mayonnaise
Salt and pepper to taste
1½ cups shredded Cheddar
cheese

Heat oil in skillet, add onions, green pepper, celery, and ham. Sauté until ham starts to brown. Reduce heat and add potatoes. Add mayonnaise and toss lightly so as not to mash potatoes. Add salt and pepper. Toss in cheese and heat until cheese begins to melt. Garnish with green onions. Serve warm. *Yield:* 6 servings.

Mrs. James V. Kestner (Dolores)
Curator, Carter House

SEASIDE BY THE SEASHORE SALAD

1 (7 ounce) package macaroni and cheese	2 Tablespoons chopped onion
	1 cup chopped celery
1 (10 ounce) package frozen green peas, cooked and drained	2 Tablespoons pimento
	1 cup mayonnaise
	Dash of paprika
1 (7 ounce) can tuna	

Prepare macaroni and cheese as directed on package. Add peas and remaining ingredients (except paprika). Sprinkle paprika on the top. Chill overnight. *Yield:* 8 to 10 servings.

Mrs. Faye Yates
Nashville, Tennessee

SHRIMP WITH RICE SALAD

1 cup uncooked rice	1 (4 ounce) jar olives, chopped
1 pound boiled shrimp, peeled	1 cup mayonnaise
1 bunch green onions, chopped	Lettuce leaves

Cook rice according to package directions. Add shrimp, onions, olives, and mayonnaise, mixing well. Serve on lettuce leaf. *Note:* This makes a nice summer luncheon served with asparagus spears, cherry tomatoes, and melba toast. *Yield:* 4 to 6 servings.

Mrs. Douglas York (Vicki)

PATY'S CREAMY CUCUMBER DRESSING

1 medium cucumber, peeled and sliced	2 Tablespoons prepared horseradish
1 (12 ounce) carton cottage cheese	½ teaspoon dillweed

Combine all ingredients in blender, process until smooth. Store in air-tight container in refrigerator. *Yield:* 2 cups.

Mrs. Thomas Wilz (Paty)
Dayton, Ohio

HONEY DRESSING

⅔ cup sugar
1 teaspoon dry mustard
1 teaspoon paprika
1 teaspoon celery seed
¼ teaspoon salt

⅓ cup honey
⅓ cup vinegar
1 Tablespoon lemon juice
1 Tablespoon grated onion
1 cup salad oil

Mix dry ingredients. Blend in honey, vinegar, lemon juice, and onion. Add oil in slow stream, beating constantly. *Yield:* 2 cups.

Mrs. William Miller (Laura May)

ROQUEFORT DRESSING

1 quart mayonnaise
1 pound Roquefort cheese
1 (13 ounce) can evaporated milk

1 teaspoon garlic powder
Juice of 2 lemons
½ teaspoon salt
¼ teaspoon pepper

In a large mixing bowl, combine mayonnaise and cheese, cream well. Add remaining ingredients. Mix well. Refrigerate. *Yield:* 2 cups.

Mrs. Larry Nichols (Ellen)

Variation: Omit salt and pepper.

Mrs. James Williams (Lois)

AUNT SALLY'S SALAD DRESSING

1 cup tomato soup
1 cup salad oil
1 cup vinegar
1 large onion, grated
1 cup sugar

3 teaspoons salt
½ teaspoon paprika
1½ teaspoons dry mustard
1½ teaspoons Worcestershire sauce

Combine all ingredients, mix well. Store in air-tight container. Shake well before serving.

Mrs. Donald Miller (Sally)

BARBECUE SAUCE

¼ cup vinegar
½ cup water
2 Tablespoons sugar
1 Tablespoon prepared
  mustard
½ teaspoon black pepper
¼ teaspoon red pepper

1½ teaspoons salt
1 thick slice lemon
1 sliced onion
¼ cup butter or margarine
½ cup catsup
2 Tablespoons
  Worcestershire sauce

In saucepan mix vinegar, water, sugar, mustard, peppers, salt, lemon, onion, and butter. Simmer uncovered for 20 minutes. Add catsup, Worcestershire and bring to a boil. *Yield:* 1½ cups.

Mrs. Ralph Volpe (Louise)
Brentwood, Tennessee

MUSTARD SAUCE

¾ cup mayonnaise
1 Tablespoon mustard
½ small onion, minced

Dash of red pepper
1½ teaspoons lemon juice
¼ cup butter

Melt butter in double boiler. Add other ingredients. Be very careful or it will curdle. Great over broccoli, limas, etc.

Mrs. Owen Waldrop (Becky)

MEXICAN HOT SAUCE

2 cups chopped and drained
  tomatoes
¼ cup chopped onion
2 teaspoons hot green pepper,
  seeded

1 clove garlic, minced
¼ teaspoon salt
¼ teaspoon chili powder
⅛ teaspoon ground cumin

In a saucepan, combine ingredients. Simmer uncovered for 30 minutes. Serve hot or cold with meat or tacos. *Yield:* 2 cups.

Mrs. James Maupin (Sara)

CLAM SAUCE

2 Tablespoons butter
3 Tablespoons olive oil
3 cloves garlic, minced
¾ cup chopped parsley
½ teaspoon sweet basil
2 (8 ounce) cans clams,
  minced and drained,
  reserve liquid

¼ teaspoon pepper
¼ teaspoon salt
Juice of 1 lemon
½ cup white wine
1 (8 ounce) package linquine,
  cooked
½ cup Parmesan cheese

Melt butter and add olive oil. Sauté garlic in butter and oil until tender. Add parsley, sweet basil, and clam juice. Stir over low heat until real hot. Add clams, salt, and pepper. Stir in lemon juice and wine. Heat until real hot. DO NOT BOIL. Serve over linquine and top with Parmesan cheese. *Yield:* 4 servings.

Mrs. William E. Ward, III (Maggie)
Nashville, Tennessee

SPAGHETTI SAUCE

5 stalks celery
2 green peppers
3 large onions
2 small cloves garlic
1 (9¼ ounce) can pear-shaped
  tomatoes
1 (18 ounce) can tomato paste
1 (10 ounce) can tomato puree
3 Tablespoons sugar

2 teaspoons salt
½ teaspoon pepper
6 whole peppercorns
1 heaping teaspoon oregano
1 teaspoon spaghetti sauce
  seasoning
2 teaspoons basil
½ teaspoon bayleaf

Puree celery, peppers, onion, and garlic in blender with a small amount of water. Add remaining ingredients and pour in a large heavy pot. Combine all spices in a small bowl and add to tomato mixture. Cook slowly for 4 hours, stirring occasionally. Add 4 pounds browned ground beef before cooking, if a meat sauce is preferred.

Mrs. David Porter (Fay)

HERBED MAYONNAISE

1½ cups mayonnaise
2 Tablespoons finely chopped
  fresh parsley
1 Tablespoon finely chopped
  fresh chives

1 teaspoon dried whole
  tarragon
¼ teaspoon dried dillweed

Combine all ingredients in container of electric blender. Blend on low speed 1 minute or until smooth. Chill thoroughly. Serve with raw vegetables or on beef, poultry, or ham sandwiches. *Yield:* 1⅓ cups.

Donald Westfall
Brentwood, Tennessee

GOVERNOR McCORD'S BY GUESS BY GOSH SAUCE

4 ounces cream cheese
2 Tablespoons bottled chili
  sauce
½ teaspoon horseradish

½ teaspoon grated onion
Dash hot sauce
Salt to taste

Mix in electric mixer or food processor. *Yield:* 4 servings.

Mrs. Robert H. Hutcheson, Sr. (Elisabeth)
From collection of Dr. R.H. Hutcheson, Sr.
Commissioner of Public Health under 5 Tennessee Governors.

RHUBARB SAUCE

1 Tablespoon cornstarch
½ cup sugar
½ cup water

1 pound rhubarb (cut ½ inch
  pieces)

Dissolve cornstarch and sugar in water. Add rhubarb. Cover and cook slowly on low heat, until rhubarb is soft (about 15 minutes). Stir occasionally. Serve warm or cold as side dish with entree.

Don Westfall
Brentwood, Tennessee

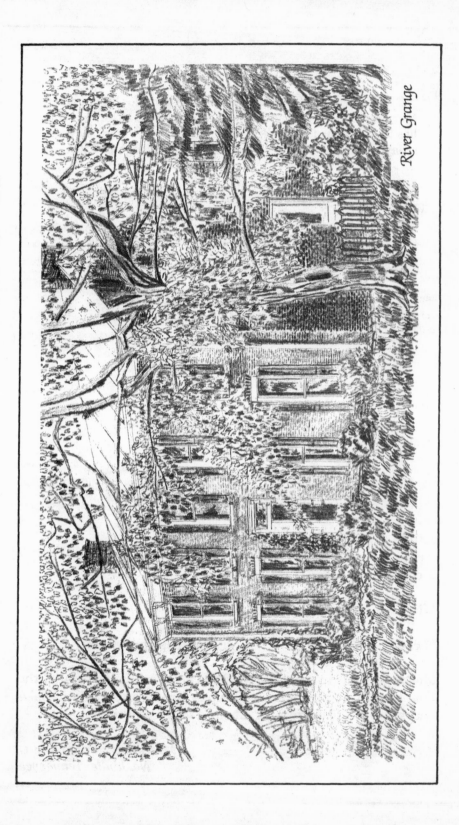

River Grange

RIVER GRANGE

Colonel Nicholas Tate Perkins built this home for his daughter, Mary Tate and her husband Thomas Moore around 1826. The name has been changed three different times. River Grange is owned today by Mr. and Mrs. Livingfield Moore and daughter, Ellen.

Vegetables

SUNDAY'S DELIGHT
Excellent with poultry.

2 (10½ ounce) cans tomato
   puree
2 cups brown sugar

¼ cup water
Salt and pepper to taste

Mix and boil slowly for 15 minutes.

¾ cup butter

3 to 4 cups bread cubes

Melt butter in 1½ quart casserole. Add bread cubes and toss lightly. Pour tomato mixture over bread cubes. Not necessary to stir. Bake uncovered at 325 degrees for 1 hour. *Yield:* 4 to 6 servings.

Mrs. John Sevier (Angie)
Nashville, Tennessee

BARBECUED BAKED BEANS

1 (16 ounce) can green lima
  beans
2 (16 ounce) cans pork and
  beans
1 (16 ounce) can red kidney
  beans
1 large onion, chopped
5 slices bacon, cut into
  pieces

¾ cup brown sugar
¾ cup catsup
1 Tablespoon Worcestershire
  sauce
1 cup shredded Cheddar
  cheese

In large bowl, mix ingredients. Pour into 13x9x2 inch pan and bake at 325 degrees for 1½ hours. Stir occasionally while baking. *Yield:* 10 to 12 servings.

Mrs. Harry Gramann (Marilyn)

Variation: Sauté onions in bacon grease before adding other ingredients. Increase sugar and catsup to 1 cup each and omit cheese.

Judy Lochman

GREEN BEAN CASSEROLE

1 (8 ounce) can French style
  green beans
½ onion, chopped
5 or 6 stalks of celery,
  finely chopped
1 can bean sprouts

1 (8 ounce) can water
  chestnuts, sliced thin
1 (10¾ ounce) can cream of
  chicken soup
⅓ cup shredded cheese
1 cup French fried onion rings

Place vegetables in layers in 2 quart casserole. Pour soup in and mix. Sprinkle cheese over mixture and top with onion rings. Bake at 350 degrees for 30 minutes. *Yield:* 8 to 10 servings.

Mrs. Gary A. Neill (Debbie)
Brentwood, Tennessee

MARINATED GREEN BEANS

4 slices bacon
½ cup sugar
½ cup vinegar

1 (16 ounce) can cut green beans

Brown bacon in pan, remove and set aside. Add sugar and vinegar to bacon grease and stir. Add green beans. Simmer about 20 minutes. Then add crumbled bacon and simmer about 5 minutes. *Note:* This is always a favorite. I usually double it. *Yield:* 4 servings.

Mrs. Thomas P. Anderson, Jr. (Sylvia)

CHEESE BUTTERBEANS
Very good!

1 (10 ounce) package frozen butterbeans
1 (6 ounce) roll garlic cheese

2 Tablespoons margarine
Garlic salt to taste

Cook butterbeans as directed on package and drain. Combine with melted garlic cheese to consistency desired. Add margarine and garlic salt. *Yield:* 6 servings.

Mrs. Tandy Rice (Frances)

LIMA BEAN CASSEROLE

2 Tablespoons butter
1 Tablespoon flour
1 green pepper, chopped
1 small onion, chopped

1 can tomato soup
1 stalk celery, chopped
1 (16 ounce) can lima beans
Cracker crumbs

Melt butter; add flour and all other ingredients except beans and cracker crumbs. Cook until thick. Add to beans and place in 2 quart casserole. Cover with cracker crumbs. Bake at 350 degrees for 30 to 45 minutes. *Yield:* 6 servings.

Mrs. Alva Jefferson (Lillian)

BEAN CASSEROLE

1 (16 ounce) can French style green beans, drained
1 (16 ounce) can English peas, drained
1 (10 ounce) package frozen baby lima beans, cooked and drained

2 hard-cooked eggs
1 cup mayonnaise
2 Tablespoons sandwich dressing
1 teaspoon Worcestershire sauce
1 can onion rings

In a buttered 2 quart baking dish place green beans, peas, and lima beans. Grate eggs over this. Combine mayonnaise, dressing, and Worcestershire sauce; pour over vegetables. Cover with onion rings. Bake at 325 degrees for 20 minutes. Do not overbake as this causes casserole to water. *Note:* I use Durkee's dressing. *Yield:* 10 servings.

Mrs. Clifton York (Frances)
Nashville, Tennessee

BROCCOLI CASSEROLE

2 (10 ounce) packages broccoli, cooked and drained
¾ cup mayonnaise
1 (10¾ ounce) can cream of mushroom soup
2 eggs, beaten
1 medium onion, grated

½ teaspoon salt
⅛ teaspoon pepper
1 cup Cheddar cheese, shredded
1 cup cracker crumbs
¼ cup butter

Mix broccoli, mayonnaise, soup, eggs, onion, salt, and pepper. Pour mixture into a large casserole. Sprinkle with cheese and cracker crumbs. Dot with butter. Bake at 350 degrees for 45 minutes. *Yield:* 6 servings.

Mrs. Robert Pilling (Nancy)

Variation: Omit butter and cracker crumbs.

Cathy Bucek
Brentwood, Tennessee
Mrs. William Gardner (Margaret)

BROCCOLI AND RICE CASSEROLE

1 cup cooked white rice
1 (10 ounce) package frozen
  chopped broccoli
½ cup water
½ cup chopped onion

½ cup chopped celery
½ cup margarine
1 small jar cheese, softened
1 (10¾ ounce) can cream of
  mushroom soup

Prepare rice. Boil water and pour over broccoli. Break broccoli apart and drain. Add rice to broccoli. Sauté onion and celery in margarine. Add to broccoli and rice mixture. Then add softened cheese and soup. Bake in a 1½ quart casserole at 350 degrees for 30 minutes. *Yield:* 8 to 10 servings.

Mrs. Gary A. Neill (Debbie)
Brentwood, Tennessee

Variation: Use ¼ cup chopped pimentos and 1 (8 ounce) can chopped water chestnuts, cream of chicken soup instead of cream of mushroom soup.

Mrs. Barbara Bracey

Variation: Omit celery. Use Cheddar cheese instead of softened cheese. Use cream of chicken soup instead of cream of mushroom soup.

Miss Lottie Lunn

HUNGARIAN CAULIFLOWER

1 head cauliflower, cut into
  flowerettes
¼ cup butter or more if desired

Salt and pepper to taste
1 cup bread crumbs, more if
  desired

Parboil cauliflower in salted water. Drain; set aside. Melt butter on low heat; add bread crumbs to brown. Toss cauliflower in buttered bread crumbs. Salt and pepper to taste. *Yield:* 4 to 6 servings.

Mrs. James Danyi (Anna)
Dayton, Ohio

APPLE CARROT CASSEROLE

5 Tablespoons sugar
2 teaspoons flour
1 teaspoon nutmeg
5 large carrots, sliced
   crosswise and cooked tender

5 large apples, peeled,
   cored, and sliced
¼ cup butter or margarine
½ cup orange juice

Mix sugar, flour, and nutmeg; set aside. Layer carrots and apples in a 2 quart dish. Sprinkle each layer with flour mixture. Dot with butter and pour orange juice over all. Bake at 350 degrees for 30 to 40 minutes. *Yield:* 4 to 6 servings.

Mariellen Perkinson
Brentwood, Tennessee

GOLDEN CARROT BAKE

3 cups shredded carrots
2 cups cooked rice
1½ cups shredded processed
   cheese
1½ cups milk
2 beaten eggs

2 Tablespoons minced onions
1 teaspoon salt
¼ teaspoon pepper
½ cup shredded processed
   cheese

Combine carrots, rice, 1½ cups cheese, milk, and eggs; stir in onion, salt, and pepper. Pour mixture into a greased 1½ quart casserole dish. Sprinkle remaining ½ cup cheese on top. Bake at 350 degrees for 50 to 60 minutes. *Yield:* 6 servings.

Mrs. Syd Oliver, Sr. (Thelma)
Nashville, Tennessee

CARROT PUDDING

2 cups cooked, mashed carrots
1 teaspoon salt
½ cup sugar
¼ cup butter or margarine
1 cup milk

3 eggs, well beaten
2 Tablespoons flour
1 teaspoon baking powder
¼ teaspoon cinnamon
½ cup chopped pecans

Mix all ingredients. Bake in greased 1½ quart casserole at 350 degrees for 1 hour. If not nicely brown on top, place under broiler for a minute or two. *Yield:* 6 servings.

Mrs. Richard Lane (Susan)

Variation: Omit milk and pecans.

Mrs. William Gentry (Edna)

OVERNIGHT MARINATED ASPARAGUS

1½ pounds asparagus spears
   or 2 (10 ounce) packages
   frozen asparagus
1 small green pepper, chopped
4 to 5 green onions with tops,
   sliced
1 stalk celery, chopped
¾ cup vegetable oil

½ cup white wine vinegar
⅓ cup sugar
1 teaspoon salt
½ teaspoon pepper
½ teaspoon dry mustard
1 clove garlic, finely
   chopped
½ cup imitation bacon bits

Heat 1 inch salted water (½ teaspoon salt to 1 cup water) to boiling in deep narrow pan. Place asparagus upright in pan. Heat to boiling; cook uncovered for 5 minutes. Cover and cook just until crisp-tender, 5 to 7 minutes; drain. Place in 13x9x2-inch baking dish. Sprinkle green pepper, onions, and celery over asparagus. Shake oil, vinegar, sugar, salt, pepper, mustard, and garlic in tightly covered container; pour over vegetables. Cover and refrigerate at least 8 hours but no longer than 24 hours. Just before serving, remove to serving platter or salad plates with slotted spoon. Sprinkle with bacon bits. *Yield:* 8 servings.

Bettina Funte

ASPARAGUS CASSEROLE

½ pound shredded sharp
  Cheddar cheese
2 cups cracker crumbs
1 (16 ounce) can asparagus,
  drained but reserve ½ can
  juice

2 boiled eggs, sliced
1 (10¾ ounce) can mushroom
  soup
½ cup butter, melted

Mix asparagus juice and soup. In a separate bowl mix cheese and crackers. In a 2 quart casserole put a layer of cheese and crackers, asparagus, eggs, and soup. Continue layering, ending with cracker crumbs on top. Pour melted butter over entire mixture. Bake at 350 degrees for 30 minutes. *Yield:* 10 to 12 servings.

Mrs. T. P. Anderson (Adeline)
Nashville, Tennessee

Variation: Use 2 cans asparagus tips, 2 cans cream of mushroom soup, 3 to 4 eggs. Omit butter and cracker crumbs.

Mrs. Bette Whitley

MISS VIRGINIA'S ASPARAGUS CASSEROLE

1 (16 ounce) can asparagus tips
1 (16 ounce) can asparagus
  pieces
½ cup dry milk
4 Tablespoons flour
1 envelope cream of chicken
  soup mix

1 cup margarine or butter
8 hard-boiled eggs, chopped
1 chopped pimento
1 teaspoon salt
2 cups cracker crumbs
2 cups shredded cheese,
  aged preferred

Drain asparagus. Pour juice into pitcher and add dry milk. In a mixing bowl, place flour, soup mix, and margarine. Add liquid, stirring until smooth. Cook until thick. Stand asparagus spears around edge of a 2 quart square casserole. Pour drained asparagus tips over bottom. Add chopped eggs and pimento. Add sauce, salt, and coarse cracker crumbs. Bake at 350 degrees until bubbly (15 minutes). Remove when ready to serve and cover with cheese. Add hot milk if mixture seems dry. Should be moist. *Note:* I prefer to roll small cheese crackers to a coarse size. *Yield:* 8 servings.

Virginia C. Jefferson

BAKED CORN PUDDING

4 Tablespoons butter
3 Tablespoons flour
2 cups milk
2 (17 ounce) cans cream style
  corn

2 Tablespoons sugar
2 teaspoons salt
½ teaspoon pepper
4 well beaten eggs

Melt butter, add flour, mixing well. Add milk gradually and bring to a boil, stirring constantly. Add corn, sugar, salt, and pepper. Remove from heat, add eggs and pour into a greased 3 quart casserole. Bake at 350 degrees until firm, about 45 minutes. *Yield:* 12 servings.

Mrs. Cliff Allen (Pauline)
Memphis, Tennessee

Variation: Omit butter and pepper.

Mrs. Robert E. Wells (Cooper)

SUZY'S CORN PUDDING

½ cup corn meal
1 teaspoon salt
¼ teaspoon soda
½ teaspoon baking powder
1 (17 ounce) can cream corn

½ cup buttermilk
2 Tablespoons butter
2 eggs, beaten
½ teaspoon Worcestershire
  sauce

Sift meal with dry ingredients. Add remaining ingredients and bake in moderate to hot oven (350 to 400 degrees) for 45 minutes. *Note:* Too low heat tends to make it soggy. *Yield:* 6 servings.

Mrs. Thomas Gore, III (Suzy)

CORN CASSEROLE

2 (17 ounce) cans creamed corn
2 eggs, well beaten
½ cup corn oil
½ cup corn meal

1 teaspoon baking powder
½ Tablespoon garlic salt
1 small can green chilies
1 cup sharp shredded cheese

Mix all ingredients except cheese. Pour into a 2 quart casserole; sprinkle cheese over top. Bake at 350 degrees for 30 minutes. *Yield:* 6 to 8 servings.

Mrs. John B. Molitor (Ruth)

BAVARIAN CABBAGE

1 small onion, chopped
½ head of cabbage, chopped
Dash salt and pepper

½ teaspoon sugar
½ cup chicken broth
½ cup caraway seed

Place onion in large skillet, add cabbage on top of onions. Sprinkle with salt, pepper, and sugar. Pour on chicken broth. Sprinkle on caraway seeds. Cover and cook on low heat, 35 to 40 minutes. Mix only before serving. *Yield:* 6 servings.

Mrs. Sam P. Holt (Frances)

ITALIAN EGGPLANT CASSEROLE

1 medium eggplant	1 teaspoon garlic salt
1 (8 ounce) can tomato sauce	1 onion, minced
Parsley flakes to taste	1 (8 ounce) package mozzarella
Pepper to taste	cheese, shredded
1 teaspoon oregano	½ cup grated Parmesan cheese

Peel eggplant and cut into ½ inch slices. Place ⅓ of eggplant slices in a greased 2 quart casserole. Pour ⅓ of tomato sauce over eggplant. Add parsley flakes and pepper. Sprinkle with ⅓ of oregano, garlic salt, onion and mozzarella cheese. Repeat layers, ending with mozzarella cheese. Sprinkle with Parmesan cheese. Bake 20 to 25 minutes at 400 degrees. *Yield:* 6 to 8 servings.

Mrs. James Maupin (Sara)

EGGPLANT WHATEVER
Very low in calories!

1 medium to large eggplant	2 tomatoes (or more) peeled
1 Tablespoon lemon juice	and chopped or
1 to 2 Tablespoons butter	1 (15 ounce) can
1 medium to large onion,	1 Tablespoon vinegar
chopped	Salt and pepper to taste

Peel eggplant and cut into 1 inch cubes. Sprinkle with lemon juice; set aside. In 8 inch skillet, melt enough butter to cover the bottom. Add onions and sauté until clear. Add tomatoes, bring to a boil. Add eggplant, vinegar, salt, and pepper. Reduce heat. Cover and simmer until eggplant is tender (5 to 10 minutes). Good served with rice and/or soy sauce. Also, very good served cold. *Note:* The tomatoes need to be juicy, so that there will be liquid to cook the eggplant. Yellow squash or zucchini may be substituted for the eggplant, or a combination of squash and eggplant is good. *Yield:* 4 to 6 servings.

Mrs. Robert A. Plummer (Mary M.)

MAKE AHEAD MUSHROOMS

3 slices white bread
1½ pounds fresh mushrooms
  or 3 medium size canned
  mushroom caps
1 medium onion

1 cup chopped celery
2 eggs
1½ cups milk
Cracker crumbs
Butter or margarine

Butter 10 inch square baking dish. Cube bread and place on bottom of dish. Remove stems from fresh mushrooms, or drain canned mushrooms. Place mushroom caps over bread. Chop onion and celery and place over mushrooms. Beat eggs with milk and pour over layered casserole. Refrigerate at least 4 hours. Sprinkle cracker crumbs over top and dot with butter. Bake at 350 degrees for 45 minutes. *Yield:* 6 to 8 servings.

Mary Lee Gladieux

HOT MUSHROOMS

¾ cup salad oil
3 Tablespoons soy sauce
⅛ cup Worcestershire
  sauce
1 teaspoon salt

3 Tablespoons lemon juice
¼ teaspoon garlic powder
1 teaspoon pepper
⅓ cup red wine
1½ pounds mushrooms

Mix all ingredients except mushrooms in a skillet. Wash and dry mushrooms. Place mushrooms, stems up, in skillet. Cook on medium heat for 15 minutes. Turn and cook 10 minutes. Let cool. Refrigerate overnight. Reheat to serve. *Yield:* 6 servings.

Mrs. Jim Roberts (Margaret)

PARTY POTATOES

8 to 10 medium potatoes
1 (8 ounce) carton sour cream
1 (8 ounce) package cream
  cheese
4 Tablespoons butter or
  margarine

⅓ cup chopped chives or
  1 Tablespoon dried chives
Salt and pepper to taste
Paprika

Peel potatoes and boil until tender. Beat sour cream and cream cheese together; add hot potatoes and beat until smooth. Add butter, chives, salt, and pepper. Pour into a well greased 2 quart casserole. Dot with butter and sprinkle with paprika. Bake at 350 degrees for 25 minutes.

Mrs. John Sevier (Angie)
Nashville, Tennessee

Variation: Substitute American cheese for cream cheese. Add ⅓ cup chopped onion. Omit chives and paprika.

Mrs. Owen Waldrop (Becky)

CRAB STUFFED POTATOES

4 medium baking potatoes
½ cup butter
2½ cups half-and-half
2⅛ teaspoons red pepper
1 teaspoon salt

4 teaspoons grated onion
1 cup shredded sharp cheese
1 (6½ ounce) can crabmeat
½ teaspoon paprika

Wash, but do not grease potatoes. Bake at 325 degrees. When half done, pierce with a fork. When potatoes are done, cut in half and scoop out pulp. Reserve potato shells. Mix potato pulp and all ingredients except crabmeat and paprika, beating well. Fold in crabmeat. Refill the potato shells and sprinkle with paprika. Preheat oven to 450 degrees and bake for 15 minutes. *Yield:* 8 servings.

Mrs. Michael Connelly (Bonnie)

OZARK POTATO CASSEROLE

2 pounds frozen hash browns,
   thawed
¼ cup melted margarine
½ cup onions, chopped
1 (10¾-ounce) can cream
   chicken soup
1 cup sour cream

1 teaspoon salt
¼ teaspoon pepper
10 ounces sharp Cheddar
   cheese, shredded
2 cups crushed cornflakes
¼ cup melted margarine

Sauté onions in ¼ cup margarine. Mix all ingredients except cornflakes and pour into greased 3 quart casserole. Cover with cornflakes mixed with ¼ cup margarine. Bake 1 hour at 350 degrees.
Yield: 6 to 8 servings.

Mrs. Dale Pewitt (Amy)
Mrs. Jesse Short, Jr. (Alma)

Variation: Use 2 (10¾ ounce) cans potato soup and 1 cup grated
Parmesan cheese. Omit butter, onion, cream chicken soup, and cornflakes.

Paty Wilz
Dayton, Ohio

Variation: Use crushed rice chex as topping instead of cornflakes.

Carol Winscott
Nashville, Tennessee

TWICE BAKED POTATOES

8 large baking potatoes
1 (3 ounce) package cream
  cheese, softened
6 Tablespoons butter

Salt and pepper to taste
1½ cups hot milk
1 (8 ounce) package Cheddar
  cheese, shredded

Scrub potatoes and prick with a fork, rub with oil and bake 1 hour at 425 degrees. While hot, cut potatoes in half, lengthwise, and spoon out pulp (be careful not to ruin shells). Place pulp in large bowl, beat with above ingredients except milk and Cheddar cheese. Gradually add the hot milk until desired consistency. Add 4 ounces Cheddar cheese and beat. Scoop potatoes back into the shells and sprinkle the remaining cheese on top. Reheat at 350 degrees for 15 to 20 minutes. These can be prepared ahead and frozen if desired. *Yield:* 8 servings.

Mable Gladieux

POTATO FILLING
Excellent served with fowl.

2½ cups seasoned mashed
  potatoes, hot
¾ cup celery, chopped
½ cup onion, chopped
4 Tablespoons butter or
  margarine
1 (7 ounce) package herb
  stuffing

1 egg, well beaten
1 Tablespoon parsley
½ teaspoon poultry seasoning
½ teaspoon thyme
¼ teaspoon sage (optional)

Prepare potatoes. Sauté celery and onions in butter until tender. Prepare stuffing according to directions. Combine stuffing with other ingredients, stir, and place in 1½ quart casserole. Bake 350 degrees for 30 minutes. *Yield:* 6 to 8 servings.

Mary Nowak

JALAPEÑO POTATOES

4 medium potatoes, sliced
1 (2 ounce) jar pimento
1 small bell pepper, chopped
½ cup butter
1 Tablespoon flour

1 cup milk
½ (6 ounce) roll garlic cheese
½ (6 ounce) roll jalapeño cheese
Salt and pepper to taste

Layer sliced potatoes, pimento, and bell pepper in a 3 quart baking dish. Over low heat melt butter. Add flour, milk and mix until smooth. Stir in cheeses until melted. Salt and pepper to taste. Pour over potatoes and bake for 45 minutes at 350 degrees. *Yield:* 6 servings.

Mrs. Allan W. Castle (Evelyn)
Nashville, Tennessee

SWEET POTATO SOUFFLE

3 cups cooked, mashed sweet
  potatoes
½ cup butter
1 cup milk

2 eggs
1½ cups sugar
½ teaspoon nutmeg
½ teaspoon cinnamon

Mix sweet potatoes, butter, and milk. Add eggs, sugar, nutmeg, and cinnamon. Pour into casserole.

Topping:
½ cup self-rising flour
½ cup sugar
½ cup butter

½ teaspoon nutmeg
½ teaspoon cinnamon
1 cup chopped pecans

In separate mixing bowl combine topping ingredients. Mix by hand and pour over sweet potatoes. Bake uncovered for 1 hour at 350 degrees. *Yield:* 12 to 14 servings.

Mrs. Allan W. Castle (Evelyn)
Nashville, Tennessee
Mrs. Robert T. Embry (Bettye)

SWEET POTATO BALLS
Unusually delicious.

4 to 5 large sweet potatoes	Large marshmallows
Sugar to taste	1 (7 ounce) can coconut
¾ cup butter	Chopped nuts (optional)
1 teaspoon rum flavoring	

Boil sweet potatoes until tender. Add sugar, butter, and flavoring. Mix and place in refrigerator overnight. Next day, take marshmallows and roll in cold sweet potatoes, then in coconut. Place balls in 13x9 baking dish and heat at 350 degrees for ½ hour. Nuts may be sprinkled on top. *Yield:* 6 servings.

Mrs. Jerry R. Marlin (Louise)

SUNDAY SWEET POTATOES

3 cups cooked, mashed yams, fresh or canned	¼ cup milk
⅓ cup melted butter or margarine	1 teaspoon vanilla
2 eggs	1 cup miniature marshmallows
1 cup sugar	1 (8 ounce) can crushed pineapple, drained

Topping:

1 cup coconut	1 cup chopped pecans

In a large mixing bowl, beat hot yams. Add butter and mix well. Add eggs, one at a time, beating well after each addition. Add sugar, milk, and vanilla, beating well. Stir in marshmallows and pineapple. Pour into a 2 quart baking dish. Mix coconut and pecans and sprinkle over potatoes. Bake 15 minutes at 300 degrees. *Yield:* 8 to 10 servings.

Mrs. Sam H. Gardner (Juanita)

GREEK SPINACH PIE

1 (11 ounce) package pie crust mix
1½ pounds fresh spinach or 2 (10 ounce) packages frozen chopped spinach

2 Tablespoons butter or margarine
½ cup chopped onion
1 clove garlic, chopped

Prepare pie crust according to directions. Line ungreased 10 inch pie plate. Cook spinach and drain. Sauté onion and garlic in 2 tablespoons butter. Stir in cooked spinach.

Sauce:
3 Tablespoons butter
3 Tablespoons flour
1½ cups milk
1½ teaspoons salt

¼ teaspoon pepper
6 eggs, beaten
8 ounces grated mozzarella cheese

In saucepan, melt butter, stir in flour. Gradually stir in milk over low heat until bubbly and thick. Add salt, pepper, and spinach. Blend eggs and cheese into the mixture. Pour into pie shell. Bake at 350 degrees for 40 to 45 minutes until puffy and firm in center. *Yield:* 8 servings.

Mrs. Joseph Mueller (Eileen)

WELSH RAREBIT SPINACH CASSEROLE

2 (10 ounce) boxes frozen chopped spinach
1 box frozen Welsh rarebit
1 (6 ounce) can water chestnuts, sliced

8 slices bacon, cooked and crumbled

Cook spinach according to directions. Thaw rarebit. Mix spinach, water chestnuts, and bacon. Stir in ⅓ of the rarebit and put into 1 quart casserole. Top with the remaining rarebit. Bake 30 minutes at 325 degrees. *Yield:* 6 servings.

Carrie Miley
Manitou Beach, Michigan

SPINACH ARTICHOKE CASSEROLE

2 (10 ounce) packages chopped
  spinach
2 (16 ounce) cans artichoke
  hearts
1 (8 ounce) can water
  chestnuts, sliced
2 (8 ounce) packages cream
  cheese
½ cup butter

2 Tablespoons green onion
1 clove garlic
1 teaspoon ground pepper
  or lemon pepper
⅛ teaspoon salt
⅛ teaspoon accent seasoning
Dash red pepper
Buttered cracker crumbs

Cook spinach according to directions and drain. Butter a 3 quart casserole. Add layer of artichokes, slightly chopped. Then layer of water chestnuts. Melt cream cheese and butter in double boiler over low heat. Mix with spinach. Add onion, garlic, and seasonings. Pour into casserole over artichokes and water chestnuts. Sprinkle with cracker crumbs and bake at 350 degrees for 35 minutes. *Yield:* 16 to 20 servings.

Mrs. Jim Crowell (Mary Ann)

MARY LEA'S SPINACH CASSEROLE

1 (10 ounce) package frozen
  spinach, cooked and drained
8 ounces sour cream
¾ package onion soup mix

½ cup water chestnuts, sliced
  and drained
Cracker crumbs
American cheese

Mix first 4 ingredients in a 1½ quart casserole. Top with crumbs and cheese. Bake at 325 degrees until brown, about 30 minutes. *Yield:* 4 to 6 servings.

Mrs. Richard Roselle (Mary Lea)

SPINACH SUPREME

2 (10 ounce) packages frozen
   chopped spinach
4 Tablespoons butter
2 Tablespoons flour
½ cup evaporated milk
2 Tablespoons chopped onion
½ cup vegetable liquor
½ teaspoon black pepper
¾ teaspoon celery salt

¾ teaspoon garlic salt
½ teaspoon salt
1 (6 ounce) roll jalapeño cheese
1 teaspoon Worcestershire
   sauce
Red pepper to taste
Buttered bread or cracker
   crumbs

Cook spinach according to directions on package. Drain and reserve liquor. Melt butter in saucepan over low heat. Add flour, stirring until blended and smooth, not brown. Blend in milk and stir until smooth. Add onion and cook until soft. Add liquor slowly, stirring constantly. Cook until smooth and thick. Continue stirring and add seasonings. Cut cheese into small pieces and stir into mixture until melted. Combine with cooked spinach. Pour into 2 quart casserole and top with buttered crumbs. The flavor is improved if kept in refrigerator overnight. Heat and serve. *Yield:* 6 servings.

Mrs. Earl Vinson (Vivian)
Petal, Mississippi

CHEESY SPINACH CASSEROLE

1 whole onion, chopped
½ cup butter
2 (10 ounce) packages frozen
   chopped spinach, thawed
1 package shredded
   Cheddar cheese

½ pound Monterey Jack
   cheese
1 egg

Sauté onion in butter. Add spinach and mix well. Put ½ spinach mixture in a pie pan and cover with Cheddar cheese. Top remaining spinach and cover with thinly sliced Monterey Jack cheese. Pour beaten egg over top. Bake at 375 degrees for 40 minutes or until brown and bubbly. Cut into squares to serve. *Yield:* 6 to 8 servings.

Mrs. Homer Gatlin (Sue)

VEGETABLES

REBECCA'S SQUASH CASSEROLE

1½ pounds squash, cooked and
  drained
5 hard-boiled eggs, grated
3 cups thick white sauce
1 medium onion, grated

1 small box cracker crumbs
1 cup butter, melted
3 cups shredded cheese,
  loosely packed

Cook and drain squash. Mix squash, grated eggs, sauce, and onion.
Mix cracker crumbs and melted butter. Layer in a 13x9x2 inch
casserole; alternating squash mixture, grated cheese and cracker
crumbs, making 2 layers of each. Bake at 350 degrees for 30
minutes. *Note:* I use Ritz crackers. *Yield:* 8 to 10 servings.

Thick White Sauce:
4 Tablespoons butter
2 cups milk
5 heaping Tablespoons flour

⅛ teaspoon white pepper or
  black pepper
½ teaspoon salt

Mix above ingredients and cook in saucepan until thick.

Mrs. J. C. Anderson, III (Rebecca)

SUPERB SQUASH CASSEROLE

2 (10 ounce) packages frozen
  squash or 3 pounds
  fresh squash
1 large onion, chopped
3 Tablespoons margarine
2 (10¾ ounce) cans cream
  of mushroom soup

1 (8 ounce) carton sour cream
Salt and pepper to taste
1 (7 ounce) package seasoned
  stuffing mix
1 cup shredded sharp
  Cheddar cheese

Cook squash until tender. Sauté squash and onion in margarine.
Mix soup, sour cream, salt and pepper, set aside. Line a 2 to 3 quart
casserole with a layer of stuffing, layer of squash, then a layer of
soup mixture. Continue to layer in this order, ending with squash
layer. Top with cheese and bake at 350 degrees for 30 minutes until
bubbly. *Yield:* 6 to 8 servings.

Mrs. Earl A. Vinson (Vivian)
Petal, Mississippi

SQUASH-CARROT CASSEROLE

1 (7 ounce) package cornbread
  stuffing
½ cup margarine, melted
2 cups cooked and mashed
  yellow squash
1 (10¾ ounce) can cream of
  chicken soup
1 cup sour cream
2 medium carrots, grated
1 (2 ounce) jar pimento
1 medium onion, chopped
Salt and pepper to taste

Mix stuffing and margarine. Reserve 1 cup mixture and use remaining mixture to line 2 quart casserole. Combine remaining ingredients and pour over stuffing. Top with reserved stuffing and bake at 350 degrees for 30 minutes. *Yield:* 6 servings.

Mrs. William Gentry (Edna)

SQUASH PATTIES

1 cup flour
1 teaspoon sugar
½ teaspoon salt
¾ cup milk
1 egg
¼ cup vegetable oil
3 cups grated yellow squash
1 medium onion, chopped
2 to 3 teaspoons crushed red
  pepper

Combine flour, sugar, salt, milk, egg, and oil. Beat with an electric mixer until smooth. Add squash, onion, and pepper, stir in well. Drop mixture by tablespoonful into a hot, greased skillet. Cook until golden brown, turning once. Drain on paper towel. *Yield:* 2 dozen.

Mrs. Sam L. Pratt, Jr. (Carolyn)

SQUASH-BELL PEPPER CASSEROLE

6 cups thinly sliced yellow
  squash
1 large onion, chopped
2 medium bell peppers,
  chopped

4 Tablespoons bacon drippings
1 teaspoon salt
½ teaspoon pepper
Bread crumbs

Cook squash until tender in boiling water. Brown onion and green peppers in bacon drippings. Combine squash, onion, bell peppers, salt, and pepper. Place in a 2 quart casserole dish. Top with bread crumbs. Bake at 350 degrees for 15 minutes. *Yield:* 4 to 6 servings.

Mrs. Felix Durham (Frances)

ZUCCHINI AND TOMATOES

½ pound bacon
1 cup minced onion
2 pounds zucchini, sliced
  ¼ inch thick
6 sliced tomatoes

2 cups cracker crumbs
1 pound shredded Cheddar
  cheese
Salt and pepper to taste

Fry bacon and cut into pieces or crumble. Sauté onion in 3 tablespoons bacon drippings. Arrange in ungreased 3 quart casserole. Alternating layers of zucchini, tomatoes, bacon, cracker crumbs, onion, and cheese. Repeat layers three times, ending with cheese. Salt and pepper while alternating layers. Bake 1 hour at 325 degrees. *Yield:* 8 to 10 servings.

Mrs. Jimmy Williams (Nancy)

TOMATO CASSEROLE

1 (16 ounce) can stewed
tomatoes
½ bell pepper, chopped
½ onion, chopped
3 slices bread, toasted and
cubed

½ pound mozzarella cheese,
cubed
4 Tablespoons butter

Combine first 5 ingredients in a casserole. Mix well. Pat with butter. Cook at 300 degrees for 20 minutes. *Yield:* 6 servings.

Mrs. Sam P. Holt (Frances)

BAKED APRICOTS
Unusual. Good for brunch or luncheon.

2 large cans peeled apricots,
drained well
Light brown sugar

1 large box crackers,
crushed
½ cup butter

In a greased 2 quart baking dish, put a layer of apricot halves. Cover with brown sugar, then a layer of crackers and dot thickly with butter. Repeat this to the top of dish, and bake slowly at 300 degrees for 1 hour. It should be thick and crusty on top. *Note:* I use Ritz crackers. *Yield:* 10 to 12 servings.

Mrs. T. G. Sheppard (Diana)
Brentwood, Tennessee

HOT FRUIT COMPOTE

1 (16 ounce) can applesauce
1 (20 ounce) can pineapple
  chunks, drained and save
  juice
1 (17 ounce) can apricot halves
1 banana sliced

2 Tablespoons butter, melted
2 Tablespoons flour
¼ teaspoon cinnamon
¼ teaspoon nutmeg
½ cup of pineapple juice

In greased casserole, layer applesauce, pineapple chunks, apricot halves, and banana. Mix butter, flour, cinnamon, nutmeg, and pineapple juice in small saucepan and cook until thick. Pour over layered fruit. Bake at 350 degrees until bubbly. *Note:* Cherries and nuts can be added if desired. *Yield:* 10 servings.

Bettina Funte

BAKED FRUIT
Great with ham!

1 (16 ounce) can fruit cocktail,
  drained
1 (16 ounce) can pineapple
  chunks, drained
1 (16 ounce) can sliced peaches,
  drained

1 (6 ounce) jar maraschino
  cherries, drained
1 cup brown sugar
Crushed cracker crumbs
1 cup melted butter

Mix fruits with brown sugar. Top with cracker crumbs. Pour melted butter over top. Bake at 350 degrees for 30 to 40 minutes. *Note:* I use Ritz crackers. *Yield:* 8 servings.

Mrs. Ben Armistead (Tina)
Concord, Tennessee

Otey-Campbell House

OTEY—CAMPBELL HOUSE

The construction of this home dates back to the 1830's or early 1840's. A one story Greek Revival porch gives a look of simplicity to this home. It is owned by Mrs. James H. Campbell.

Main Dish Casseroles

GROUND BEEF CASSEROLE

Meat Sauce:
1 pound chuck
2 Tablespoons margarine
2 Tablespoons chopped green
  peppers

1 small onion, chopped
2 (8 ounce) cans tomato
  sauce

Brown meat in margarine. Add green peppers, onion, and tomato sauce. Simmer until cooked down a little.

1 (8 ounce) package
  cream cheese
1 cup cottage cheese

½ cup sour cream
1 (8 ounce) package medium
  noodles

Blend cream cheese, cottage cheese, and sour cream. Grease a 2 quart baking dish and preheat oven to 350 degrees. Layer noodles, cheese mixture, and then meat sauce. Repeat until all ingredients are used. Bake 30 minutes. *Yield:* 8 servings.

Mrs. William F. Holt (Frances)
Nashville, Tennessee

TOMATO BEEF CASSEROLE

2 ounces medium noodles
½ pound ground beef
1 medium onion, chopped
1 (10¾ ounce) can tomato soup
½ cup water

½ cup green beans, cooked
  and drained
½ cup Cheddar cheese,
  shredded
Salt and pepper to taste

Cook noodles in lightly salted water and drain. Brown beef and onions, stirring frequently to separate. Add soup, water, beans, noodles, salt and pepper. Pour into a 1 quart casserole, and top with cheese. Bake at 375 degrees about 25 minutes until hot and bubbly. *Yield:* 4 to 6 servings.

Louise Lunn

CORN BREAD PIE

1 pound ground beef
1 large onion, chopped
1 (10¾ ounce) can tomato soup
2 cups water
1½ teaspoons salt
¾ teaspoon pepper
1 Tablespoon chili powder
1 cup whole kernel corn,
  drained
½ cup chopped green pepper
¾ cup yellow cornmeal
1 Tablespoon sugar
1 Tablespoon flour
1½ teaspoons baking powder
1 beaten egg
½ cup milk
1 Tablespoon melted fat

Brown beef and onion in a skillet. Add soup, water, 1 teaspoon salt, pepper, chili powder, corn, and green pepper and mix well. Simmer for 15 minutes and pour into a greased 2 quart casserole. Sift cornmeal, sugar, flour, remaining salt and baking powder into a bowl. Add egg and milk and stir lightly. Add the fat and mix. Spread over beef mixture. Bake at 350 degrees for 20 to 25 mintutes. *Yield:* 6 to 8 servings.

Mrs. Bobby Lofton (Betty)

BEEF AND RICE CASSEROLE

1 pound ground beef
2 onions, chopped
1 cup celery, chopped fine
1 cup water
1 (10¾ ounce) can cream of
  mushroom soup
1 (10¾ ounce) can cream of
  chicken soup
2 Tablespoons soy sauce
½ cup rice, uncooked
1 (5 ounce) can Chinese noodles

Brown ground beef with onions. Add celery, water, soups, soy sauce, rice, and mix well. Turn into 2 quart casserole and bake at 250 degrees for 30 minutes. Then top with noodles and bake at 350 degrees for 30 minutes. *Yield:* 4 to 6 servings.

Mrs. Donna Brown
Huntsville, Alabama

LOUISIANA RED BEANS AND RICE

1 cup red kidney beans, washed and sorted
1 quart cold water
½ pound smoked sausage, cut in small pieces
1 medium-sized yellow onion, peeled and coarsely chopped
1 clove garlic, peeled and chopped
1 stalk celery, coarsely chopped
1 bay leaf, crumbled
¼ teaspoon cumin
¼ teaspoon pepper
1 Tablespoon light brown sugar
½ to 1 teaspoon chili powder or to taste (optional)
½ teaspoon salt or to taste
4 cups hot boiled rice
2 Tablespoons minced parsley

Soak beans overnight in 2 cups water. Drain, measure soaking water and add enough cold water to make two cups. Place beans and water in heavy saucepan, cover and simmer 45 minutes. Add all but the last 3 ingredients, cover and simmer 30 to 45 minutes longer until tender. Season to taste with salt. Ladle over rice. Sprinkle with parsley and serve. *Yield:* 4 cups.

Hellen Garrett
Monroe, Louisiana

SAUSAGE STRATA

6 slices of bread (any kind, any thickness—variety makes it better!)
1 pound sausage
1 teaspoon dry mustard
1 cup shredded sharp Cheddar cheese
3 eggs, beaten
1¼ cups milk
½ cup half-and-half
½ teaspoon salt
1 teaspoon Worcestershire sauce

Preheat oven to 350 degrees. Trim bread and place in bottom of 10x14 inch greased casserole. Brown sausage and drain. Add dry mustard to browned sausage; spoon over bread and sprinkle cheese on top of this. Combine eggs, milk, half-and-half, salt, and Worcestershire sauce and pour over top. Bake at 350 degrees for 30 to 35 minutes. This recipe can be made in advance. *Yield:* 6 servings.

Mrs. William W. Wells (Joan)

CALICO BEANS

1 pound ground beef, browned
½ cup onion, chopped
½ cup brown sugar
1 Tablespoon vinegar
1 (15 ounce) can kidney beans

1 cup bacon, cooked and
   chopped
½ cup catsup
1 Tablespoon mustard

Mix all ingredients together in a Dutch oven. Bake uncovered at 350 degrees for 35 to 45 minutes. *Yield:* 8 servings.

Mrs. Sam L. Pratt, Jr. (Carolyn)

PIONEER BEANS

1 pound dried lima beans
1½ pounds smoked sausage,
   sliced
1 bunch green onions, chopped

½ teaspoon garlic powder
4 beef bouillon cubes
1 teaspoon liquid pepper sauce
6 cups water

Combine all ingredients in large saucepan. Mix well. Bring to a boil. Cover and simmer on low for 2 to 3 hours, or until beans are tender, stirring occasionally. Add water if necessary. Serve with corn bread and tossed salad. *Yield:* 6 servings.

Mrs. Ron Seltz (Mary Anne)

BAKE BEAN CASSEROLE

1 pound ground beef
½ pound bacon, chopped
½ cup onion
½ cup catsup
1 teaspoon salt
2 Tablespoons vinegar
¾ cup brown sugar

1 Tablespoon prepared
   mustard
1 (16 ounce) can red kidney
   beans, drained and washed
1 (16 ounce) can butter beans,
   drained and washed
1 (16 ounce) can baked beans

Brown beef, bacon, and onion. Drain excess fat. Add remaining ingredients. Mix well. Pour into bean pot or casserole. Cover and bake at 350 degrees for 40 minutes. *Yield:* 6 servings.

Mrs. John Iacobucci (Mary Ann)

MUSCOTELLI

2 pounds ground beef
1 large green pepper, chopped
2 large onions, chopped
1 (2½ ounce) jar button
  mushrooms
1 cup mushrooms, stems
  and pieces
1 (6 ounce) can tomato paste
1 (28 ounce) can tomatoes

1 (15 ounce) can tomato sauce
1 (10¾ ounce) can tomato soup
1 teaspoon chili powder
2 Tablespoons Worcestershire
  sauce
1 (8 ounce) package shell
  noodles, cooked
8 ounces sharp coon cheese,
  shredded

Brown ground beef; drain and set aside. Sauté pepper and onion in beef drippings and drain. Combine all ingredients and pour into greased 4 quart casserole. Bake 50 minutes at 350 degrees. Sprinkle cheese on top and bake 10 minutes at 400 degrees. If desired, add dry red pepper flakes. *Yield:* 10 to 12 servings.

Mrs. James Williams (Lois)

OLIVE ENCHILADAS

½ cup oil
2 Tablespoons flour
2 (10 ounce) cans of enchilada
  sauce
⅔ cup water
Salt to taste
2 pounds ground beef

3 large onions, finely chopped
1 (6 ounce) can black olives,
  chopped
2 pounds Monterey Jack
  cheese, shredded
2 dozen corn tortillas

Heat oil in 2 quart saucepan, then add flour stirring constantly until lightly browned. Add sauce, water, and season with salt. Stir and boil for 5 minutes. Brown ground beef in large frypan, add onions, olives, and 1 cup of the shredded cheese; remove from heat. Fry each of the tortillas briefly, turning once in hot oil, then dip in sauce. Roll each tortilla with hamburger filling and put in large 13x9x2 inch casserole or pan. Cover enchiladas with remaining grated cheese and bake in preheated 350 degree oven for 30 to 45 minutes. This recipe can be made the day before and baked accordingly. *Yield:* 10 to 12 servings.

Mrs. Gordon C. Anderson (Helen Joy)

MAIN DISH CASSEROLES

STUFFED PEPPER CUPS

6 medium green peppers
1 pound ground beef
½ cup onion, chopped
1 Tablespoon fat
2 cups or 1 (16 ounce) can
  stewed tomatoes

¾ cup packaged precooked rice
2 Tablespoons Worcestershire
  sauce
Salt and pepper
1 cup shredded sharp cheese

Cut off tops of green peppers; remove seeds and membranes. Precook green pepper cups in boiling salted water (about 5 minutes), drain. (For crisp peppers omit precooking.) Sprinkle with salt inside. Brown meat and onions in hot fat; add tomatoes, rice, and Worcestershire sauce. Salt and pepper to taste. Cover and simmer until rice is almost tender, about 5 minutes. Add cheese. Stuff peppers and stand upright in 10x6x1½ inch baking dish. Bake uncovered at 350 degrees for 25 minutes or until hot. Sprinkle with more cheese. *Yield:* 6 servings.

Mrs. Thomas L. Garrett (Hellen)
Monroe, Louisiana

STUFFED PEPPERS NEW ORLEANS

3 large green peppers
2½ cups cooked rice
1½ cups (6 ounces) crawfish
  tails
2 eggs, slightly beaten
½ cup onion, finely chopped
½ cup celery, finely chopped

2½ Tablespoons melted butter
  or margarine, divided
1 Tablespoon lemon juice
½ teaspoon salt
Dash of red pepper
½ cup rice cereal, crushed

Cut peppers in half lengthwise; remove seeds and membranes. Cook in boiling salted water 2 to 3 minutes. Drain. Combine rice, crawfish, eggs, onions, celery, 2 tablespoons butter, lemon juice, salt, and pepper. Fill pepper halves with rice mixture. Combine cereal crumbs with remaining butter. Sprinkle over peppers. Bake at 350 degrees for 30 minutes or until heated through. *Yield:* 6 servings.

Mrs. Ronald L. Barrett (Betty)

MANICOTTI

Sauce:

1 pound ground beef, browned
½ cup minced onion
¼ cup chopped green pepper
1 (12 ounce) can tomato paste
2 cups water

1½ teaspoons salt
½ teaspoon pepper
1 teaspoon sugar
1½ teaspoons Italian
   seasoning

Combine all ingredients and simmer 15 minutes.

Filling:

1 (16 ounce) carton cottage
   cheese
1 (8 ounce) package shredded
   mozzarella cheese

8 to 9 manicotti noodles,
   cooked

Combine cheeses and fill shells. Place in 13x9x2 inch pan. Pour sauce over and bake at 350 degrees for 30 minutes. *Yield:* 8 servings.

Mrs. Phil Davis (Sue)
Chicago, Illinois

BARBECUED MEATBALLS

1 cup bread crumbs
½ cup milk

1 pound ground beef
1 teaspoon salt

In a medium mixing bowl, combine all ingredients and shape into 2 inch balls. Place into an 8x8x2 inch baking dish.

Sauce:

1½ teaspoons Worcestershire
   sauce
¼ cup vinegar
1 Tablespoon sugar

½ cup catsup
½ cup water
½ cup onion, chopped

In a small mixing bowl, combine all ingredients and pour over meatballs. Bake uncovered for 45 minutes at 375 degrees. *Yield:* 4 servings.

Mrs. Gary Gaines (Andra)

THELMA'S "HALLOWEEN CARNIVAL" SPAGHETTI

2½ pounds (about 6 cups)
 onions, chopped
3 green peppers, chopped
¾ pound margarine
5 pounds ground beef
½ gallon tomato puree

4 (10¾ ounce) cans tomato
 soup
⅓ bottle Worcestershire sauce
Salt and pepper to taste
3 to 3½ pounds cooked
 spaghetti

Brown onion and green pepper in margarine. Add meat and cook until well done. Add puree, soup, Worcestershire sauce, salt, and pepper. Cook slowly about 1 hour. DO NOT BOIL. Simmer in heavy saucepan. Add cooked spaghetti. *Yield:* 25 servings.

To serve 100 use the following and cook as above:

3 pounds margarine
10 pounds onions, (about 25)
12 green peppers
20 pounds ground beef
2 gallons tomato puree
7 (10¾ ounce) cans tomato
 soup

1 bottle Worcestershire sauce
Salt and pepper to taste
12 to 15 pounds spaghetti,
 cooked

Thelma Alexander (deceased)

ITALIAN SPAGHETTI

4 medium onions, chopped
2 cloves garlic, chopped
1 to 2 Tablespoons oil
1 pound ground beef

2 (6 ounce) cans tomato paste
1 Tablespoon sugar
Salt and pepper to taste
2 (6 ounce) cans tomato puree

Sauté onions and garlic in oil. In another skillet, brown and drain ground beef. Combine onions, garlic, and ground beef. Add tomato paste. Mix and cook for about 2 minutes. Add sugar, puree, salt, and pepper. Simmer for about 4 hours. *Note:* This sauce can also be used for meatballs. *Yield:* 6 servings.

Mrs. James Pewitt (Thelma)

SYMPHONY CASSEROLE

8 ounces noodles, boiled, drained well
1 pound sausage, cooked, crumbled, and drained
1 (12 ounce) can whole corn, drained
1 (8 ounce) can tomato sauce
2 cups shredded Cheddar cheese (reserving 1 cup for topping)
1 teaspoon mustard
1 cup pitted ripe olives
1 Tablespoon fresh or dried minced parsley
½ teaspoon onion powder
½ teaspoon celery salt
½ teaspoon pepper
1 (10¾ ounce) can cream of mushroom soup

Combine the first 12 ingredients in a 13x9x2 inch casserole, generously sprayed with non-stick spray. Top with remaining 1 cup cheese. Bake at 350 degrees for 1 hour. *Yield:* 6 servings.

Mrs. Robert H. Hutcheson (Nancy)

HAM AND CHEESE NOODLE CASSEROLE

1 (8 ounce) package wide noodles
2½ cups (¾ pound) diced, cooked ham
8 ounces shredded American cheese
2 green peppers, chopped
2 Tablespoons chopped onion
1 teaspoon salt
1 cup sour cream
2 green pepper rings, reserved from green peppers

Cook noodles according to directions; drain. In a large bowl toss together noodles, ham, cheese, green pepper, onion, and salt. Gently blend in sour cream. Turn into 1½ quart casserole. Bake 25 to 30 minutes at 375 degrees until cheese melts and casserole is heated through. Top with green pepper rings. *Yield:* 6 servings.

Mrs. Syd Oliver, Sr. (Thelma)
Nashville, Tennessee

TURKEY, BROCCOLI, RICE CASSEROLE

3 cups chopped, cooked
turkey or chicken
½ cup chopped onion
½ cup chopped celery
½ cup sliced mushrooms
1 (10¾ ounce) can cream of
mushroom soup

1 (10¾ ounce) can cream of
celery soup
1 (10 ounce) package frozen
broccoli
1 cup uncooked converted rice

Combine all ingredients in slow cooker. Stir to mix well. Cover and cook on high for 3 hours. *Yield:* 12 servings.

Mrs. Steven Allbrooks (Pam)

CHICKEN BROCCOLI CASSEROLE

2 (10 ounce) packages frozen
chopped broccoli, cooked
and drained
8 chicken breasts, cooked
and chopped
2 (10¾ ounce) cans cream of
chicken soup

1 cup mayonnaise
1 cup shredded Cheddar
cheese
2 to 3 cups corn bread stuffing

Place broccoli evenly in a 13x9x2 inch dish. Spread chicken pieces over top. Mix cream of chicken soup and mayonnaise. Spread over chicken. Sprinkle cheese over sauce. Mix 2 to 3 cups stuffing according to package instructions. Spread over top. Bake at 300 degrees for 1 hour. This is better if made a day ahead and refrigerated. *Yield:* 8 servings.

Mrs. Tim Beringer (Linda)
Akron, Ohio

Variation: Use 1 Tablespoon lemon juice and ¼ teaspoon curry powder. Substitute stuffing with ½ cup buttered bread crumbs.

Mrs. Thomas Van Olst (Vonnie)
Hendersonville, Tennessee

CHICKEN DIVAN

2 (10 ounce) packages frozen
broccoli
3 whole chicken breasts
2 (10¾ ounce) cans cream of
chicken soup
1 cup sour cream
1 cup mayonnaise

1 cup shredded, sharp Cheddar
cheese
1 Tablespoon lemon juice
1 teaspoon curry powder
Grated Parmesan cheese
Paprika
Butter

Cook chicken breasts. Cook broccoli. Mix soup, sour cream, mayonnaise, Cheddar cheese, lemon juice, and curry powder. Drain broccoli and arrange on bottom of a flat, greased 3 quart casserole. Sprinkle generously with Parmesan cheese. Remove skin from chicken and cut into pieces and place over broccoli. Sprinkle again with Parmesan. Pour sauce over all. Sprinkle with Parmesan and paprika. Dot with butter. Bake uncovered at 350 degrees for 30 to 40 minutes. (This is a great dish to make ahead and refrigerate until time to bake). *Yield:* 6 to 8 servings.

Mrs. Hampton Pitts (Debbie)
Nashville, Tennessee

CALICO CASSEROLE

2 chicken bouillon cubes
4 cups water
8 ounces spaghetti
½ cup onion, chopped
¼ cup green pepper, chopped
2 Tablespoons butter
½ teaspoon celery salt
½ teaspoon paprika

1 (4 ounce) can mushrooms,
stems and pieces
½ cup sliced ripe olives
3 Tablespoons chopped
pimento
2 cups chicken, diced
1 cup Cheddar cheese,
shredded

In 3 quart saucepan dissolve bouillon cubes in water. Cook spaghetti in bouillon until barely tender. Sauté onions and green pepper in butter; add celery salt and paprika. Combine all ingredients except cheese; pour into buttered casserole. Top with shredded cheese. Bake at 350 degrees for 1 hour. *Note:* Canned, diced chicken or tuna may be substituted. *Yield:* 6 to 8 servings.

Mrs. Rodney Vickery (Nancy)

CHICKEN BREAST SUPREME

4 chicken breasts
1 package prepared bread
 dressing
1 cup hot chicken stock
½ cup margarine, melted
1 (10 ounce) package frozen
 broccoli

2 (10¾ ounce) cans cream of
 chicken soup
2 cups milk
1 (10¼ ounce) can green peas
½ cup sliced almonds

Simmer chicken in enough salted water to cover meat. When tender, remove meat from bones and cut into very large chunks. Set aside. Measure 1 cup of chicken stock and mix with prepared dressing; add margarine. Cook broccoli according to directions. Don't overcook! Mix soup and milk; set aside. In a large buttered casserole, place layer of chicken, dressing, broccoli, peas, and ½ of soup. Remove ¾ cup of dressing from remaining dressing. Continue layers until all but the reserved ¾ dressing is used. Pour on remaining soup. Top with remaining dressing and almonds. Bake at 350 degrees for 45 minutes. May be made the day before and baked just before serving. *Yield:* 6 to 8 servings.

Mrs. Sam Gardner (Juanita)

COMPANY CHICKEN CASSEROLE

3 cups cooked, diced chicken
1 (10¾ ounce) can cream of
 chicken soup
½ cup mayonnaise
1 (16 ounce) can French green
 beans, drained
1 (8 ounce) can water
 chestnuts, sliced

1 (2 ounce) jar pimento,
 chopped
1 medium onion, chopped
1 rib celery, chopped
1 (6 ounce) package long grain
 and wild rice, cooked
Salt and pepper to taste

In large mixing bowl, combine all ingredients with rice. Place in 13x9x2 inch pyrex dish. Bake at 350 degrees for 30 minutes. *Yield:* 9 to 10 servings.

Mrs. Edwin Yarbrough (Anne)

CHICKEN AND SAUSAGE IN A SAUCE SUPREME

2 whole chickens (5 to 6 cups cooked meat)
3 bay leaves
2 cloves garlic
1 Tablespoon salt
1 pound sweet Italian sausage
2 pounds mushrooms, whole or halved
¾ cup butter
3 shallots or 5 green onions, chopped

3 Tablespoons flour
4 cups creme fraiche or sour cream
¼ cup dry sherry
¼ to ½ teaspoon freshly grated nutmeg (if canned, use less)
Salt and white pepper to taste
1 cup freshly grated Parmesan cheese (about 6 ounces)

Place chickens in a large pot with water to cover. Add bay leaves, garlic, and salt. Cook until tender, about 1½ hours. Remove chicken from water and cool. Skin and bone chicken and cut into bite size pieces. Cook sausage and drain. Set aside. Sauté mushrooms in ½ cup butter on high temperature. Do not overcook. Set aside. In a large pan, sauté shallots or onions in remaining ¼ cup butter until tender. Add flour and cook 1 minute. Add creme fraiche or sour cream and blend well. Add mushrooms, chicken, sausage, sherry, nutmeg, salt, and pepper. Blend well. Spoon mixture into a 3 quart casserole. Sprinkle with cheese. Bake at 350 degrees for about 20 minutes, or until slightly brown and bubbly. *Note:* To make creme fraiche, for each cup mix 1 cup whipping cream with 1 tablespoon buttermilk or sour cream in a glass container and leave at room temperature overnight or until thickened. Store in refrigerator. (Créme fraiche will not separate in cooking as sour cream might.) *Yield:* 6 to 8 servings.

Mrs. Robert H. Wickham (Cindy)

CHICKEN-ASPARAGUS CASSEROLE

5 cups chicken, cooked and
  cubed
4 (10¾ ounce) cans cream of
  mushroom soup
¾ cup slivered almonds

3 (8 ounce) packages
  asparagus, cooked and
  drained
½ cup chopped pimento
1 (3 ounce) can onion rings

Combine chicken, soups, and almonds and spread in 13x9x2 inch pan. Spoon asparagus and pimento over chicken mixture. Cover and bake at 350 degrees for 60 minutes. Uncover and sprinkle onion rings over all and bake 5 minutes more. *Yield:* 8 to 10 servings.

Mrs. Richard Sappenfield (Ann)
Brentwood, Tennessee

CHEESY TUNA PIE

1 (11 ounce) can condensed
  Cheddar cheese soup
4 eggs, slightly beaten
¼ cup milk
2 Tablespoons instant minced
  onion

¼ teaspoon hot pepper sauce
2 (7 ounce) cans tuna, well
  drained and flaked
1 (9 inch) baked pie shell
Tomato wedges
Parsley

In bowl, combine soup, eggs, milk, onion, and hot pepper sauce. Stir in tuna. Pour into pie shell. Bake at 350 degrees for 45 minutes or until knife inserted in center comes out clean. (If necessary during baking, cover edges of pie shell with aluminum foil to prevent over browning.) Let stand 5 minutes before serving. Garnish with tomato and parsley, if desired. *Yield:* 6 servings.

Mrs. Douglas P. Anderson (Mary)

Harrison House

HARRISON HOUSE

William Harrison, Sr., built this house prior to 1848; the exact date is unknown. A two story portico is supported by square columns, a common feature in the mid-state area. The home is owned by Dr. and Mrs. Charles Morton.

Meats

BEEF BRISKET

1 (4 pound) beef brisket,
  boned and trimmed
Unseasoned meat tenderizer
Seasoned salt to taste

Celery salt to taste
Garlic salt to taste
3 Tablespoons liquid smoke
¼ cup Worcestershire sauce

Sprinkle both sides of meat with tenderizer. Sprinkle liberally with seasoned salt, celery salt, and garlic salt. Pour liquid smoke and Worcestershire sauce over brisket. Cover and refrigerate 24 hours. Bake covered at 225 degrees for 6 to 8 hours. *Yield:* 6 servings.

Mrs. Larry Pendley (Paulette)
Waco, Texas

Variation: Omit meat tenderizer and seasoned salt. Use salt and pepper to taste. Last hour of cooking, pour 1 cup barbecue sauce over beef and bake at 350 degrees for 1 hour. Slice and serve sauce over each slice.

Linda Magness
Monticello, Arkansas

MARINATED CHUCK ROAST

3 to 5 pound chuck roast
Meat tenderizer
1 Tablespoon sesame seeds
2 teaspoons butter
½ cup strong coffee

½ cup soy sauce
1 Tablespoon Worcestershire
  sauce
1 Tablespoon vinegar
1 large onion, chopped

Early in the day, sprinkle meat with tenderizer. Brown sesame seeds in butter and add remaining ingredients, stirring well. Pour over roast. Let stand, turning every few hours, in refrigerator all day. Charcoal broil about 45 minutes. *Yield:* 6 servings.

Mrs. Rich McDavitt (Linda)
Brentwood, Tennessee

BARBECUE POT ROAST

3 pounds sirloin roast
3 Tablespoons shortening
3 medium onions, sliced
1 clove garlic, minced
½ cup water
1 (8 ounce) can tomato sauce
2 teaspoons salt
¼ teaspoon pepper

2 Tablespoons brown sugar
¼ teaspoon paprika
½ teaspoon dry mustard
¼ cup lemon juice
¼ cup vinegar
¼ cup catsup
1 Tablespoon Worcestershire
sauce

In large Dutch oven, brown roast in shortening. Remove roast and sauté onions and garlic. Place roast back in pan and add water and tomato sauce. Cover and cook over low heat for 1½ hours. Add remaining ingredients and recover and let cook on low heat for 1 hour or until meat is tender. *Yield:* 6 servings.

Mrs. Franklin Bracey (Barbara)

ITALIAN BEEF

2 pounds beef roast, rump or
sirloin tip
3 cloves garlic, in pieces
Salt and pepper to taste
Italian seasoning

Fennel seed
1 onion, thinly sliced
2 cups water
2 (10¾ ounce) cans beef broth
Hard rolls

Score roast with ½ inch slits. Push garlic pieces into slits. Place meat in 13x9x2 inch pan. Salt and pepper roast. Sprinkle Italian seasoning over meat and cover heavily with fennel seed. Cover meat with onion; cover pan with aluminum foil. Bake at 350 degrees for 15 minutes per pound. Let roast cool. Slice very thinly and return slices to cooking pan. Add water and broth. Add more seasonings, if desired. Make enough broth so that all meat is covered. Cover pan and refrigerate overnight to blend flavors. To serve, warm meat in broth and place on warmed hard rolls. Serve a side dish of broth for au jus. *Yield:* 6 servings.

Mrs. William Bryant (Beverly)

SLOW COOKER CHUCK ROAST

2 to 3 pound chuck roast
Salt and pepper to taste
½ cup water
½ cup red wine

2 Tablespoons brown mustard
1 package brown gravy mix
Sprinkle of garlic powder

Place roast in crockpot (slow cooker). Combine remaining ingredients and pour over roast. Cook 8 to 10 hours. *Yield:* 4 servings.

Mrs. Dale Pewitt (Amy)

FLANK STEAK

½ cup salad oil
¼ cup soy sauce
Several green onions, chopped
½ teaspoon ginger

½ teaspoon allspice
1 Tablespoon lemon juice
1 (16 ounce) flank steak

Mix all ingredients. Score flank steak. Place in marinade for several hours. Broil to desired doneness. Slice on the diagonal. *Yield:* 4 servings.

Mrs. James Rogers (Jan)

STEAK FLAMBE MOUTARDE

4 (6 ounce) pieces sirloin steak,
  1 inch thick
6 Tablespoons butter
Salt and pepper to taste
¼ cup brandy

½ cup whipping cream
3 Tablespoons Dijon mustard
2 Tablespoons sour cream
1 teaspoon Worcestershire
  sauce

Pound pieces of steak between pieces of waxed paper to ½ inch thickness. In large skillet, heat butter and sauté sirloins for 2 minutes. Turn and season with salt and pepper. Cook to desired degree of doneness (2 minutes each side for rare). Pour brandy over steaks; ignite. When flame dies, transfer steaks to warm serving platter. Add whipping cream, mustard, sour cream, and Worcestershire sauce to juices in pan. Cook and stir. Pour over steaks to serve. *Yield:* 4 servings.

Mrs. Joe Brent (Catherine)

ORIENTAL STEAK

1 pound round steak, cut in
  strips
1 clove garlic
2 Tablespoons shortening
1 can bean sprouts

1 Tablespoon soy sauce
½ teaspoon sugar
½ teaspoon salt
1 (10¾ ounce) can tomato soup
1 green pepper, cut in strips

Brown steak in shortening with garlic. Drain sprouts and save liquid. Add enough water to liquid to make 1¾ cups. Pour over meat. Add soy sauce, sugar, and salt. Simmer covered, stirring occasionally, for 1 hour or until tender. Add soup, sprouts, and green pepper. Simmer until pepper is tender. Serve over chow mein noodles. *Yield:* 4 servings.

Mrs. Sarina Sherwin
Irvine, California

STEAK AND RICE

2 pounds lean sirloin steak
1½ Tablespoons vegetable oil
2 large onions, cut in ½ inch
  slices and separated into
  rings
1 (10¾ ounce) can cream of
  mushroom soup

½ cup dry sherry
1 (4 ounce) can sliced
  mushrooms, drained; save
  liquid
1 teaspoon garlic salt
3 cups cooked hot rice

Cut steak into thin strips removing all fat. In a large skillet, brown meat in oil, using high heat. Add onions. Sauté until tender. Blend soup, sherry, mushroom liquid and garlic salt. Pour over steak. Add mushrooms and reduce heat. Cover and simmer for 45 minutes or until steak is tender. Serve over rice. *Yield:* 6 servings.

Mrs. A. C. Frensley (Betty)

TERIYAKI STEAK

¼ cup honey
½ cup chicken stock
¼ cup soy sauce
2 Tablespoons catsup

½ teaspoon powdered ginger
1 clove garlic, crushed
1 (16 ounce) flank steak

Combine all ingredients except steak. Cook over low heat for 10 minutes, cool. Pour over steak placed in a glass casserole and refrigerate overnight, or up to 48 hours. Turn steak occasionally to marinate evenly. Broil on grill about 5 minutes per side. Slice thinly on the diagonal. *Yield:* 4 servings.

Barbara (Mandrell) Dudley
Gallatin, Tennessee

BEEF BURGUNDY

2 pounds beef stew meat
1 (10¾ ounce) can cream of
 mushroom soup
1 (10¾ ounce) can onion soup

1 (4 ounce) jar sliced
 mushrooms, not drained
⅓ to ½ cup red cooking wine

Mix all ingredients except the wine in a covered casserole. Bake for 2 hours at 350 degrees. Remove from oven. Add wine, stir and return to the oven for 30 to 45 additional minutes. Serve over rice or noodles. *Note:* You may need to thicken this at the time you add the wine. *Yield:* 4 servings.

Mrs. Jim Jordan (Dianah)

NO PEEK STEW

2 pounds lean stew meat
1 (10¾ ounce) can cream of
 mushroom soup

1 package onion soup mix
1 cup water

Mix all ingredients in a pan or casserole and cover with a tight lid. Bake for 3 hours at 300 degrees. NO PEEKING! Serve with noodles or rice, buttered and sprinkled with poppyseed. *Yield:* 6 servings.

Mrs. Douglas Anderson (Mary)

BEEF STROGANOFF

1 to 1½ pounds round steak
1 Tablespoon flour
Salt and pepper to taste
1½ Tablespoons butter
1 large onion, chopped
1½ Tablespoons
   Worcestershire sauce

¼ cup beef bouillon
½ cup sherry
½ to 1 clove garlic, minced
1 (2 ounce) can mushrooms
½ cup sour cream

Cut meat into cubes and mix with flour, salt, and pepper; brown well in butter. Add onion, Worcestershire sauce, beef bouillon, sherry, garlic, and mushrooms. Bake covered for 1½ hours at 350 degrees. Just before serving, blend in sour cream. Serve over buttered noodles or rice. *Yield:* 6 servings.

Mrs. Dale Pewitt (Amy)

QUICK BEEF STROGANOFF

½ cup onions, minced
¼ cup butter
1 pound round steak, ground
1 clove garlic, minced
2 Tablespoons flour
2 teaspoons salt
¼ teaspoon pepper

¼ teaspoon paprika
1 (4 ounce) can mushrooms, drained
1 (10¾ ounce) can cream of chicken soup
1 cup sour cream
½ cup chopped chives

In large skillet, brown onion and steak in butter. Add garlic, flour, salt, pepper, paprika, and mushrooms and sauté for 5 minutes. Add soup, simmer for 10 minutes. Stir in sour cream. This can be served over rice, noodles, potatoes or toast and garnished with chopped chives. *Yield:* 4 to 6 servings.

Mrs. Ralph Kelton (Susan)
Nolensville, Tennessee

BEEF CURRY

½ cup margarine
6 medium onions, chopped
3 green peppers, chopped
4 large green tomatoes (may substitute 8 stalks celery, plus 1 Tablespoon lemon juice)

1 (6 ounce) can tomato paste
1 (14½ ounce) can tomatoes
1 pound cubed round steak
2 ounces water
1 Tablespoon curry powder

Sauté onions in margarine until brown. Add chopped peppers. Cook on medium heat 10 minutes until tender. Add green tomatoes or celery. Cook until tender. Add tomato paste and canned tomatoes. Mix well, add beef to mixture. Add water and curry powder. Cover and simmer 3 to 4 hours. Serve over rice. *Yield:* 6 servings.

Mrs. Emory Milton (Ann)
Manchester, Georgia

HAMBURGER DINNER IN FOIL

1 pound hamburger
Salt and pepper to taste
¼ cup chili sauce
1 large onion

1 large potato
2 tomatoes
2 green peppers

Divide hamburger into 4 thin meat patties. Put each patty in the center of a 12-inch square of foil. Add salt and pepper. Spread each with a tablespoon of chili sauce and cover with a thick slice of onion, potato, tomato, and green pepper. Add a little more salt and pepper. Wrap foil around contents very securely so that no broth is lost. Bake in a preheated 350 degree oven 2 to 2¼ hours. Serve in foil with green salad and favorite bread. *Note:* Carrots, turnips, cabbage, or any vegetable may be added or substituted. When fresh tomatoes are not available, a firm canned tomato may be used. The chili sauce is the secret ingredient to this dinner. *Yield:* 4 servings.

Karen Steiner

HOT CHILIES MEATLOAVES

1 pound ground beef
½ cup oats, uncooked
1 (8 ounce) can tomato sauce
4 Tablespoons hot taco sauce
1 egg
1 Tablespoon plus 1 teaspoon
  minced onion

1 teaspoon chili powder
½ teaspoon salt
⅛ teaspoon garlic powder
½ cup shredded Cheddar
  cheese

In mixing bowl, combine meat, oats, ¼ cup tomato sauce, 2 tablespoons taco sauce, egg, 1 tablespoon onion, chili powder, and salt; mix well. Shape to form 4 to 6 (4x2 inch) loaves. Place in baking dish. Bake in preheated oven at 375 degrees for 20 to 25 minutes. Combine remaining tomato sauce, taco sauce, onions, and garlic powder in small saucepan and heat. To serve, spoon sauce over meat loaves; sprinkle with cheese. *Yield:* 4 to 6 servings.

Mrs. Sam Gardner (Juanita)

MEAT LOAF

2½ to 3 pounds lean ground
  beef
1 (5.33 ounce) can evaporated
  milk
2 whole eggs
½ cup raw carrots, grated

2 teaspoons salt
3 slices bread crumbs, toasted
1 large onion, chopped
1 cup sharp Cheddar cheese,
  shredded

Mix all ingredients together for the meat loaf and place in 13x9x2 inch baking dish.

Topping:
¼ cup brown sugar
¼ cup catsup

1 Tablespoon prepared
  mustard

Mix and pour topping over meat loaf. Bake at 350 degrees for 1 hour. *Yield:* 12 servings.

Mrs. Clifton York (Frances)
Nashville, Tennessee

PATTIES PARMIGIANA

1½ pounds ground beef
1 small onion, chopped
1 teaspoon salt
1 teaspoon Worcestershire
  sauce
¼ teaspoon pepper
½ cup Parmesan cheese

¼ cup cornflake crumbs or
  bread crumbs
1 egg, slightly beaten
1 (8 ounce) can tomato sauce
1 teaspoon Italian seasoning
6 (3x3 inch) slices mozzarella
  cheese

Mix meat, onion, salt, Worcestershire sauce, and pepper. Shape mixture into 6 patties, about 3 inches. Mix Parmesan cheese and crumbs. Dip patties into egg, then coat with crumb mixture. Brown patties in large skillet over medium heat, turning once. Drain off fat, if necessary. Mix tomato sauce and Italian seasoning; pour over patties in skillet. Cover and simmer for 15 minutes. Top each patty with mozzarella cheese slice; cover and heat until cheese is melted. Serve sauce over patties. *Yield:* 6 servings.

Mrs. William Bryant (Beverly)

HUNGARIAN CABBAGE ROLLS

1½ pounds ground meat (beef,
  pork, or veal)
¼ cup rice
1 medium onion, chopped
1 teaspoon pepper

1 teaspoon paprika
1 (46 ounce) can tomato juice
1 head cabbage
1 (16 ounce) can sauerkraut
2 teaspoons salt

Mix meat, rice, onion, pepper, paprika, and salt. Add 1 cup tomato juice; mix well. Parboil cabbage to soften leaves. Fill each cabbage leaf with heaping tablespoon meat mixture and roll up leaf. In large kettle put ½ can of sauerkraut. Layer cabbage rolls on top. Put remaining sauerkraut on top of cabbage rolls. Over this, pour equal parts of tomato juice and water to cover cabbage rolls. Simmer until rice is tender (approximately 1 hour after broth begins to simmer on top of stove). *Note:* Cabbage rolls can be made ahead and frozen before being cooked when stored without liquid being poured over them. *Yield:* 6 to 8 servings.

Mrs. Donald Westfall (Nancy)

PORK CHOP SKILLET

4 pork chops
2 Tablespoons flour
3 Tablespoons oil
½ cup Parmesan cheese
½ teaspoon salt
¼ teaspoon pepper

4 potatoes, peeled and thinly
  sliced
2 medium onions, sliced
3 beef bouillon cubes
¾ cup hot water

Roll chops in flour. Brown in hot oil. Combine cheese, salt, and pepper. Leaving chops in skillet sprinkle 2 tablespoons cheese mixture over chops. Layer potatoes over cheese. Sprinkle 2 more tablespoons of cheese mixture on potatoes. Add sliced onion. Dissolve bouillon in water and pour over all. Sprinkle with remaining cheese. Cover and simmer 30 minutes or until vegetables are tender. *Yield:* 4 servings.

Mary Camm

CONSOMMÉ CASSEROLE

½ cup rice
6 pork chops, browned in oil

1 (10¾ ounce) can beef
  consommé

Pour rice into buttered casserole and add browned pork chops. Pour can of soup over all. Bake at 350 degrees for 1 hour. *Yield:* 4 servings.

Sue P. Johnson

YUMMY PORK CHOPS

4 pork chops
1 large onion, cut in 4 slices
1 large tomato, cut in 4 slices

2 cups instant rice, uncooked
1 (10¾ ounce) can tomato soup

Brown chops on both sides. Drain excess fat. Place thick slice of onion on each pork chop. Top with tomato slices. Add ½ cup instant rice to each chop. Pour tomato soup over chops. Cover and simmer for 1 hour. *Note:* Salad and bread make this a complete meal. *Yield:* 4 servings.

Mrs. Tandy Rice (Frances)

ORANGE PORK CHOPS

4 loin pork chops
2 Tablespoons flour
¾ teaspoon salt
⅛ teaspoon pepper
2 Tablespoons oil

1 garlic clove, crushed
Grated rind of 1 orange
½ cup orange juice
½ cup gin

Dredge pork chops in flour; season with salt and pepper. Brown chops in oil on both sides. Sprinkle chops with garlic and orange rind. Pour orange juice and gin over them. Cook in covered skillet over low heat, turning occasionally until tender. The sauce will have cooked and thickened slightly. Serve chops with sauce and rice. *Yield:* 4 servings.

Mrs. Michael Connelly (Bonnie)

CHOP SUEY

1 cup carrots
1 cup green beans
1 cup celery

½ cup onion, cut in strips
¼ cup chicken or pork,
  cut in strips

Cut carrots, green beans, and celery in narrow strips at an angle. Pan fry celery, onions, and chicken. Add carrots and green beans and fry 2 minutes.

Gravy:
¼ teaspoon salt
⅛ teaspoon pepper
1 Tablespoon soy sauce
¼ teaspoon sugar

2 Tablespoons cornstarch
1 teaspoon liquor
2 cups chicken stock

Mix salt, pepper, soy sauce, sugar, cornstarch, liquor, and chicken stock in separate pan. Pour gravy over vegetables. Bring to a boil and simmer for 1 minute. *Yield:* 4 servings.

Mrs. James Pewitt (Thelma)

MEATS

PORK BARBECUE

4 pounds pork shoulder	2 teaspoons chili powder
1 cup water	1 teaspoon salt
1 onion, finely chopped	½ teaspoon black pepper
1 cup catsup	1 teaspoon paprika
1 cup water	¼ teaspoon garlic salt
¼ cup vinegar	1 teaspoon hot sauce
1 Tablespoon Worcestershire sauce	¼ teaspoon red pepper

Cut pork into small cubes and cook in water until tender. A pressure cooker makes it better. While meat is cooking, mix remaining ingredients in saucepan and cook for about 1 hour over low heat. When pork is tender, drain, and put in food processor and add sauce. Shred and mix in processor. Cook barbecue over low heat for 1 hour and serve on hamburger buns or corn bread. *Yield:* 8 servings.

Mrs. David Myers (Carla)

SWEET AND SOUR SPARERIBS

2 pounds spareribs, cut in 1 inch pieces	4 teaspoons soy sauce
1 teaspoon salt	1 teaspoon liquor
2 Tablespoons cornstarch	Vegetable oil

Marinate ribs with salt, cornstarch, soy sauce, and liquor for about 10 minutes. Brown ribs in generous amount of oil. Remove and drain.

Sweet and Sour Sauce:

2 cups sugar	1 slice fresh ginger
1 cup vinegar	

Add spareribs to sugar, vinegar, and ginger mixture. Bring to a boil and simmer for 35 to 45 minutes or until ribs are tender. *Yield:* 4 to 6 servings.

Mrs. James Pewitt (Thelma)

LITTLE MAMA'S BARBECUED LEG OF LAMB

1 leg of lamb
2 or 3 large onions, sliced
2 Tablespoons oil or butter
¾ cup vinegar
2 Tablespoons Worcestershire
sauce

1 Tablespoon sugar
1 Tablespoon onion juice
1 bay leaf
Juice of 1 lemon
½ teaspoon red pepper

Place leg of lamb on rack in roasting pan. Slice onions and place on the leg of lamb. In mixing bowl, combine oil, vinegar, Worcestershire sauce, sugar, onion juice, bay leaf, lemon juice, and red pepper. Pour over lamb and cover with a "tent" of foil. Baste often. Bake at 200 to 250 degrees according to weight of lamb. *Yield:* 8 servings.

Mrs. B. H. Burt (Teeta)

TARRAGON-LEMON LAMB

1½ cups lemon juice
2 teaspoons tarragon
1 teaspoon salt
½ teaspoon pepper
1 leg of lamb, 6 to 7 pounds

2 cloves garlic, slivered
1 small bunch parsley
1 (15 ounce) can whole apricots
1 (15 ounce) can spiced crab
apples

Combine lemon juice, tarragon, salt, and pepper. Marinate leg of lamb for several hours, turning occasionally. With sharp knife, make several slits in lamb, insert slice of garlic and additional tarragon, if desired. Place roast, fat side up, on a rack in a low pan. Cook at 325 degrees for 20 minutes per pound or until meat thermometer registers 175 degrees (medium). Baste occasionally with lemon marinade. Garnish with parsley, apricots, and spiced crab apples. *Note:* Very good served with a tossed salad with oil and lemon juice, a loaf of crusty French bread and a good rosé wine and coffee. *Yield: 6 to 8 servings.*

Carrie Miley
Manitou Beach, Michigan

MEATS

SPAGHETTI WITH VEAL SAUCE

2 pounds boneless veal, cut
   in thin strips
¼ cup flour
¼ cup olive oil
2 medium size green peppers,
   chopped
1 (4 ounce) can sliced
   mushrooms, drained
2 (28 ounce) cans tomatoes,
   undrained

2 (8 ounce) cans tomato sauce
1 teaspoon dried whole basil
1 teaspoon dried whole
   oregano
1 teaspoon garlic powder
Hot cooked spaghetti
Grated Parmesan cheese

Dredge veal in flour; sauté in oil until no longer pink. Add green peppers and cook, stirring occasionally until tender. Stir in remaining ingredients except spaghetti and cheese and simmer 1 hour. Serve sauce over spaghetti; sprinkle with Parmesan cheese. *Yield:* 8 servings.

Mrs. J. C. Anderson, III (Rebecca)

BARBECUE VEAL

3 pounds veal shoulder
2 Tablespoons shortening
Salt and pepper to taste
1 (8 ounce) can tomato sauce
½ cup catsup
½ cup water
1 medium onion, chopped

½ cup celery, chopped
2 Tablespoons brown sugar
1 Tablespoon prepared
   mustard
1 Tablespoon Worcestershire
   sauce
Hot cooked rice

Cut veal into 1 inch cubes. Brown well on all sides. Season with salt and pepper. Combine browned veal, tomato sauce, catsup, water, onion, celery, brown sugar, mustard, and Worcestershire sauce in 2 quart casserole. Cover and bake at 350 degrees for 1 hour and 45 minutes. Remove cover and bake for 15 minutes. Serve over rice. *Note:* If you reduce quantity of meat, do not reduce sauce. *Yield:* 6 servings.

Mrs. John Iacobucci (Mary Ann)

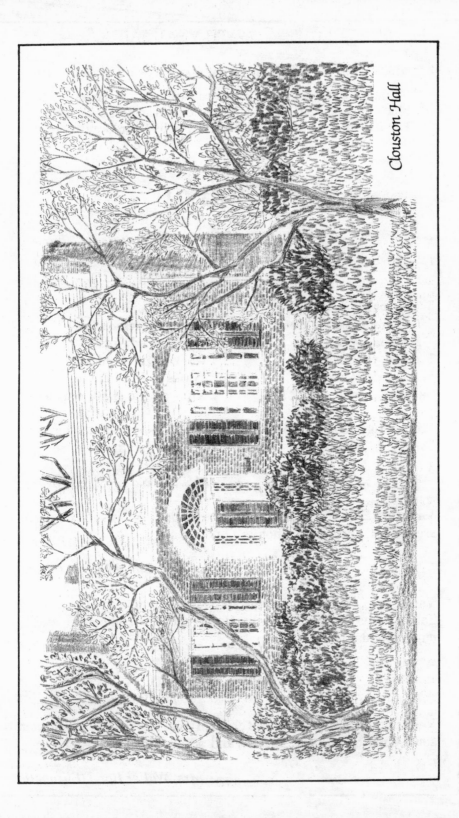

Clouston Hall

CLOUSTON HALL

Edward G. Clouston is thought to have built this home in the 1830's. Joseph Reiff designed this Middle Tennessee style home. The exterior has Federal lines. It is owned by Bunn Gray.

Poultry

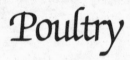

HOT CHICKEN SALAD

3 cups chicken, cooked	½ cup mayonnaise
2 (10¾ ounce) cans cream of chicken soup	½ teaspoon lemon juice
	2 hard-boiled eggs
1 onion, chopped	1 to 1½ cups shredded cheese,
¾ cup celery, chopped	Swiss or Cheddar
Salt and pepper to taste	2 cups potato chips, crushed

Mix all ingredients. Top with cheese and crushed potato chips and bake at 375 degrees for 40 minutes. *Yield:* 6 servings.

Mrs. Ronald L. Barrett (Betty)

Variation: Substitute cracker crumbs for potato chips and 6 eggs instead of 2. Add 1 cup almonds. Omit cheese.

Mrs. David Gentry (Susan)

Variation: Omit cream of chicken soup, onion, and eggs. Add 2 Tablespoons chopped pimento, ⅓ cup chopped bell pepper, and ⅓ cup almonds.

Mrs. Gerald Sieberling (Bernice)
Director, Carnton Association, Inc.

Variation: Substitute cream of chicken soup for cream of mushroom soup. Omit onions, lemon juice, and potato chips.

Mrs. Walter Bond (Elizabeth)

HUTCH'S CHICKEN LIVERS WITH SHERRY

1½ pounds chicken livers
2 Tablespoons lemon juice
½ cup flour
¼ cup olive oil

½ cup dry sherry
Salt and pepper to taste
2 cups hot cooked rice

Pour lemon juice over livers, roll in flour, and sauté gently in oil. When done, add sherry, cover pan and cook slowly over low heat for 5 minutes. Season with salt and pepper. Serve over hot rice. *Yield:* 4 servings.

From the collection of Dr. R.H. Hutcheson, Sr. (Deceased)

GRANDMA BAKER'S CHICKEN POT PIE
Old family recipe. Excellent!

1 (6 to 7 pound) hen, cut into
   pieces

3 quarts boiling water
Salt to taste

Boil hen until done. Remove chicken pieces and place in baking dish. Skim off some fat from broth and put over chicken. Reserve remaining broth. Add salt to chicken and cover. Place in oven at 300 to 350 degrees and brown slightly.

Pot Pie:
2 cups flour
½ teaspoon baking powder
1 teaspoon salt
Shortening (the size of an egg)

1 egg
Water
2 to 3 potatoes, diced
3 Tablespoons chopped parsley

Mix flour, baking powder, and salt. Blend in shortening, egg, and just enough water to hold; form a gentle dough. Roll about ¼ inch thick. Cut strips about 1 inch wide. Cut strips into 1 to 2 inch pieces. Bring chicken broth to a boil. Add potatoes and parsley. Drop dough pieces into broth and stir while adding. Cover and cook 15 to 20 minutes. Chicken and pot pie can be served in a large dish together or separately. *Yield:* 6 servings.

Ira V. Miller
Dayton, Ohio

CHRISTY'S CHICKEN FRUIT SALAD

3 whole chicken breasts,
  skinned
1 (15¼ ounce) can pineapple
  chunks in unsweetened
  juice

1 medium unpeeled apple
1 cup seedless grapes, halved
¼ cup mayonnaise
Lettuce leaves

Place chicken in 1½ cups water in a Dutch oven; cover and cook 15 to 20 minutes until tender. Drain and remove chicken from bone, coarsely chop and set aside. Drain pineapple and reserve juice. Coarsely chop apple, dip in pineapple juice to prevent browning. Combine chicken, pineapple, apple, grapes and mayonnaise; mix well. Cover and chill 2 hours. Serve on lettuce leaves. *Yield:* 6 servings.

Christy Wilz
Dayton Ohio

CHINESE CHICKEN CASHEW

1½ pounds uncooked chicken
  breast, cut into bite sized
  pieces
2 slightly beaten egg whites
½ cup cornstarch
6 Tablespoons cooking oil
2 slices fresh ginger root,
  minced
1 Tablespoon white wine
2 teaspoons sugar

½ cup cashew nut pieces
3 Tablespoons soy sauce
1 cup chicken stock
1 Tablespoon cornstarch
1 (6 ounce) package frozen
  Chinese pea pods, broken
  in half
1 (16 ounce) can bean sprouts,
  drained

Dip chicken pieces in egg whites and coat with cornstarch. Heat oil in frying pan or wok. Add ginger root and chicken. Stir fry. When chicken changes color, add wine, sugar, nuts and soy sauce. Lower heat and stir in chicken stock mixed with 1 tablespoon cornstarch. Add frozen pea pods and bean sprouts. Cover and simmer ten minutes. Serve with fried rice. *Yield:* 4 servings.

Mrs. Francis DeCoster (Donna)

PARTY CHICKEN
This is "always" a party favorite.

1 cup butter or margarine
6 to 8 chicken breasts (with ribs)

Lemon-pepper seasoning salt
¼ cup sherry

Melt butter in 9x13 inch casserole in oven at 350 degrees. Sprinkle chicken with seasoning. Remove dish from oven and roll chicken in melted butter. Pour sherry over each piece. Bake covered, skin side up, at 350 degrees for 1 hour.

2 (10¾ ounce) cans cream of chicken soup
1 cup sour cream
½ cup mayonnaise

1 teaspoon paprika
1 Tablespoon parsley flakes
4 cups cooked white rice

Remove chicken and let cool. Remove meat from bones. Pour off liquid into large mixing bowl. Add soup to chicken liquid. Stir in sour cream, mayonnaise, paprika, and parsley flakes. Mix well. In buttered 9x13 inch dish, place rice and pour over half of the sauce. Layer chicken over rice and pour remaining sauce over chicken. Bake at 350 degrees for 40 minutes. *Note:* This takes some time to prepare, but it is worth it. May be prepared the night before. *Yield:* 6 servings.

Linda P. Tarkington

MARINATED CHICKEN WINGS

2 pounds chicken wings
1 cup catsup
¼ cup honey

¼ cup soy sauce
¼ cup lemon juice

Remove tips from chicken wings and discard. Cut wings into 2 pieces. Combine catsup, honey, soy sauce and lemon juice. Pour mixture over chicken wings in a large bowl. Marinate in refrigerator overnight. Remove chicken wings from marinade and place them in a large baking pan. Bake at 275 degrees for 1 hour, basting occasionally. Serve warm. *Yield:* 6 to 8 servings.

Mrs. Ray Tucker (Susan)

FRUITED CHICKEN

¾ cup sifted flour
¼ teaspoon salt
¼ teaspoon celery salt
¼ teaspoon garlic salt
¼ teaspoon ground nutmeg
2 broiler-fryer chickens, cut up

½ cup butter or margarine
1 (20 ounce) can pineapple tidbits
3 Tablespoons flour
1 Tablespoon sugar
2 Tablespoons soy sauce

In a plastic bag, mix ¾ cup flour, salt, celery salt, garlic salt and nutmeg. Shake chicken, a few pieces at a time, in flour mixture until coated. Melt butter in large skillet and brown chicken on all sides. Place chicken in a large baking dish. Drain pineapple, reserving 1 cup syrup. Sprinkle pineapple over chicken. Stir 3 tablespoons flour and sugar into butter remaining in skillet. Add reserved pineapple juice and soy sauce, cook and stir until mixture thickens and bubbles. Spoon evenly over chicken and pineapple. Cover and bake at 350 degrees for 1 hour. *Yield:* 6 to 8 servings.

Mrs. Philip Miller (Nancy)

ORIENTAL CHICKEN

1 (6 ounce) package long-grain and wild rice with seasoning packet
1 (10¾ ounce) can cream of mushroom or cream of celery soup
1¼ cup water
1 Tablespoon soy sauce

1 Tablespoon onion, finely chopped
1 (16 ounce) can Chinese vegetables, drained
6 chicken breasts
Salt and pepper to taste
2 Tablespoons margarine or butter

Pour rice into 2 quart baking dish. Mix seasoning packet, soup, water, soy sauce, onion, and vegetables. Pour over rice. Place chicken breasts on top and salt and pepper. Dot with margarine. Bake at 350 degrees for 1 hour and 15 minutes. This can be prepared and refrigerated until ready to bake. *Note:* Pork chops can be substituted for chicken breasts; or use any other chicken parts. *Yield:* 6 servings.

Mrs. Douglas C. York (Vicki)

SOUR CREAM CHICKEN

1 (3 pound) chicken, cut up
½ cup butter or margarine
2 Tablespoons flour
1 pint sour cream
¼ pound fresh mushrooms or 1 (4 ounce) can mushrooms
1 teaspoon salt
½ teaspoon pepper
3 Tablespoons chopped parsley
½ green pepper, chopped
1 onion, chopped
¼ cup water
1 teaspoon paprika

Brown chicken in butter. Place in 2 quart casserole. Reheat butter in skillet and blend in flour. Cook, stirring until light brown. Cool thoroughly. Gradually add sour cream to flour-butter mixture. Mix well. Add mushrooms, salt, pepper, parsley, green pepper, onion and water to sour cream. Pour sour cream mixture over chicken. Sprinkle with paprika. Cover and bake for 1 to 1½ hours at 325 degrees. *Yield:* 4 to 6 servings.

Mary Lee Gladieux

CHICKEN-DRESSING CASSEROLE

1 package corn bread stuffing mix
½ cup butter or margarine, melted
1 chicken, stewed, deboned; reserve broth
1 large can mushrooms, sliced
1 (10¾ ounce) can cream of chicken soup
2 cups chicken broth
1 small carton sour cream
Salt and pepper to taste

Mix cornbread crumbs with melted butter or margarine. Put ⅔ into bottom of 13x9 inch dish. Layer chicken and mushrooms. Mix soup with 1½ cups broth and sour cream. Pour over chicken and mushroom layer. Season to taste. Top with remaining crumbs. Pour ½ cup broth over top. Bake at 350 degrees for approximately 1 hour or until brown. If it becomes too dry, pour over more broth. *Yield:* 8 to 10 servings.

Mrs. Steve Roussel (Janie)

CHICKEN FLAUTAS

Filling for flautas:

3 Tablespoons butter
¼ cup flour
¼ teaspoon salt
1 cup chicken broth
1 Tablespoon parsley

1 Tablespoon lemon juice
1 teaspoon grated onion
1½ cups cooked chicken
24 corn tortillas

In saucepan, melt butter and blend in flour and salt. Cook and stir until mixture thickens. Add broth, parsley, lemon juice, onion. Stir in chicken and cool. Place 1 tablespoon chicken mixture on each tortilla. Roll and place, seam side down, in hot oil (350 degrees). Fry for 1 to 2 minutes and turn until crisp. Serve hot with avocado sauce.

Sauce:

2 ripe avocados, mashed
½ cup dairy sour cream
1 teaspoon lime juice

¼ teaspoon onion salt
1 Tablespoon taco sauce

Mix all ingredients well. *Yield:* 24 servings.

Mrs. David P. Gaines (Donna)
Brentwood, Tennessee

CRACKER CHICKEN CASSEROLE

1 (8 ounce) box snack crackers, crumbled
6 chicken breasts, or 1 whole chicken, stewed and cut into bite sized pieces
1 (10¾ ounce) can cream of mushroom soup

1 (10¾ ounce) can cream of chicken soup
1 (8 ounce) carton sour cream
1 (8 ounce) can sliced water chestnuts, drained
1 cup margarine, melted

Line 9x13x2 inch casserole with ½ of the cracker crumbs. Mix chicken, soups, sour cream, and water chestnuts in large mixing bowl. Spoon mixture over cracker crumbs. Top mixture with remaining cracker crumbs and pour melted margarine over top. Bake in 375 degree oven for 30 minutes. *Yield:* 10 to 12 servings.

Mrs. Archie Hughes (Ruby)

HUTCH'S CHICKEN AND DUMPLINGS

Dumplings:

1 cup sifted flour
¼ teaspoon baking powder
¼ teaspoon salt

1 egg, beaten with 1
   Tablespoon butter

Combine flour, baking powder, salt, egg and butter mixture. Stir until moist, then knead. Roll thinly and cut into 1 or 2 inch dumpling strips. Remove chicken from broth and add dumplings one at a time, stirring with a fork to keep from sticking. Cook 20 minutes.

Chicken:

1 large chicken
1 onion, sliced
2 teaspoons salt
½ teaspoon ground ginger

½ teaspoon marjoram
1 carrot, sliced
4 cups water

Stew chicken, onions, spices and carrots in water in a covered pot until tender. Remove chicken to cook dumplings. Debone chicken. Combine meat with cooked dumplings and broth. Serve hot. *Yield:* 4 servings.

Mrs. Robert H. Hutcheson (Elisabeth)

CHICKEN WITH RICE

½ cup margarine
½ cup almonds
½ cup chopped onions
1 (3 ounce) can mushrooms
½ cup lemon juice

¼ cup cooking sherry
Pinch of salt, pepper,
   basil, rosemary, paprika
6 chicken breasts
3 cups cooked rice

Melt margarine in skillet, lightly brown almonds; remove. Add onions, mushrooms, lemon juice, sherry, and herbs. Sauté until onions are tender. Place chicken breasts in baking dish, pour mixture over chicken. Cover and bake at 350 degrees for 1 hour, basting occasionally. To serve, remove chicken breasts, add rice and stir. Place chicken on top of rice. *Yield:* 6 servings.

Mrs. Billy Blankenship (Betty)

CHICKEN TETRAZINNI

6 ribs celery, chopped
2 onions, chopped
3 Tablespoons butter
1 pint chicken stock
1 Tablespoon Worcestershire sauce
Salt and red pepper to taste
1 cup mushroom soup, condensed
½ pound sharp cheese
½ pound spaghetti
1 large hen, boiled and shredded
1 small bottle stuffed olives, sliced
1 cup broken pecans

Cook celery and onion in butter until tender. Add chicken stock and seasonings. Simmer 15 minutes. Add slowly to mushroom soup; then add cheese. Set aside. Boil and blanch spaghetti. Add to stock and let stand 1 hour. Add chicken and olives. Pour into 9x13x2 inch casserole. Sprinkle pecans on top and heat thoroughly. *Note:* May top with Chinese noodles if desired. *Yield:* 12 to 15 servings.

Mrs. James Short (Mary Catherine)
Mrs. Thomas J. Turbeville (Mary Otha)

MEXICAN CHICKEN CASSEROLE

8 to 10 chicken breasts
Salt and pepper to taste
1 pint chicken broth
2 medium onions
2 (10¾ ounce) cans cream of chicken soup
2 cans green chilies
½ pint sour cream
1 package flour tortillas
1 (8 ounce) package cream cheese
1 to 2 cups shredded Cheddar cheese

Boil chicken breasts and debone. Salt and pepper. Boil chopped onion in pint of broth; add soup, chilies, and sour cream. Put some of the soup mixture into greased 3 quart casserole. Layer tortillas (broken into bite size pieces), cream cheese, and chicken. Pour remaining soup mixture over top. Sprinkle shredded Cheddar cheese on top and bake at 350 degrees for about 45 minutes. *Yield:* 8 servings.

Mrs. Jim Roberts (Margaret)

180

MISS DAISY'S CREAM CHICKEN
A favorite at Miss Daisy's Tea Room.

Sauce:

½ cup butter
½ cup flour
1 teaspoon salt

2 cups chicken stock
2 cups light cream
2 cups milk

Melt butter. Add flour and salt; cook until bubbly. Add chicken stock. Stir with wire whisk until smooth. Add cream and milk. Simmer 30 minutes. Add following ingredients and heat thoroughly when ready to serve:

4 cups chicken, cooked and chopped
1 (8 ounce) can mushroom pieces, drained
1 (8 ounce) can water chestnuts, sliced and drained

1 (2 ounce) jar pimento, drained and chopped
¼ cup sherry

This is great served over corn meal muffins. *Yield:* 6 to 8 servings.

Mrs. Wayne King (Daisy)

QUICK AND EASY CHICKEN POT PIE

1 whole chicken, stewed and deboned, reserve broth
2 cups chicken broth
1 (10¾ ounce) can cream of chicken soup

Salt and pepper to taste
Celery salt (optional)
1½ cups biscuit mix
1½ cups milk
Butter or margarine

Place deboned chicken in bottom of greased 13x9x2 inch pan or pyrex dish. Mix broth and soup together and pour over chicken. Season to taste. Mix biscuit mix and milk together. (Will form thin mixture). Carefully pour over soup and chicken mixture. Dot with butter. Bake 1 hour at 350 degrees or until brown. *Yield:* 6 to 8 servings.

Mrs. Ben Armistead (Tina)
Concord, Tennessee

JANIE'S CHICKEN BREASTS

1 (3 ounce) package dried, pressed, sliced beef	Salt and pepper
6 chicken breasts	6 slices bacon

Line the bottom of 9x13 inch casserole with ½ of sliced beef. Remove skin and debone chicken breasts. Salt and pepper and wrap each breast with a slice of bacon. Place chicken on top of beef layer. Top with remaining ½ of sliced beef.

1 (10¾ ounce) can cream of mushroom soup	1 (8 ounce) carton sour cream

Mix equal amounts of mushroom soup and sour cream. Pour over the chicken. Bake at 350 degrees for 1 to 1½ hours. *Yield:* 6 servings.

Mrs. Tom Neal (Betty)

Variation: Substitute cream of mushroom soup with Golden mushroom soup. Omit sour cream.

Mrs. Tandy C. Rice (Frances)

CHICKEN CONFETTI

4 to 5 pounds broiler fryer chicken	1 teaspoon salt
¼ cup salad oil	⅛ teaspoon pepper
½ cup chopped onion	2 Tablespoons parsley
1 clove garlic, minced	1 teaspoon basil
1 (8 ounce) can tomato sauce	8 ounces spaghetti, cooked and drained
1 (6 ounce) can tomato paste	Grated Parmesan cheese
2 (16 ounce) cans tomatoes	

Cook chicken in oil and remove. Sauté onion and garlic, and remove grease. Add tomato sauce, paste, tomatoes, and spices. Simmer for 1 hour. Pour over cooked spaghetti. Top with Parmesan cheese. *Yield:* 4 servings.

Mrs. H. J. O'Donnell (Susie)

CURRIED CHICKEN #1

1 to 3 pound hen
4 to 6 extra chicken breasts
Chicken broth
1 cup white wine
1 (6 ounce) box wild rice
1 (6 ounce) box white rice
1 cup sour cream
1 (10¾ ounce) can cream of
  mushroom soup
2 (8 ounce) cans water
  chestnuts, sliced

1 onion, chopped
4 ribs celery, chopped
2 Tablespoons butter or
  margarine
1 teaspoon curry powder
Salt and pepper to taste
1 (4½ ounce) jar sliced
  mushrooms, drained

Cook and remove meat from bones. Into chicken broth, add wine and cook rice in broth according to package directions. Add sour cream, soup, and water chestnuts to rice. Sauté onion and celery in butter until tender. Add this to rice mixture with curry powder, salt, pepper, and mushrooms. Pour into 9x13x2 inch dish and bake at 350 degrees for 30 minutes. *Yield:* 10 to 12 servings.

Mrs. Malcolm Beasley (Bonnie)
Nashville, Tennessee

CURRIED CHICKEN #2

1 (10 ounce) box frozen broccoli
  spears
4 chicken breasts cooked
  and sliced
1 (10¾ ounce) can cream of
  chicken soup

½ cup mayonnaise
½ teaspoon lemon juice
½ teaspoon curry powder

Cook broccoli, drain. Place in buttered pyrex dish. Layer chicken over broccoli. Mix soup, mayonnaise, lemon juice, and curry powder. Pour this sauce over chicken, covering well. Cook at 350 degrees for 30 minutes or until bubbly. *Yield:* 4 servings.

Mrs. Owen Waldrop (Becky)

COMPANY CHICKEN

3 whole chicken breasts, split
Dash of salt, pepper, and
  paprika
½ cup butter or margarine
¼ teaspoon sweet basil
¼ teaspoon rosemary
½ cup chopped onion
1 (4 ounce) can sliced
  mushrooms, drained

½ cup slivered almonds
¼ cup cooking sherry
Juice of ½ lemon
1 (10¾ ounce) can cream of
  mushroom soup
3 cups hot cooked rice

Place chicken, skin side up, in a greased shallow baking dish. Sprinkle with salt, pepper, and paprika. Melt butter or margarine in large saucepan, add remaining ingredients except rice. Stir until blended; pour over chicken. Bake at 350 degrees for 1 hour and 15 minutes. When ready to serve, remove chicken from baking dish. Mix gravy and rice together and place chicken breasts on mound of rice. *Yield:* 6 servings.

Mrs. Sam L. Pratt, Jr. (Carolyn)

CHICKEN SUPREME

4 whole chicken breasts or
  8 halves, deboned
8 Swiss cheese slices (use ½
  if long)

8 ham slices, thinly sliced
8 bacon slices

Place cheese and ham slices inside flat chicken breast. Roll and wrap with bacon around roll, secure with toothpick.

Mix:
1 (10¾ ounce) can cream of
  mushroom soup

1 (8 ounce) carton sour cream

Combine soup and sour cream. Pour over chicken rolls that have been placed in casserole dish. Bake covered 2 hours at 275 degrees, uncover and bake for 1 additional hour. *Yield:* 4 servings.

Mrs. J. W. Cross, III (Caroline)

LEEKA'S FRIED CHICKEN

1 small fryer, disjointed   Vegetable oil
Salt   Paprika and pepper
Flour

Soak chicken 6 to 8 hours in salt water in the refrigerator. Drain well, salt lightly, and dredge in flour. Place in hot oil at least 2 inches deep in an iron skillet, placing meatier pieces in center with bony pieces on the outside. Sprinkle liberally with pepper and paprika. Cook for 1 minute. Turn heat down, cover skillet and let cook 12 to 15 minutes. Remove cover, turn pieces over, turn heat up, pepper and paprika liberally again, and cook for 1 minute. Cover, turn heat down and cook for 12 to 15 minutes. Remove from skillet and drain on paper toweling before serving, either warm or cold. *Note:* Small chickens are best for frying. They are more flavorful and tender. *Yield:* 4 to 5 servings.

Mrs. Cortez E. Isaacs (Aleectrice)

CHICKEN WITH GREEN NOODLES

1 (4 to 5 pound) hen cooked,   1 (10¾ ounce) can cream
  deboned, cubed; reserve   of mushroom soup
  stock   1 large (8 ounce) can
1 package green noodles   mushrooms
½ cup margarine   1 small jar stuffed olives
1 cup green pepper, chopped   sliced (optional)
1 cup celery, chopped   Crushed cheese crackers
1 cup onion, chopped   Melted butter
8 ounces processed cheese

Prepare hen. Cook noodles in reserved stock. Melt margarine in skillet. Sauté pepper, celery, and onion about 10 minutes. Add cheese, soup and mushrooms. Blend well. Add olives. Layer noodles and chicken in greased 3 quart casserole. Pour sauce over layers. If mixture seems too thick, add a little of the reserved stock, (½ cup). Sprinkle crackers, which have been moistened with melted butter, over top of casserole. Bake 30 minutes at 350 degrees or until it bubbles. *Yield:* 12 servings.

Mrs. Stewart Campbell, Jr., (Mary)
Spring Hill, Tennessee

TURKEY DELIGHT CASSEROLE

6 slices white bread
6 Tablespoons mayonnaise
1½ pounds cooked turkey cut
   into ½ inch cubes (about
   4 cups)
½ pound fresh mushrooms,
   sliced
2 Tablespoons butter
1 (8 ounce) can water
   chestnuts, drained and
   sliced

1 (8 ounce) package sharp
   American cheese slices
1 cup milk
4 eggs
1 (10¾ ounce) can cream of
   mushroom soup
1 (10¾ ounce) can cream of
   chicken or celery soup
¼ teaspoon salt

Spread each slice of bread with 1 tablespoon mayonnaise. Arrange in well buttered baking dish 13x9x2 inch. Cover with turkey. Cook and stir mushrooms in butter until tender. Add water chestnuts and heat thoroughly. Sprinkle over turkey, cut cheese slices diagonally in half. Arrange in 2 rows (points overlapping in same direction) on mushrooms and water chestnuts. Mix milk, eggs, soups and salt; pour over casserole and cover. Refrigerate at least 6 hours; no longer than 20 hours. Heat oven to 350 degrees. Bake 45 minutes. Let stand 20 minutes before serving. *Yield:* 8 servings.

Mrs. Joseph Mueller (Eileen)
Pekin, Illinois

CHICKEN PARMESAN

1½ cups bread crumbs
½ cup Parmesan cheese
1 Tablespoon salt
1 teaspoon pepper

6 chicken breasts or 3 whole
   breasts (deboned and
   skinned)
1 cup butter

Combine bread crumbs, cheese, salt and pepper. Dip chicken breasts in the melted butter and then into breadcrumbs, being careful to coat them heavily. Place in long baking dish and bake at 350 degrees for approximately 30 minutes uncovered. Do not turn chicken. *Note:* I use Italian Progresso bread crumbs. *Yield:* 4 to 6, depending on size of portions.

Mrs. T. G. Sheppard (Diana)
Brentwood, Tennessee

CHICKEN-KRAUT CASSEROLE

1 (12 ounce) can sauerkraut, rinsed and drained
6 chicken breasts or mixed parts
1 (16 ounce) can whole cranberry sauce

½ (8 ounce) bottle French dressing
1 package dried onion soup mix

Place kraut in bottom of 9x13 inch casserole dish. Place chicken pieces on top. Set aside. Mix together cranberry sauce, dressing and soup mix. Pour over chicken and kraut. Refrigerate for 24 hours. Bake uncovered at 250 to 275 degrees for 2 hours or until chicken is very tender. Delicious reheated. *Yield:* 6 servings.

Mrs. T. W. Perkinson (Martha)
Brentwood, Tennessee

ELLEN MARY CHICKEN

Salt and pepper to taste
2 Tablespoons oil
8 chicken breasts
1 large onion, sliced
1 (10¾ ounce) can cream of mushroom soup
1 (10¾ ounce) can cream of celery soup

¼ cup margarine
1 teaspoon horseradish
1 Tablespoon Worcestershire
½ cup lemon juice
1 (10 ounce) can rotel tomatoes
1 (2 ounce) jar pimentos

Salt and pepper breasts and brown lightly in small amount of oil. Slice onion and place in Dutch oven or crockpot. Prepare sauce of all other ingredients. Pour over chicken and onion. Cook on low heat 1½ to 2 hours. Serve over rice. *Yield:* 8 servings.

Louise Long
Nashville, Tennessee

MUSHROOM, CHEESE AND TURKEY STRATA

1 pound small fresh
mushrooms or 2 cans (6 to 8
ounces each) whole
mushrooms
¼ cup butter or margarine,
melted
½ cup minced onion
1 small clove garlic, crushed
10 slices white bread

1 cup shredded American
cheese
2 cups diced cooked turkey
or chicken
5 eggs, beaten lightly
2¾ cups milk
¾ teaspoon salt
⅛ teaspoon ground black
pepper

Rinse and pat dry fresh mushrooms or drained canned mushrooms. In a medium skillet, heat butter. Add mushrooms, onions and garlic. Sauté 3 minutes. Trim and discard crusts from bread slices. Cut each slice into a 3 inch circle; set aside. Tear remaining bread into small pieces and place in a buttered 3 quart casserole. Arrange alternate layers of cheese, turkey and sautéed mushrooms in the casserole. Overlap bread circles around outer edge of the casserole. Combine eggs, milk, salt and black pepper, pour over casserole ingredients, completely moistening the bread. Bake, uncovered, in a preheated 350 degree oven for 1 hour and 15 minutes or until bread is lightly browned. *Note:* Serve as a main dish for lunch or supper. *Yield:* 6 servings.

Mrs. J. P. Dawson (Sara)
Columbia, Tennessee

STICKY CHICKEN

6 to 8 chicken breasts
⅓ cup margarine or butter
½ cup honey

¼ cup prepared mustard
1 teaspoon salt
1 teaspoon curry powder

Place chicken breasts in a 9x13x2 glass baking dish. Melt butter, add honey, mustard, salt, and curry powder. Pour over chicken in dish and bake at 325 degrees for 1 hour and 15 minutes. This is great served over rice with the remaining sauce. *Yield:* 6 to 8 servings.

Mrs. Phil Mikesell (Judy)

Marshall House

MARSHALL HOUSE

The Marshall House was built in 1805 and is an example of early town house construction in Middle Tennessee. The house is owned by Mr. and Mrs. James Farrell.

Game and Seafood

BARBECUED WILD RABBIT AND TOMATO GRAVY

2 wild rabbits

Parboil rabbits until tender. Drain rabbit, saving broth. Place rabbit pieces in a broiler pan, baste top side with barbecue sauce, brown under broiler then reserve pieces and repeat.

Barbecue Sauce:

1 (8 ounce) can tomato sauce 1 clove garlic
¼ cup honey   ½ teaspoon ginger
¼ cup lemon juice   ½ teaspoon Tabasco
1 Tablespoon soy sauce   ¼ teaspoon dry mustard
1 Tablespoon Worcestershire
 sauce

Combine all ingredients in a bowl and mix well.

Tomato Gravy:

1 (10¾ ounce) can cream of 3 to 4 Tablespoons flour
 tomato soup

Mix broth with soup. Add flour to thicken. Bring to a boil, stirring to avoid lumping until thickened. Serve gravy over creamed potatoes or cornbread cakes. *Yield:* 6 servings.

Mrs. Marvin Wallace (Alice)

PLANTATION QUAIL

½ cup bacon, cubed
8 quail
Salt and pepper
6 Tablespoons flour
¼ cup finely chopped onion

¼ cup finely chopped celery
3 cups chicken broth
½ bay leaf
1 Tablespoon chopped parsley
Rice

Sauté bacon until brown; remove from skillet. Place lightly salted and peppered quail in drippings and brown. Add flour, onions, and celery; stir. Add all remaining ingredients except rice; add bacon. Cover and simmer 30 minutes, turning occasionally, until tender. More broth may be added, if necessary. Serve over hot, cooked rice. *Yield:* 4 to 5 servings. *Note:* This makes an elegant breakfast dish. Dove breast may be substituted or included with quail.

Mrs. Herbert E. Patrick (Lyn)
Savannah, Tennessee

SHERRIED QUAIL CASSEROLE

6 quail, quartered
¼ cup butter
½ cup chopped onion
½ cup chopped celery

1 Tablespoon cornstarch
1 cup chicken broth
2 Tablespoons sherry
2 Tablespoons chopped parsley

Sauté quail in butter for 10 minutes. Remove quail and sauté onion and celery in butter remaining in skillet for 5 minutes. Add cornstarch dissolved in chicken broth and cook, stirring constantly, until thickened. Stir in sherry and parsley. Arrange quail in shallow casserole and pour sauce over them. Bake at 350 degrees for 15 minutes. Arrange parsley on top if desired for color. *Yield:* 6 servings.

Mrs. David Pittman (Sydney)

EASY VENISON (OR BEEF) CASSEROLE

1½ pounds of venison or round
   steak
1 (10¾ ounce) can beef
   consommé
½ cup red wine
¼ cup fine dry bread crumbs

¼ cup flour
¾ teaspoon salt
⅛ teaspoon pepper
1 medium onion, sliced
1 (4 ounce) can mushrooms

Cut venison into 2 inch cubes. Combine consommé, wine, bread crumbs, and flour. Add salt, pepper, onion, and mushrooms. Mix with meat and pour into covered baking dish. Bake at 300 degrees for 3 hours. Serve over rice or noodles. *Yield:* 6 servings.

Mrs. William T. Batson (Linda)

ORLEANS SHRIMP

¼ cup butter
¼ cup olive oil
½ cup flour
1 cup chopped green onions
1 (16 ounce) can whole peeled
   tomatoes, drained (reserve
   ½ cup juice)
Salt to taste

Red and black pepper to taste
2 pounds boiled shrimp,
   peeled and deveined
2 cups sour cream
¼ cup dry white wine
¼ cup Parmesan cheese
2 Tablespoons capers
Pastry shells or toast

Melt butter in skillet and add olive oil and flour. Brown slowly on medium heat until dark. Using blender, combine green onions and tomatoes with salt and pepper to make purée. Transfer roux to heavy Dutch oven and add tomato purée. Simmer for 20 minutes, stirring occasionally. Add remaining ingredients and cook for 1 to 2 minutes. Stir to mix. Cook just long enough to heat thoroughly. Use the ½ cup tomato juice to make the desired consistency or for reheating. Serve on pastry shells or toast. *Yield:* 6 to 8 servings. *Note:* May be frozen for short period.

Mrs. Richard Dodson (Carolyn)

GRILLED SHRIMP

1 teaspoon dry mustard
½ cup salad oil
3 Tablespoons vinegar
2 Tablespoons lemon juice
1 teaspoon Worcestershire
  sauce
2 Tablespoons prepared
  horseradish

½ teaspoon sugar
¼ cup tomato catsup
¼ teaspoon pepper
3 drops hot pepper sauce
1 teaspoon salt
2 pounds jumbo shrimp,
  deveined

Blend mustard with oil to make a smooth paste. Add all remaining ingredients except shrimp; mix well. Add shrimp. Marinate shrimp at least 2 hours or overnight in refrigerator. Grill 9 inches above charcoal 15 minutes, turning occasionally. *Note:* Put on bamboo skewers or shish kebab skewers to keep from falling through grill. *Yield:* 4 servings.

Mrs. Jerry Holcomb (Tinker)

Variation: For marinade use 2 cups oil, 1 clove garlic, 1 teaspoon salt, 1 teaspoon pepper, 3 Tablespoons chili sauce, 1 Tablespoon Worcestershire sauce, 3 Tablespoons cider vinegar and ¼ cup fresh chopped parsley. Marinate shrimp, then grill.

Mrs. Donald Hillenmeyer (Chris)

BAKED SHRIMP

5 pounds shrimp, unpeeled
1 (16 ounce) bottle Italian
  salad dressing
1 pound butter or margarine

1 Tablespoon red pepper
1 Tablespoon black pepper
1 Tablespoon salt

Melt butter and dressing together. Add remaining ingredients. Pour over unpeeled shrimp and bake 1 hour at 350 degrees. Serve with green salad and French bread. *Yield:* 6 servings.

Helen Griffin
Petal, Mississippi

CANTONESE SHRIMP
Dieters' Delight

2 pounds raw, peeled and
  deveined shrimp
2 Tablespoons margarine
2 cup diagonally sliced celery
2 cups sliced onions
1 (6½ ounce) can sliced water
  chestnuts

2 cups frozen broccoli pieces
1 cup sliced green bell pepper
¼ teaspoon pepper
¼ cup soy sauce
1¼ cups chicken broth
2 Tablespoons cornstarch

Sauté shrimp in margarine in electric skillet at 300 degrees for 2 to 3 minutes until shrimp are pink. Add celery and onions. Cook for 4 minutes over medium heat. Add water chestnuts, broccoli, and bell pepper. Cook for 4 minutes. In separate bowl, add pepper, soy sauce, chicken broth, and cornstarch. Add liquid mixture to shrimp and vegetables. Stir until sauce clears and thickens. Serve over hot cooked rice. Great for those on a diet. Do not over cook. Vegetables should be crunchy. *Yield:* 6 to 8 servings.

Erika Engel
Mobile, Alabama

BAKED SHRIMP CREOLE

1 cup chopped celery
½ cup chopped green pepper
1 large onion, chopped
1 Tablespoon butter or
  margarine
1 pound cooked shrimp
1 cup cooked rice
1 (10¾ ounce) can tomato soup

1 (6 ounce) can chopped
  mushrooms with juice
⅛ teaspoon thyme
1 teaspoon red pepper
1 pound sharp Cheddar cheese,
  shredded
½ cup Parmesan cheese

Sauté celery, green pepper, and onion in margarine until soft. In large mixing bowl, add remaining ingredients, saving ½ cup of Cheddar cheese and Parmesan cheese for topping. Pour into greased 2-quart casserole dish. Bake at 350 degrees for 45 minutes. *Yield:* 8 servings.

Mrs. Larry Nichols (Ellen)

SEAFOOD CASSEROLE

2 pounds frozen haddock
1 Tablespoon shrimp boil
  seasoning
3 (10¾ ounce) cans cream of
  shrimp soup

1 long roll of crackers,
  crumbled

Thaw haddock. Bring a large pan of water to boil and add 1 table-spoon of shrimp boil seasoning. Poach fish for 15 minutes. Remove the fish and break into pieces (like crabmeat). Mix fish and cream of shrimp soup and pour into 13x9x2 inch dish and sprinkle with cracker crumbs. Dot with butter. Bake at 350 degrees for 45 minutes. *Yield:* 8 servings. *Note:* I use Ritz crackers.

Mrs. C. D. Berry, IV (Kathy)

LOBSTER THERMIDOR

2 Tablespoons butter
2 Tablespoons flour
1 cup stock (1 cup boiling
  water poured over 2 chicken
  bouillon cubes)
1 cup half-and-half
1 egg yolk

2 cups lobster meat
¼ cup wine (sherry)
3 hard-boiled eggs (optional)
1 cup mushrooms (optional)
Dash red pepper
Dash paprika
1 cup buttered bread crumbs

Melt butter in top of double boiler; add flour and mix. Add stock and cook until thick. Mix half-and-half and beaten egg yolks with a few spoonfuls of sauce. Stir and add back to sauce. Cook until thick, never letting water boil too hard. Remove from heat. Add lobster meat, wine, hard-boiled eggs, mushrooms, red pepper, and paprika. Pour into buttered 2-quart casserole. Sprinkle with buttered bread crumbs. Bake at 300 degrees for 15 to 20 minutes until bubbly and bread crumbs are brown. *Yield:* 4 to 6 servings.

Mrs. H. Grady DeVan, Jr. (Ann)

SALMON SUPREME CASSEROLE

1 (7¾ ounce) can pink salmon,
  drained and flaked
½ cup uncooked macaroni
½ cup creamed cottage cheese
½ cup sour cream
½ small onion, minced
1 Tablespoon chopped parsley

¼ teaspoon salt
1/16 teaspoon pepper
1 cup buttered bread crumbs
  (optional)
1 cup crushed corn flakes
  (optional)
Paprika

Cook macaroni in boiling salted water until almost tender; drain.
Combine flaked salmon, cottage cheese, sour cream, onion, parsley,
salt, and pepper in large mixing bowl. Add macaroni and mix well.
Pour into a greased 1-quart casserole. Top with buttered bread
crumbs, crushed corn flakes, and paprika. Bake in a pre-heated 350
degree oven for 35 to 40 minutes. *Yield:* 4 servings.

Mariellen Perkinson

TROUT MARGUERY

4 fillets of trout
3 Tablespoons olive oil
2 egg yolks, beaten
1 cup butter, melted
1 Tablespoon flour
¼ cup dry white wine
1 Tablespoon lemon juice

1 cup shrimp, cooked and
  chopped
½ cup crabmeat
½ cup mushrooms, sliced
Paprika
Salt and pepper to taste

Salt and pepper fillets. Place in baking pan and add olive oil. Bake at
375 degrees for 20 minutes. As fish bakes, prepare sauce. Place egg
yolks in top of double boiler over hot water and add melted butter,
stirring constantly until mixture thickens. Blend in flour. Add wine,
lemon juice, shrimp, crabmeat, mushrooms, paprika, salt and
pepper to taste. Stir and cook for 15 minutes. Place fish on platter
and cover with sauce. *Yield:* 4 servings.

Mrs. H. L. Malone (Lib)

GOURMET HALIBUT

3 pounds frozen Halibut,
  ¾ inch thick
⅓ cup lemon juice
¼ cup melted butter
½ teaspoon salt

½ teaspoon pepper
½ (10¾ ounce) can cream of
  shrimp soup
½ cup sour cream
½ cup tiny shrimp, canned

Cut fish into 6 pieces. Soak overnight or for 3 to 4 hours in lemon juice. Turn fish over occasionally. The next day drain off juices and save. Pour melted butter, salt, and pepper over fish and broil 10 minutes. Take out and baste with remaining juices. Cool slightly. Make sauce from shrimp soup and sour cream. Spoon over top of fish. Bake at 325 degrees for 30 minutes. Brown tiny shrimp; sprinkle over top of fish. Broil for 5 minutes and serve. *Yield:* 6 servings.

Mrs. Robert Olson (Janie)
Washington, D.C.

MINCED CLAM AND EGGPLANT CASSEROLE

1 medium eggplant, peeled
  and cubed
¼ cup margarine
Salt and pepper to taste
1 cup cracker crumbs

1 (6½ ounce) can clams,
  undrained
½ cup buttered cracker crumbs
Paprika

Soak eggplant in salt water for 20 minutes. Drain and cook until tender. Drain again and mash with margarine, salt and pepper. Stir in cracker crumbs and clams. Pour into 1-quart casserole and top with buttered cracker crumbs and paprika. Bake at 350 degrees for 35 minutes or until golden brown. *Yield:* 4 to 6 servings.

Nancy P. Conway

OYSTERS AU PAINRE

8 large or 12 medium freshly
  shucked oysters
¼ cup melted butter
Salt to taste
Celery salt to taste

Freshly ground black pepper
  to taste
Bread crumbs
Salad oil or melted butter
Paprika

Drain oysters and dry well on paper towel. Dip in butter; sprinkle
with salt, celery salt, and lots of freshly ground pepper. Dip in bread
crumbs; sprinkle lightly with melted butter and paprika. Place
under preheated broiler and broil on both sides only until crumbs
are lightly brown. Avoid overcooking. *Yield:* 8 to 12 appetizers.
Note: For bread crumbs, I use Progresso Redi Flavored Bread
Crumbs Italian style.

Mrs. James B. White (Virginia)

SCALLOPS IN WINE

1 pound scallops
1 cup white wine
¼ cup water
1 medium onion, chopped
1 bay leaf
3 sprigs parsley
1 stalk celery
6 peppercorns
Salt and pepper to taste

¼ pound mushrooms, chopped
1 Tablespoon lemon juice
3 Tablespoons butter,
  melted
3 Tablespoons flour
1 cup milk
1 egg yolk, beaten
1 cup buttered bread crumbs

Cook scallops with wine, water, onion, bay leaf, parsley, celery,
peppercorns, salt, and pepper for 10 minutes. Remove scallops to
drain. Simmer remaining liquid down to ½ cup. Sauté mushrooms
in lemon juice for 4 minutes. Blend butter and flour; add milk and
reserved liquid from scallops. Cook until thickened. Pour slowly
over egg yolk. Combine sauce, mushrooms, and scallops in a
casserole. Top with buttered bread crumbs and bake at 400 degrees
for 15 minutes or until heated through. Brown bread crumbs under
broiler. Serve immediately over rice. *Yield:* 4 servings.

Mrs. Joseph Barker (Sherry)

COQUILLES ST. JACQUES

1½ pounds fresh scallops
¾ cup white wine
1 Tablespoon lemon juice
½ teaspoon salt
¼ cup butter
1 cup sliced green onion
   or shallots

1 clove minced garlic
¼ cup flour
⅛ teaspoon nutmeg
Dash of white pepper
1 cup milk
1 cup bread crumbs
2 Tablespoons melted butter

Halve any large scallops. In a saucepan, combine scallops, wine, lemon juice, and salt. Bring to a boil. Reduce heat; cover and simmer 2 to 4 minutes or until scallops are opaque in appearance. Drain, reserving 1 cup of the wine mixture. Add water if necessary to make 1 cup. Melt ¼ cup butter and sauté the green onion and garlic until tender. Blend in flour, nutmeg, and pepper. Add milk and the reserved 1 cup wine mixture all at once. Cook, stirring constantly, until thickened and bubbly. Add scallops and heat. Spoon mixture into 6 buttered shells or ramekins. Toss bread crumbs with butter and sprinkle over top. Bake at 400 degrees for 10 minutes or until brown. *Yield:* 6 servings.

Mrs. William E. Ward, III (Maggie)

CRAB CASSEROLE

4 slices of bread, cubed
1 (6½ ounce) can crabmeat
½ cup celery, chopped
¼ cup mayonnaise
1 cup milk
2 eggs, well beaten

½ can cream of mushroom
   soup
1 medium onion, chopped
⅛ teaspoon garlic salt
1 cup sharp Cheddar cheese,
   shredded

Butter 2-quart casserole. Layer all bread cubes in the bottom of the dish. Layer crabmeat on top of bread cubes. In a large mixing bowl combine celery, mayonnaise, milk, eggs, soup, onion, and garlic salt; mix well. Pour this mixture over crabmeat and fork this into bread and crab layers. Top with cheese. Bake at 300 degrees for 1 hour. *Yield:* 6 servings.

Mrs. J. B. Ellis (Evelyn)
Huntsville, Alabama

BAKED FLOUNDER WITH SHRIMP SAUCE
A must for seafood lovers.

8 flounder fillets (bass, trout,
or pompano may be
substituted)

Place each fillet on a piece of aluminum foil and spread each with shrimp sauce. Wrap so that no steam will escape. Bake at 350 degrees for 45 minutes. Serve directly from foil.

Shrimp sauce:

1¾ cups milk	Dash red pepper
3 Tablespoons flour	¾ teaspoon salt
1 cup butter or margarine	½ garlic clove, minced
4 Tablespoons chopped green pepper	2 beaten egg yolks
1 Tablespoon chopped pimento	¾ cup heavy cream
½ cup chopped onion	1½ cups chopped mushrooms
1 teaspoon Worcestershire sauce	2½ pounds chopped, cooked shrimp

Using double boiler, make a thick sauce by melting butter and adding flour and milk. Then add green pepper, pimento, onion, Worcestershire sauce, red pepper, salt and garlic clove. Mix egg yolks and cream. Add to sauce. Then stir in mushrooms and shrimp. *Yield:* 8 servings.

Mrs. Lenox Rawlings (Libby)

CRABMEAT SALAD
Quick, Easy, and Rich!

1 (6½ ounce) can crabmeat
1 (10½ ounce) can cut asparagus
1 (4½ ounce) can chopped ripe olives

2 Tablespoons chopped sweet pickle relish
2 Tablespoons mayonnaise

Check crabmeat for shell. Drain crabmeat, asparagus, olives, and pickle relish in a strainer for about 10 minutes. Place in small mixing bowl and mix together, mashing the asparagus. Add mayonnaise and chill. *Note:* Can be used for party sandwiches by adding a little more mayonnaise so that the mixture will be of a spreading consistency. *Yield:* 3 to 4 servings.

Mrs. Robert Plummer (Mary)

Walker-Ridley
House

Cakes and Frostings
Scratch and Mix

ITALIAN CREAM CAKE

½ cup margarine
1½ cups vegetable shortening
2 cups sugar
5 egg yolks
2 cups flour
1 teaspoon soda

1 cup buttermilk
1 teaspoon vanilla
1 cup chopped pecans
1 (3½ ounce) can coconut
5 egg whites, stiffly beaten

Cream margarine with shortening. Add sugar and beat until mixture is smooth. Add egg yolks and beat well. In a separate bowl combine flour and soda; add to creamed mixture alternating with buttermilk. Stir in vanilla. Add pecans and coconut. Fold in egg whites. Pour batter into 3 greased and floured 8 inch pans. Bake at 350 degrees for 30 minutes.

Cream Cheese Frosting:
1 (8 ounce) package cream
   cheese, softened
¼ cup margarine
1 (16 ounce) box powdered
   sugar

1 teaspoon vanilla
¼ cup chopped pecans

Beat cream cheese and margarine until smooth. Add powdered sugar and mix well. Add vanilla and mix well. Frost cake. Sprinkle pecans on cake. *Yield:* 12 to 14 servings.

Mrs. W. W. Kennedy (Lucy)
Brentwood, Tennessee

CARROT PINEAPPLE CAKE

1½ cups flour
1 cup sugar
1 teaspoon baking powder
1 teaspoon ground cinnamon
½ teaspoon salt
⅔ cup oil

2 eggs
1 cup finely shredded
  raw carrots
½ cup crushed pineapple with
  syrup
1 teaspoon vanilla

Stir together dry ingredients. Add oil, eggs, carrots, pineapple, and vanilla; mix until all are moistened. Beat with electric mixer 2 minutes at medium speed. Pour batter into greased and lightly floured 9x9x2 inch pan. Bake at 350 degrees about 35 minutes. Frost with cream cheese frosting.

Cream Cheese Frosting:
1 (3 ounce) package cream
  cheese, softened
4 Tablespoons butter or
  margarine, softened
1 Tablespoon vanilla

Dash of salt
2½ cups sifted powdered
  sugar
½ cup chopped pecans

Cream together cream cheese and butter. Beat in vanilla and salt. Gradually add powdered sugar, blend well. Stir in pecans. *Yield:* 12 to 14 servings.

Mrs. C. W. French (Louise)
Nashville, Tennessee

CREAM CHEESE POUND CAKE

1½ cups butter or margarine
1 (8 ounce) package cream
  cheese
3 cups sugar

Dash of salt
1½ teaspoons vanilla
6 large eggs
3 cups cake flour, sifted

Cream butter, cream cheese, and sugar until light and fluffy. Add salt and vanilla, beat well. Add eggs one at a time, beating well after each addition. Stir in flour. Spoon mixture into greased 10 inch tube pan. Do not preheat oven. Bake at 325 degrees about 1½ hours. *Yield:* 16 servings.

Mrs. Emory Milton (Ann)

CREAM CHEESE CHEESE-CAKE

1 (16 ounce) carton cottage
  cheese, small curds
2 (8 ounce) packages cream
  cheese
4 beaten eggs
1 teaspoon vanilla

1½ Tablespoons lemon juice
3 Tablespoons cornstarch
3 Tablespoons flour
1½ cups sugar
½ cup butter, melted
1 pint sour cream

Cream first 2 ingredients. Add beaten eggs, vanilla, lemon juice, cornstarch, flour, and sugar. Beat well until all ingredients are well blended. In the meantime, melt butter completely and add to mixture. Fold in sour cream. Bake in a springform pan at 350 degrees for 1 hour. Turn off heat and leave in oven for 2 hours. Cool and refrigerate or freeze. If cake isn't brown on top put it under the broiler to brown after the 2 hour wait. *Yield:* 12 servings.

Mrs. H. W. Lane (Evelyn)
Hillside, New Jersey

CHOCOLATE BOURBON CAKE
Very rich mousse-like cake, perfect for a large crowd.

2 cups butter
1 cup sugar
1 cup powdered sugar
1 dozen eggs, separated
4 ounces unsweetened
  chocolate, melted
1 teaspoon vanilla extract

1 cup chopped pecans
1 dozen double ladyfingers
1 pound dry Italian macaroons
  (approximately 4 dozen),
  broken and soaked in 1 cup
  Bourbon
1½ cups heavy cream, whipped

Cream butter and sugars until light and fluffy. Beat egg yolks until light and blend into butter mixture. Beat in chocolate, add vanilla, and pecans. Beat egg whites until stiff, but not dry; fold into chocolate mixture. Line a 10 inch springform pan around sides and bottom with split ladyfingers. Alternate layers of soaked macaroons and chocolate mixture over ladyfingers. Chill overnight. Remove sides of springform pan and cover top with whipped cream. If it is frozen, add whipped cream after defrosting. Freezes well. *Yield:* 18 servings.

Mrs. Donald N. Edmands (Isabel)

PINEAPPLE SHEET CAKE

Cake:

2 cups flour
2 cups sugar
2 teaspoons baking soda
1 (20 ounce) can crushed
    pineapple

2 eggs, beaten
1 teaspoon vanilla
½ cup chopped nuts

Mix flour, sugar, and baking soda. Stir in pineapple (undrained), eggs, and vanilla. Mix well. Add nuts and pour into greased jellyroll pan (15½x10½x1 inch). Bake at 350 degrees for 25 to 30 minutes.

Icing:

1 (8 ounce) cream cheese,
    softened
2 Tablespoons margarine

1 pound box powdered sugar
3 teaspoons vanilla
½ cup chopped nuts

Mix cream cheese, margarine, powdered sugar, and vanilla until well blended. Sprinkle chopped nuts on iced cake. Keep refrigerated. *Yield:* 100 servings.

Mrs. Harv Gerecke (Mary)
Pekin, Illinois

SOUR CREAM POUND CAKE

1 cup butter or margarine
3 cups sugar
6 eggs
1 (8 ounce) carton sour cream
3 cups flour

¼ teaspoon salt
¼ teaspoon baking soda
1 teaspoon vanilla
1 teaspoon lemon extract

Melt margarine over low heat. Cream with sugar. Add 6 eggs, one at a time, beating into mixture. Next add sour cream, mixing well. In separate bowl, sift flour, salt and baking soda. Add this to the first mixture, little by little, beating well between each addition of flour mixture. Add flavoring. Pour into a greased and floured 10 inch stem pan. Cook at 300 degrees for about 1 hour or until cake is done. Turn cake out of pan immediately. *Yield:* 1 cake.

Mrs. Dean Campbell (Anna Marie)
Columbia, Tennessee

CARROT CAKE

Cake:

2 cups sugar
1½ cups vegetable oil
4 eggs, unbeaten
1 teaspoon cinnamon

3 cups raw grated carrots
½ cup chopped pecans
2 cups self-rising flour

Mix ingredients in the order listed. Pour into a greased and floured tube or bundt pan and bake for 1 hour at 350 degrees.

Icing:

1 (16 ounce) box powdered
   sugar
½ cup butter or margarine

2 teaspoons vanilla
1 (8 ounce) package cream
   cheese

Mix sugar, butter, vanilla, and cream cheese. Ice cooled cake. *Note:* I have found it helps to put this cake in the freezer for a couple of hours before icing. *Yield:* 12 to 14 servings.

Mrs. Jimmy Jordan (Dianah)

APPLE CAKE

1 cup salad oil
2 cups sugar
3 eggs
3 cups flour
1 teaspoon soda

1 teaspoon salt
1 teaspoon cinnamon
1 teaspoon vanilla
3 cups chopped raw apples
1 cup nuts

Measure oil into large bowl, add sugar and eggs. Beat until creamy. Sift dry ingredients together, then add a little at a time to the creamy mixture. Beat well. Fold in apples and nuts. Spread evenly in a greased 13x9x2 inch pan. Bake 55 minutes at 350 degrees.

Icing:

1 cup brown sugar, packed
   firmly

¼ cup milk
½ cup margarine

Combine ingredients and cook for 2½ minutes. Spoon over cake while still warm in pan. *Yield:* 12 to 14 servings.

Mrs. Walter Bond (Elizabeth)

CHERRY CONFETTI CAKE

3 cups sifted flour
2 teaspoons baking powder
1 teaspoon salt
1 cup butter, softened
4 cups sifted powdered sugar
1 teaspoon almond extract

4 eggs
1 cup milk
½ cup chopped almonds
1 cup maraschino cherries, finely cut, allowing some juice to remain

In a medium mixing bowl sift the first 3 ingredients. In another mixing bowl, cream butter and gradually add powdered sugar, creaming well. Add extract and eggs, one at a time, creaming well after each addition. Add dry ingredients and milk alternately to the creamed mixture, beginning and ending with the dry ingredients. Use low speed, blend thoroughly after each addition. Fold in almonds and maraschino cherries. Pour into well greased and lightly floured 10 inch tube pan. Cut gently through batter to break air bubbles. Bake at 350 degrees for 60 to 65 minutes.

Topping:
½ cup melted butter
½ cup sugar

1 teaspoon cinnamon

After cake is removed from pan, but still warm, spread top and sides with melted butter and sprinkle with a mixture of sugar and cinnamon, patting it into the melted butter. *Yield:* 12 to 14 servings.

Mrs. Michael Connelly (Bonnie)

LAVINIA'S POUND CAKE

1 cup butter, melted or softened
2 cups sugar
5 eggs

2 teaspoons vanilla
3 cups self-rising flour
1 cup milk

Preheat oven to 350 degrees. Grease and flour 10 inch tube pan. Cream butter and sugar. Add eggs and vanilla; mix well. Add flour and milk alternately and mix until smooth. Pour into tube pan and bake at 350 degrees for 1 hour. Serve plain, with fresh fruit or with ice cream. *Yield:* 12 to 14 servings.

Mrs. Kerry A. Perkinson (Susan)

ORANGE APPLE CAKE

2½ cups flour, sifted
1 teaspoon pumpkin pie spice
1 teaspoon baking powder
1 teaspoon soda
1 teaspoon salt
½ cup shortening
1¾ cups sugar

3 eggs
1 teaspoon vanilla
½ cup milk
2 cups peeled, grated apples
1 cup seedless raisins
1 cup pecans, chopped

Sift flour, spice, baking powder, soda, and salt together. Set aside. Cream shortening and sugar. Add eggs; beat well until light and fluffy. Add vanilla, milk, and apples. Add sifted dry ingredients to creamed mixture. Stir well. Add raisins and pecans and blend well. Pour into 3 greased and floured 8 inch round pans and bake at 350 degrees for 35 minutes. Cool and frost with Orange Butter Icing.

Orange Butter Icing:
½ cup butter, softened
1 (16 ounce) box powdered
  sugar
¼ cup orange juice

4 teaspoons grated orange peel
1 teaspoon salt
1 teaspoon vanilla

Cream butter and powdered sugar. Add orange juice, orange peel, salt, and vanilla. Blend completely. Frost cake. *Yield:* 24 servings.

Mrs. William F. Greenwood, Jr. (Sandra)

POUND CAKE

1 cup butter, (no substitution)
  soften at room temperature
3 cups sugar
6 eggs

1 teaspoon vanilla
3 cups cake flour, sifted 3
  times
½ pint whipping cream

Cream butter and sugar. Add eggs, one at a time, blending well. Add vanilla. Alternately add flour and whipping cream. Put in a well greased 10 inch bundt or tube pan. Bake at 250 degrees for 2 hours or until toothpick comes out clean. Do not open door during the 2 hour cooking time. *Yield:* 12 to 14 servings.

Mrs. Robert Sevier (Paula)
Brentwood, Tennessee

GRANDMOTHER SHAVER'S JAM CAKE

1 cup butter
2 cups sugar
2 cups blackberry jam
3 eggs, beaten
1 cup buttermilk
3½ cups flour

1 teaspoon soda
1 teaspoon cinnamon
1 teaspoon allspice
1 teaspoon baking powder
1 teaspoon nutmeg
1 teaspoon cloves

Cream butter. Add sugar and jam. Mix well. Add eggs and buttermilk. Sift flour and other dry ingredients and add to mixture. Beat well. Bake in 2 greased 9 inch cake pans at 350 degrees for 30 minutes.

Caramel Icing:
1 cup buttermilk
2 cups sugar
½ teaspoon soda

½ cup butter
½ cup brown sugar
1 teaspoon vanilla

Combine all ingredients in saucepan and cook to soft ball stage on low heat and test in cold water. Stir mixture constantly. When soft ball stage is reached, remove from heat. Beat until creamy and ready to spread. It takes about 20 to 30 minutes to make. *Yield:* 12 servings.

Mrs. Ed Anderson (Mary Jane)

PLUM CAKE

2 cups sugar
1 cup vegetable oil,
   less 1 Tablespoon
3 eggs
2 (4½ ounce) jars plum baby
   food

2 cups sifted self-rising flour
1 teaspoon cloves
1 teaspoon cinnamon
1 teaspoon nutmeg
1 teaspoon allspice
1 cup chopped nuts

Mix all ingredients well. Pour into greased and floured tube pan. In cold oven, bake at 300 degrees for 1½ hours. Cool. Remove from pan. *Yield:* 12 to 14 servings.

Mrs. Ben Armistead (Tina)
Concord, Tennessee

BLACKBERRY CAKE
An old family recipe.

1½ cups sugar	1 teaspoon cinnamon
1 cup cooking oil	1 teaspoon nutmeg
2 cups flour	1 teaspoon allspice
3 eggs	1 teaspoon salt
1 cup buttermilk	1 teaspoon soda
2 cups blackberry jam or preserves	1 teaspoon vanilla

Grease and flour 10 inch tube pan or 13x9x2 inch pan. Mix all ingredients and bake 40 minutes at 325 degrees.

Filling:

½ cup butter	½ teaspoon vanilla
1 cup sugar	1 Tablespoon white corn syrup
½ cup milk	

Combine ingredients; bring to a boil and pour onto hot cake while syrup is hot. Punch holes in cake with knife for syrup to penetrate. *Yield:* 12 to 14 servings.

Mrs. Bobby Stratton (Margie)

DR. BIRD CAKE

2 cups sugar	1½ cups oil
3 cups flour	1½ teaspoons vanilla
1 teaspoon soda	2 cups diced bananas
1 teaspoon cinnamon	1 (8 ounce) can crushed
1 teaspoon salt	pineapple with juice
3 eggs	

Mix dry ingredients. Make a well in center and into it, break eggs, add oil, vanilla, bananas, then pineapple. Stir, do not beat, until blended well. Pour into 9 or 10 inch tube pan. Bake at 350 degrees for 1 hour and 20 minutes. Cake will crack slightly on top. Cool in pan on rack. Remove when cold. Keeps well in refrigerator. Wrap well. *Yield:* 12 to 14 servings.

Miss Julie Westfall

PRUNE CAKE

2 cups flour	1 teaspoon cinnamon
1½ cups sugar	1 teaspoon allspice
1 cup vegetable oil	1 teaspoon soda
3 eggs	1 teaspoon vanilla
1 cup buttermilk	1 cup prunes, cooked, chopped

Mix flour and sugar. Add oil and eggs to sugar mixture, beating well after each addition. Add buttermilk, cinnamon, allspice, soda, and vanilla, blending well. Fold in prunes. Bake in two 9 inch round cake pans at 325 degrees for 40 minutes.

Icing:

½ cup butter	¼ cup milk
1 cup brown sugar	1¾ cups powdered sugar

Melt butter; add sugar. Cook 2 minutes. Add milk and boil 1 minute. Let cool and add powdered sugar. *Yield:* 14 to 16 servings.

Mrs. Margaret Darnell
Shelbyville, Tennessee

APRICOT SHEET CAKE

3 cups flour	Dash of salt
1 cup butter or margarine	1 (12 ounce) jar peach or
3 egg yolks	apricot preserves
¼ cup milk	3 egg whites
¼ cup sugar	½ cup sugar
2 teaspoons baking powder	½ to 1 cup crushed nuts

Work flour and butter by hand until mixed thoroughly. Add egg yolks, milk, ¼ cup sugar, baking powder, and salt. Mix well and pat dough into 15x10x1 inch jelly roll pan, spreading evenly in pan for crust. Spread peach or apricot preserves over dough. Beat egg whites until stiff. Add ½ cup sugar and beat until sugar is mixed in well. Spread egg whites over preserves so edges of dough are sealed. Sprinkle egg whites with crushed nuts. Bake at 350 degrees for 40 minutes. *Yield:* 35 to 50 servings.

Mrs. Donald Westfall (Nancy)
Brentwood, Tennessee

214

BROWN BOTTOM CUPCAKES

Batter:

1½ cups flour
1 cup sugar
¼ cup unsweetened chocolate, melted
1 teaspoon soda
½ teaspoon salt
1 cup water
⅓ cup cooking oil
1 teaspoon vinegar
1 teaspoon vanilla

Mix all ingredients in a large mixing bowl. Beat well. Fill lined muffin tins ⅓ full.

Filling:

1 (8 ounce) package cream cheese
1 egg
⅛ teaspoon salt
⅓ cup sugar
1 cup chocolate chips

Combine cream cheese, egg, salt, and sugar. Beat well. Stir in chocolate chips. Place a heaping teaspoon of filling mixture on batter in each muffin cup. Bake at 350 degrees for 30 minutes. *Yield:* 24 servings.

Mrs. Gayle Weber (Mary Alice)
Fairview, Tennessee

AUNT MARY'S DEVIL'S FOOD CAKE

2½ cups flour
3 heaping Tablespoons cocoa
½ cup butter
2 cups sugar
3 eggs
1 cup buttermilk
½ cup warm water
1½ teaspoons baking soda
1½ teaspoons vanilla

Sift flour with cocoa. Cream butter and add sugar; beating until creamy. Add eggs, one at a time, beating well after each addition. Add buttermilk, alternating with flour mixture. Leave a little flour mixture to add to ½ cup warm water, which has baking soda dissolved in it. Add vanilla and mix well. Pour into 2 (9 inch) greased cake pans. Bake at 350 degrees for 30 minutes. *Yield:* 12 to 16 servings.

Katherine Keller
Dayton, Ohio

CHOCOLATE SYRUP CAKE

½ cup margarine
1 cup sugar
4 eggs
1 cup flour

1 teaspoon baking powder
Pinch of salt
1 (16 ounce) can chocolate
  syrup

Cream margarine and sugar. Add eggs, one at a time. Beat well. Sift flour, baking powder, and salt. Add to creamed mixture, alternately with chocolate syrup. Bake for 30 minutes or until done at 350 degrees in a greased and floured 8x12x2 inch pan.

Icing:
½ cup margarine
1 cup sugar
⅓ cup evaporated milk

½ cup chocolate chips
1 teaspoon vanilla
1 cup chopped nuts

Bring to a boil; margarine, sugar, and evaporated milk. Cook 2 or 3 minutes, stirring constantly. Turn off heat and add chocolate chips, stirring until chips melt. Add vanilla and nuts. Pour immediately over warm cake. When cool, cut into squares. *Yield:* 20 to 24 servings.

Mrs. James Short (Mary Catherine)

CHESS CAKE

It's great served hot and with ice cream. Your children will love this one!

2 cups flour
2 teaspoons baking powder
½ teaspoon salt
1 (16 ounce) box brown sugar

1 cup margarine, melted
4 egg yolks, beaten
1 cup pecans
4 egg whites, stiffly beaten

Mix flour, baking powder, salt, and brown sugar. Add melted margarine and egg yolks. Add nuts. Fold in stiffly beaten egg whites. Bake in a 13x9x2 inch pan at 350 degrees for 30 minutes. *Yield:* 12 to 14 servings.

Mrs. Richard Goodwin (June)

APPLE-COCONUT CAKE

Cake:

3 eggs
1¼ cups oil
2 cups sugar
2½ cups self-rising flour
2 medium apples, peeled,
   cored, chopped

1 cup shredded coconut
1 cup chopped walnuts or
   pecans

Grease and flour a 10 inch tube pan and preheat oven to 350 degrees. Blend eggs, oil, and sugar until creamy. Add flour a little at a time. Blend well. Batter will be stiff. Fold in apples, coconut, and nuts. Pour into tube pan and bake for 1 hour. Cool about 30 minutes and remove from pan.

Topping:

¼ cup butter
½ cup brown sugar

⅓ cup milk

Mix butter, sugar, and milk in a saucepan. Boil for 3 minutes and pour over warm cake. *Yield:* 12 to 14 servings.

Mrs. C. W. French (Louise)
Nashville, Tennessee

FRUIT CAKE

½ pound candied pineapple
   (8 ounces)
½ pound candied cherries
   (8 ounces)
½ pound pecans (8 ounces)

1 pound dates
1 (3½ ounce) can coconut
1 (14 ounce) can sweetened
   condensed milk
¼ teaspoon salt

Cut up fruit and nuts coarsely and mix. Add coconut. Add sweetened condensed milk and salt. Line 9x5x3 inch baking pan with brown paper. Press mixture into pan. Bake 1 hour at 300 degrees. *Yield:* 12 to 14 servings.

Mrs. Farris Galbraith (Kitty)

COLA CAKE

2 cups flour	2 eggs, beaten
2 cups sugar	1 teaspoon baking soda
1 cup margarine	1 teaspoon vanilla
3 Tablespoons cocoa	1½ cups miniature
1 cup cola	marshmallows
½ cup buttermilk	

Combine flour and sugar. Heat margarine, cocoa, and cola until mixture boils. Pour mixture over flour and sugar. Blend and add buttermilk, eggs, soda, and vanilla. Fold in marshmallows. Beat well by hand and pour into 13x9x2 inch pan. Bake 30 to 40 minutes at 350 degrees. Frost while hot. *Note:* If center of cake is a little undercooked after alloted cooking time, turn off oven and allow cake to set in oven for 5 to 10 minutes.

Cola Icing:

½ cup margarine	1 (16 ounce) box powdered
3 Tablespoons cocoa	sugar
6 Tablespoons cola	1 cup chopped nuts, if desired

Combine margarine, cocoa, and cola. Bring to boil in small saucepan. Pour over powdered sugar and mix well. Fold in nuts. Spread on hot cake. *Yield:* 12 to 14 servings.

Mrs. Billy Blankenship (Betty)

Variation: Add 1 teaspoon vanilla to frosting.

Mrs. Jimmy Darnell (Sherri)

PEANUT BUTTER ICING

¼ cup brown sugar	½ cup cream
¾ cup white sugar	½ cup peanut butter

Mix and boil brown and white sugar and cream until smooth, stirring constantly. Remove from heat. Add peanut butter and beat until thick. Thin with more cream if necessary. *Yield:* 2 cups.

Mrs. Ira V. Miller (Mary K.)
Dayton, Ohio

PINEAPPLE CAKE

2 eggs, beaten
1 (20 ounce) can of crushed
  pineapple, undrained
2 cups flour
1 cup sugar

1 cup brown sugar, firmly
  packed
2 teaspoons baking soda
1 cup chopped nuts

Beat eggs in a bowl. Add pineapple, flour, sugar, brown sugar, and baking soda. Mix well by hand. Add nuts. Spread in a 13x9x2 inch pan. Bake at 350 degrees for 30 minutes.

Icing:
1 (3 ounce) package cream
  cheese, softened
¼ cup margarine

1 teaspoon vanilla
2 cups powdered sugar
½ teaspoon ground ginger

Mix cream cheese with margarine and vanilla. Add powdered sugar and ground ginger. Ice when cake is cool. *Yield:* 16 servings.

Mrs. Don Savage (Lillian)
Ms. Dollie Steed
Nashville, Tennessee

SOUR CREAM COCONUT CAKE
Delicious for the holidays.

1 (16 ounce) carton sour cream
1 (14 ounce) package frozen
  coconut

2 cups sugar

On the first day, mix sour cream, coconut, and sugar. Refrigerate.

1 (18½ ounce) box butter cake
  mix

On the second day, bake cake according to directions. When cooled, remove from pans and cut each layer in half to make a 4 layer cake. Spread each layer with sour cream mixture and then ice the top and sides. Sprinkle extra coconut on the top. Keep refrigerated. *Yield:* 12 to 16 servings.

Mrs. W. C. Gatlin (Annie Mae)

BUTTER CAKE

1 (18½ ounce) yellow cake mix   ½ cup margarine
3 eggs

Combine cake mix, eggs, and margarine. Mix by hand and pour into a 13x9x2 inch pan.

Spread:
1 (16 ounce) box powdered   2 eggs
    sugar
1 (8 ounce) package cream
    cheese

Mix powdered sugar, cream cheese, and eggs thoroughly. Pour over cake mixture. Bake at 350 degrees for 40 to 45 minutes. *Yield:* 12 to 16 servings.

Mrs. Dale Vincent (Charlotte)
Earlington, Kentucky

Variation: Submitted as Chess Bars.

Mrs. Kerry A. Perkinson (Susan)

ORANGE ANGEL FOOD CAKE AND SAUCE

1¼ cups orange juice   2 Tablespoons butter
1 egg yolk   2 half pints whipping cream,
3 Tablespoons cornstarch   whipped
½ cup sugar   1 angel food cake
⅛ teaspoon salt

Heat ¼ cup orange juice in double boiler and add egg yolk slowly. Return to double boiler and add cornstarch, sugar, and 1 cup orange juice. Cook, stirring constantly, until thick. Remove from heat and add salt and butter. Cool thoroughly. Add half pint whipping cream. Split cake and fill with orange filling. Put cake together and frost with remaining half pint whipping cream. Refrigerate until served. *Yield:* 12 to 16 servings.

Mrs. E. A. Rowe (Lucille)
Martin, Tennessee

STRAWBERRY PECAN CAKE

1 (18½ ounce) white cake mix
1 (3 ounce) package strawberry
  gelatin
1 cup salad oil
½ cup milk

4 eggs
1 cup coconut
1 cup chopped pecans
1 cup frozen strawberries,
  thawed

Combine cake mix and dry gelatin in mixer. Add remaining ingredients, in order listed, adding eggs one at a time. Pour into 3 greased and floured 9 inch cake pans. Bake for 20 to 25 minutes at 350 degrees.

Strawberry Frosting:

½ cup margarine
1 (16 ounce) box powdered
  sugar

½ cup strawberries, drained
½ cup coconut
½ cup chopped pecans

Cream margarine and sugar. Add remaining ingredients and spread on cake. *Yield:* 12 servings.

Mrs. Michael Lynch (Donna)

MOUND CAKE

1 (18½ ounce) chocolate cake
  mix
24 large marshmallows

½ cup milk
½ cup sugar
1 cup coconut

Prepare cake mix as directed and bake in a 13x9x2 inch pan. Let cool. In saucepan, melt marshmallows with milk and sugar. Add coconut and pour over cake.

Topping:

½ cup margarine
1 (6 ounce) package chocolate
  chips

2 to 2½ cups sugar
1 cup milk

Melt margarine and chocolate chips. Add sugar and milk. Boil until soft ball stage, beat until thick. Pour over cake. Let cool. *Yield:* 12 to 16 servings.

Mrs. James Rogers (Janice)

RUM CAKE

½ cup chopped nuts
1 (18½ ounce) box butter
  golden cake mix
½ cup oil
4 eggs

1 (3¾ ounce) package instant
  vanilla pudding
½ cup rum
½ cup water

Spread nuts in bottom of a tube pan. Mix remaining ingredients and pour over nuts. Bake at 350 degrees 50 to 60 minutes.

Glaze:
1 cup sugar
½ cup butter

¼ cup water
¼ cup rum

Boil sugar, butter, and water for 3 to 4 minutes. Add rum. Pour over cake. Pick cake with toothpick to allow glaze to soak through. Leave cake in pan until all glaze has soaked in and then turn onto cake plate. *Note:* This cake freezes well. *Yield:* 12 to 16 servings.

Mrs. Don Waters (Carolyn)

POPPY SEED CAKE

1 (18½ ounce) package
  yellow cake mix
1 (3¾ ounce) package instant
  butterscotch pudding

4 eggs
¾ cup oil
1 cup water
2 ounces poppy seeds

In a large mixing bowl, mix all ingredients with electric mixer until well mixed (about 2 minutes). Pour all of batter into a greased and floured 10 inch bundt pan. Bake at 350 degrees for 45 to 60 minutes. (This time depends on your oven). Let cake cool for 15 minutes in pan; remove from pan and cool. Delicious with a whipped topping or vanilla ice cream. *Yield:* 12 to 16 servings.

Mrs. Mark Eberle (Emily)
Westfield, Pennsylvania

PLANTATION CAKE

½ cup chopped pecans

3 Tablespoons brown sugar

Cake:
1 (18½ ounce) yellow
  cake mix
1 (3¾ ounce) package instant
  vanilla pudding
4 eggs

½ cup sour cream
½ cup cooking sherry
½ cup oil
¼ cup poppy seeds

Grease tube or bundt pan with margarine and sprinkle with chopped pecans and brown sugar. Combine the cake mix, instant pudding, eggs, sour cream, sherry, oil, and poppy seeds. Stir until well blended. Beat 2 minutes. Bake 50 minutes at 350 degrees. Cool and remove from pan. *Yield:* 12 to 16 servings.

Ginger Houlton

CHOCOLATE CHIP CAKE

1 (18½ ounce) yellow cake mix
4 eggs
1 (3¾ ounce) package vanilla
  instant pudding
1 cup corn oil
1 cup milk

1 (4 ounce) package sweet
  cooking chocolate, grated
1 (6 ounce) package chocolate
  chips
¼ cup powdered sugar

In mixing bowl, combine cake mix, eggs, pudding, corn oil, and milk. Mix 5 minutes at medium speed. Set aside 2 tablespoons grated chocolate for topping. Add remaining grated chocolate and chocolate chips to batter. Mix gently. Pour mixture into greased and floured tube pan and bake in pre-heated oven at 350 degrees for 1 hour. Let cool in pan. Remove from pan and sprinkle powdered sugar and reserved chocolate over top. *Yield:* 12 to 16 servings.

Arvemia Wilburn

MANDARIN ORANGE CAKE
(ORANGE-PINEAPPLE CAKE)

Cake:

1 (18½ ounce) butter cake mix   ½ cup oil
4 eggs
1 (11 ounce) can mandarin
   oranges, drained

Combine cake mix, eggs, oranges, and oil. Mix well and pour into 3 greased and floured 9 inch cake pans. Bake at 350 degrees for 20 to 25 minutes. Cool.

Icing:

1 (3 ounce) box vanilla instant   1 (8 ounce) can crushed
   pudding mix   pineapple, drained
1 (12 ounce) carton prepared   ¼ cup chopped nuts
   whipped topping

Combine pudding, whipped topping, and pineapple. Mix well; use to fill and ice cake layers. Sprinkle top of cake with chopped nuts. Refrigerate. *Yield:* 12 to 16 servings.

Mrs. Henry Sparkman (Monta)

Variation: Eggs can be separated and egg whites beaten and folded in. Do not drain oranges when doing this.

Lois Oakman

PISTACHIO CAKE

1 (18½ ounce) box yellow cake
   mix
1 (3¾ ounce) package instant
   pistachio pudding

3 eggs
½ cup chopped walnuts
½ cup oil
1 cup club soda

Mix all ingredients well. Bake in a buttered and floured bundt pan at 350 degrees for 50 minutes. Cool 10 to 15 minutes. Invert.

Frosting:
½ pint whipping cream
½ pint half-and-half
1 (3¾ ounce) package pistachio
   instant pudding

¼ cup chopped walnuts

Mix all ingredients and beat until thick. Frost cake. Put remainder in center of cake. Sprinkle chopped walnuts on top. Refrigerate. *Yield:* 12 to 16 servings.

Mrs. Richard F. Roselli

SNOWBALL CAKE

2 envelopes plain gelatin
2 Tablespoons cold water
1 cup boiling water
½ cup sugar
1 (20 ounce) can crushed
   pineapple, undrained

2 teaspoons lemon juice
½ teaspoon salt
1 (15 ounce) carton non-dairy
   whipped topping
1 angel food cake
1 cup shredded coconut

Mix gelatin in cold water to dissolve, then add boiling water. Add sugar, pineapple, lemon juice, and salt. Mix and refrigerate until slightly set. Fold in ½ of the whipped topping. Break cake into small pieces. Pour gelatin mixture over and stir well. Line a large bowl with waxed paper. Pour mixture into bowl and press firmly. Cover with waxed paper and refrigerate overnight. Turn out onto cake plate and ice with remaining whipped topping and coconut. *Yield:* 12 servings.

Martha Rosalyn Gardner

CRÈME de MENTHE CAKE

1 package white pudding cake mix

3 Tablespoons crème de menthe (syrup or liqueur)

1 (16 ounce) can hot fudge topping

3 Tablespoons crème de menthe

1 (8 ounce) container non-dairy whipped topping

Prepare cake according to package directions, substituting 3 tablespoons of crème de menthe for 3 tablespoons of the water. Bake in 13x9x2 inch pan and cool. Heat the fudge topping and smooth over top of cake. Cool. Fold crème de menthe into whipped topping and smooth on cake. *Yield:* 24 servings.

Mrs. Floyd Soeder (Suzanne)

CHEESE CAKE

2 packages instant cheesecake mix

1 (8 ounce) package cream cheese

½ cup heavy cream, not whipped

2½ cups milk

Prepare crumb mixture as directed on packages. Place in springform pan or 13x9x2 inch pan. Mix all the above ingredients with electric beater until smooth. Pour into prepared crust. Chill and serve. Can be prepared ahead of time. *Yield:* 12 servings.

Mrs. Al Bevilaqua (Linda)

CHEESECAKE PUFFS

2 (8 ounce) packages cream cheese, softened

¾ cup sugar

2 eggs

1 teaspoon vanilla

24 vanilla wafers

2 (31 ounce) cans cherry pie filling

Whip cream cheese, sugar, eggs, and vanilla. Put vanilla wafers in bottom of foil lined cupcake papers on a cookie sheet. Fill ¾ full with cream cheese mixture. Bake at 375 degrees for 10 minutes. Cool and then cover with cherry pie filling. Chill overnight. *Yield:* 24 servings.

Mrs. John Iocobucci (Mary Ann)

Kirkpatrick-Powell House

Pies and Pastries

LIBBY'S PEANUT BUTTER PIE
Rich, delicious, and the talk of the town.

Crust:

1½ cups chocolate wafer crumbs

⅓ cup melted butter or margarine

Preheat oven 375 degrees. Place wafers in a paper bag and roll fine with rolling pin. Measure crumbs into medium bowl and toss with melted margarine until well mixed. With back of spoon, press mixture to bottom and side of 9 inch pie plate, making small rim. Bake 8 minutes.

Filling:

½ gallon vanilla ice cream, softened

4 heaping Tablespoons super crunchy style peanut butter

2 chocolate wafer 9 inch pie crusts

In electric mixer, place ice cream and peanut butter. Mix well at medium speed. Pour into pie crusts. Freeze. Heat hot fudge sauce and spoon over individual pie serving.

Hot Fudge Sauce:

4 squares unsweetened chocolate

½ cup butter or margarine

Pinch salt

3 cups sugar

1 (13 ounce) can evaporated milk, heated

1½ teaspoons vanilla

Melt chocolate and butter in top of double boiler. Add salt; start adding sugar slowly. Add milk a little at a time. Remove from heat; add vanilla. *Yields:* 1 quart sauce. *Yields:* 16 servings.

Mrs. Lenox D. Rawlings (Libby)

PIES AND PASTRIES

CHOCOLATE PIE

1½ cups sugar
4 to 5 Tablespoons flour
¼ cup cocoa
⅛ teaspoon salt
2 cups milk
3 egg yolks, slightly beaten
1 Tablespoon butter or
  margarine

1 teaspoon vanilla extract
1 (8-inch) pastry shell, baked
3 egg whites (at room
  temperature)
6 Tablespoons sugar

Combine 1½ cups sugar, flour, cocoa, and salt; stir in milk, mixing until smooth. Cover and place over low heat, stirring constantly until smooth and thickened (about 10 minutes). Add a small amount of hot mixture to egg yolks and mix well; add yolk mixture to remaining hot mixture, mixing well. Cook 2 minutes longer, stirring constantly. Remove from heat. Stir in butter and vanilla. Pour into pastry shell. Beat egg whites until soft peaks form. Gradually add 6 tablespoons sugar, 1 tablespoon at a time; continue beating until stiff peaks form and sugar is completely dissolved. Spread meringue over filling, and seal edges well. Bake at 350 degrees for 15 minutes or until golden brown. Cool completely before serving. *Note:* If pie is to be served at room temperature, use maximum amount of flour. *Yield:* 6 servings.

Mrs. J. C. Anderson, III (Rebecca)

CHOCOLATE CHIP PIE
Not much work with lots of results!

1 (6 ounce) package semi-sweet
  . chocolate morsels
1 cup broken pecans
2 (9-inch) pie shells, unbaked

4 eggs, beaten
1 cup sugar
½ cup butter
1 cup light corn syrup

Combine chocolate morsels and pecans. Place ½ of mixture onto bottom of each unbaked pie shell. Combine eggs, sugar, butter, and corn syrup and mix well. Pour mixture over morsels and pecans in pie shells. Bake 30 to 40 minutes at 350 degrees. Pie is done when knife inserted in the center comes out clean. *Yield:* 12 to 16 servings.

Mrs. George Atwood (Sherrie)

BONNIE'S FRENCH SILK PIE

Crust:

⅓ cup butter (no substitution)   2 cups shredded coconut

Melt butter and mix with coconut until well blended. Press into a (9-inch) pie plate and chill in freezer while preparing filling.

Filling:

½ cup butter, softened   1 teaspoon vanilla
   (no substitutions)   2 eggs
¾ cup sugar
1 square unsweetened
   chocolate, melted

Cream butter and sugar well. Blend in melted chocolate and vanilla. Add eggs one at a time beating 5 minutes after each addition. Pour into coconut crust. Chill 2 to 3 hours.

Topping:

1 cup whipping cream   Shaved semi-sweet chocolate
2 Tablespoons sugar   (optional)
1 teaspoon vanilla

Whip cream with sugar and vanilla. Dollop on pie before serving. Sprinkle with chocolate. *Yield:* 6 to 8 servings.

Bonnie Adams

COCOA FUDGE PIE

½ cup butter   ½ cup sifted flour
3½ Tablespoons cocoa   1 teaspoon vanilla
1 cup sugar   ½ cup chopped pecans
2 eggs, beaten

Melt butter and cocoa together. (Use your microwave, if desired). Add sugar and remaining ingredients. Mix well. Pour into well buttered 9-inch pie pan. (Recipe may be doubled and baked in a 13x9x2 inch pan). Bake at 325 degrees for 25 minutes. (Bake 10 minutes longer if in 13x9x2 inch pan). *Yield:* 6 to 8 servings.

Mrs. Pat Hagerty (Sharon)

FRENCH SILK CHOCOLATE PIE

1 cup butter
1 cup sugar
2 (1 ounce) squares bitter
  chocolate, melted
2 teaspoons vanilla

4 chilled eggs
1 (9 inch) pie shell, baked
½ pint whipping cream,
  whipped

Use an electric mixer. Cream butter with sugar. Add chocolate and vanilla. Add chilled eggs, one at a time, beating 2 minutes at least after adding each. Pour into baked pie shell. Chill. Top with whipped cream. You may sprinkle with chopped walnuts or toasted almond slivers. *Note:* Served at the Green Parrot Restaurant in Houston, Texas. *Yield:* 8 servings.

Mrs. Stewart Campbell, Jr. (Mary)
Spring Hill, Tennessee

CHOCOLATE SUNDAY PIE
A light dessert to follow a heavy meal.

1 cup evaporated milk
½ cup water
¼ teaspoon nutmeg
3 eggs, separated
½ cup sugar
⅛ teaspoon salt
1 Tablespoon gelatin

3 Tablespoon cold water
½ teaspoon vanilla
1 (10-inch) pie shell, baked
1 cup whipped cream,
  sweetened
¼ cup grated German
  chocolate

Heat milk and ½ cup water in double boiler with nutmeg. Beat egg yolks with sugar and salt until light. Pour hot milk over the egg mixture. Return to double boiler and cook until the consistency of thick cream. Remove from heat. Add gelatin which has been soaking in the cold water for 5 minutes. Add vanilla and cool. When cool and ready to set, beat with a rotary beater and fold into egg whites which have been beaten stiff. Pour this mixture into a baked pie shell. Refrigerate. When thoroughly chilled, cover with sweetened whipped cream and sprinkle with grated chocolate. *Yield:* 8 servings.

Mrs. H. W. Lane (Evelyn)
Hillside, New Jersey

CHOCOLATE BAR PIE

6 almond chocolate bars
½ cup milk
18 large marshmallows,
  cut up

Pinch of salt
1 cup non-dairy whipped
  topping
1 (9 inch) pie shell, baked

Place chocolate bars, milk, marshmallows, and salt in double boiler. (Do not let water in bottom pan boil). Heat mixture until it is mixed well. Let cool. Fold in whipped topping. Pour mixture into baked pie shell. Refrigerate at least 1 hour or overnight. Can sprinkle almonds on top of pie. *Yield:* 6 to 8 servings.

Mrs. Gary Quick (Joan)

CHOCOLATE PECAN PIE

½ cup margarine
1 cup sugar
½ cup flour
2 eggs, beaten
1 teaspoon vanilla

¾ cup chocolate semi-sweet
  chips
1 cup pecans
1 (9-inch) pie shell, unbaked

Melt margarine and let cool in saucepan. In same pan, add sugar, flour, eggs, vanilla, chips, and pecans. Pour into pie shell. Bake at 350 degrees for 30 minutes. *Note:* For fudgier pie, melt chocolate chips in hot margarine. *Yield:* 6 servings.

Mrs. John Lowney (Beth)
Hendersonville, Tennessee

CHESS PIE

1 cup butter
3 cups sugar
2 Tablespoons vinegar
6 eggs, beaten

2 teaspoons vanilla
Pinch of salt
1 (9 inch) pie shell

Cream butter, sugar, and vinegar over low heat. Pour over beaten eggs. Stir in vanilla and salt. Pour into pie shell. Cook 1 hour at 350 degrees. *Yield:* 8 servings.

Juliet Randolph

CHOCOLATE CHESS PIE

½ cup butter
1½ (1 ounce) squares
  semi-sweet chocolate
1 cup brown sugar
½ cup white sugar

1 Tablespoon flour
2 eggs
½ egg shell of milk
1 teaspoon vanilla
1 (9-inch) pie shell, unbaked

Melt butter and chocolate; add sugars and flour. Mix well. Add eggs, milk, and vanilla. Pour into pie shell and bake at 325 degrees for 45 minutes. *Yield:* 6 servings.

Sue P. Johnson

LEMON CHESS PIE
An Old Southern Ohio Recipe.

2 cups sugar
1 Tablespoon flour
1 Tablespoon corn meal
4 eggs, unbeaten
¼ cup margarine, melted

¼ cup milk
¼ cup lemon juice
1 lemon rind, grated
1 (9-inch) pie shell, unbaked

Toss sugar, flour, and corn meal with a fork. Combine remaining ingredients and mix well. Pour into unbaked pie shell. Bake at 450 degrees for 10 minutes. Reduce heat to 350 degrees and bake for 25 additional minutes. *Yield:* 6 to 8 servings.

Mrs. James R. Kelso (Carol)

AUNT PUTT'S CHESS PIE

5 egg yolks
1 whole egg
½ cup cream
½ cup butter
2 cups sugar

1 Tablespoon flour
1 Tablespoon corn meal
2 teaspoons vanilla
1 (9 inch) pie shell, unbaked

Mix egg yolks, egg, cream, butter, sugar, flour, corn meal, and vanilla. Pour into pie shell. Bake at 350 degrees 40 to 50 minutes, until silver knife inserted in center comes out clean. *Yield:* 6 to 8 servings.

Mrs. Cortez E. Isaacs (Aleectrice)

OLD FASHIONED CHESS PIE

¾ cup white sugar
¾ cup dark brown sugar
1 Tablespoon corn meal
1 Tablespoon flour
½ teaspoon salt
1 teaspoon vinegar

2 eggs
½ cup milk
½ teaspoon vanilla
½ cup butter, melted
1 (9 inch) pie shell, unbaked

Sift together white and brown sugar, corn meal, flour, and salt. Add vinegar, eggs, milk, vanilla, and butter. Mix well and pour into an unbaked pie shell. Bake at 350 degrees for 30 to 40 minutes or until brown and settled. *Yield:* 8 servings.

Mrs. Thomas J. Turbeville (Mary Otha)
Nashville, Tennessee

SUNNY ISLAND PIE

41 vanilla wafers, finely rolled
(about 1⅔ cups crumbs)
¼ cup sugar

⅓ cup margarine, softened
¼ cup flaked coconut

In a medium bowl combine vanilla wafer crumbs and sugar. Using a pastry blender, cut in margarine to resemble coarse crumbs; toss in coconut. Press firmly against bottom and sides of a 9-inch pie plate. Bake at 375 degrees for 8 minutes or until lightly browned. Cool on wire rack.

Filling:
1 (3¾ ounce) package instant
lemon pudding mix
¾ cup milk
1½ cups sour cream

1 (8 ounce) can crushed
pineapple, drained,
reserving ¼ cup juice

To prepare instant lemon pudding: pour cold milk, sour cream, and reserved juice into bowl. Add the mix. Beat slowly with rotary beater or at lowest speed of electric mixer until will blended, about 2 minutes. Fold in pineapple. Spoon into pie crust. Chill at least 2 hours before serving. *Yield:* 8 servings.

Mrs. J. P. Dawson (Sara D.)
Columbia, Tennessee

SILLY GRANNY'S FRIED PIES

1 (12 ounce) package dried
  peaches

1 cup sugar

Wash peaches. Cook until tender and mash. Add sugar and mix well.

Biscuit Dough:
2½ cups self-rising flour
Pinch of soda
1 teaspoon baking powder

1 heaping Tablespoon lard
1 cup buttermilk

Sift flour. Make a birdnest in the middle and sprinkle with soda and baking powder. Add lard and buttermilk. Work this with hands until dough becomes thick enough to roll out. Roll out dough on floured board and cut the size of a saucer. Put a few teaspoons of peaches on one half and fold dough over. Pinch edges with a fork to seal. Fry each side in a hot skillet until golden brown. *Yield:* 12 to 14 pies.

Mrs. Leslie Darnell (Nellie)
Shelbyville, Tennessee

CARAMEL CREAM PIE

1 (14 ounce) can sweetened
  condensed milk
1 cup whipping cream,
  whipped

1 can pressurized real
  whipped cream
1 (9-inch) graham cracker crust

Place unopened can of sweetened condensed milk in pan and cover with water. Bring to a boil, cover and continue to boil for 3 hours. Check periodically and add more water if necessary to keep can covered. Chill carmelized milk, then fold into whipped cream. Pour mixture into graham cracker crust and freeze. To serve, garnish with additional whipped cream. *Note:* Must be watched closely — can of milk will explode if not covered with water. *Yield:* 6 to 8 servings.

Mrs. Nancy J. Massey
Nashville, Tennessee

CARAMEL CHIFFON PIE
Easy to make and deliciously light.

28 candy caramels
1¼ cups water, separated
1 envelope unflavored gelatin
½ teaspoon vanilla

1 cup heavy cream, whipped
¾ cup chopped pecans, separated
1 (9-inch) pie shell

Melt caramels with 1 cup water in double boiler or in saucepan over low heat. Stir occasionally until sauce is smooth. Soften gelatin in ¼ cup water. Pour gelatin into the hot caramel sauce. Add vanilla. Chill until slightly thickened. Fold in whipped cream and ½ cup nuts. Pour into pie shell; sprinkle with remaining nuts. Chill until firm. Garnish with additional whipped cream, if desired. *Yield:* 8 servings.

Mrs. Mark Levy (Cheryl)

CARAMEL PIE

3 cups sugar, divided
6 eggs, separated
3 cups milk
7 Tablespoons cornstarch

2 teaspoons vanilla
3 Tablespoons butter
2 (9-inch) pie shells, baked

In a saucepan, beat 1½ cups sugar and egg yolks; adding milk and cornstarch gradually. At the same time, brown 1½ cups sugar on medium heat in iron skillet. This will thicken and brown slightly. As sugar begins to boil, pour both mixtures together, stirring constantly. Add vanilla and butter, beating until smooth. Pour into baked pie crusts. Top with meringue. *Note:* May beat mixture with electric mixer if not smooth. *Yield:* 12 to 16 servings.

Mrs. Wilson Herbert (Ann)

Variation: This can be used also without meringue.

Mrs. Buford Burt (Teeta)

SCRUMPTIOUS PECAN PIE
Divine served with Butter Pecan Ice Cream.

1 cup dark corn syrup
3 eggs
1 cup sugar
2 Tablespoons margarine, melted
1 teaspoon vanilla

⅛ teaspoon salt
1 cup halved or chopped pecans
1 (9-inch) pie shell, unbaked
Nutmeg

Mix first 6 ingredients. Stir in pecans. Pour into unbaked pie shell. Sprinkle top with nutmeg. Bake at 400 degrees for 15 minutes. Reduce heat to 350 degrees and bake 30 to 35 minutes. Outer edge of filling should be set and center slightly soft. *Yield:* 8 servings.

Mrs. Nelson Sweeney (Beth)

FRESH LEMON MERINGUE PIE

3 or 4 lemons
1½ cups sugar
6 Tablespoons cornstarch
¼ teaspoon salt
½ cup cold water
3 eggs, separated

2 Tablespoons butter or margarine
1½ cups boiling water
¼ teaspoon cream of tartar
6 Tablespoons sugar
1 (9-inch) pie shell, baked

Grate 1 teaspoon peel from lemon and squeeze ½ cup juice. Set aside. Combine sugar, cornstarch, and salt in a saucepan and thoroughly blend in lemon juice, cold water, and beaten egg yolks until completely smooth. Add butter and stir in boiling water gradually. Bring to a boil and cook for 3 to 4 minutes, stirring constantly. Stir in grated peel and cool. Beat egg whites until frothy. Add cream of tartar and beat at high speed until soft peaks form. Add 6 tablespoons sugar gradually, beating until all sugar is used and whites are stiff, but not dry. Pour filling into baked pie shell. Spread meringue over filling, sealing carefully at edges of pastry. Bake at 350 degrees for 12 to 15 minutes or until golden brown. Cool on rack away from drafts. *Yield:* 6 to 8 servings.

Mrs. Bobby Lofton (Betty)

FRENCH MERINGUE SHELL LEMON PIE

4 egg whites ¾ cup sugar
¼ teaspoon cream of tartar

Beat egg whites and cream of tartar. Add sugar, 2 tablespoons at a time. Beat until stiff. Put in ungreased (9-inch) pie pan. Form into fluffy pie shell. It will be thick. Bake at 300 degrees for 1 hour.

Filling:
4 egg yolks 1 teaspoon grated lemon rind
½ cup sugar 1 teaspoon grated orange rind
Dash of salt 1 cup whipping cream
2 Tablespoons orange juice 2 Tablespoons powdered sugar
1 Tablespoon lemon juice ½ teaspoon vanilla

Beat egg yolks. Add sugar, salt, orange juice, lemon juice, lemon rind, and orange rind. Place in double boiler and cook over medium heat, stirring constantly until thick (about 10 minutes). Cool. Whip whipping cream with powdered sugar and vanilla. In cooled shell pour ½ whipping cream, all of the lemon filling and then remaining whipping cream. Refrigerate 12 to 24 hours. *Yield:* 6 to 8 servings.

Ida Maye Christensen

PRESIDENT TYLER'S PUDDIN' PIES

16 (2-inch) individual pastry 2 eggs
   shells ½ cup half-and-half
½ cup butter, softened ½ teaspoon vanilla
¾ cup white sugar Nutmeg
¾ cup firmly packed dark Whipping cream, whipped
   brown sugar

Bake pastry shells at 350 degrees for 4 to 5 minutes. Combine butter with white sugar and brown sugar. Cream until light and fluffy. Add eggs, half-and-half, and vanilla; beat well. Spoon filling into pastry shells and sprinkle with nutmeg. Bake at 350 degrees for 15 to 20 minutes or until set. Filling will settle while cooling. Serve with a dollop of whipped cream and a dash of nutmeg. *Yield:* 16 servings.

Mrs. Andrew W. Kennedy (Mabel)

TASTY BERRY TARTS

2 cups flour
¼ cup sugar

¾ cup butter or margarine
2 egg yolks

Combine flour and sugar. Cut butter into flour mixture. Add egg yolks. Work with hands to mix evenly. Divide dough into 48 equal walnut sized balls. Press each ball into small (1¾ inch) muffin pans. Bake at 300 degrees for 20 minutes. Cool five minutes in pan and remove.

Filling:
1 (3 ounce) package cream
  cheese
1 cup heavy cream
½ teaspoon lemon juice

½ teaspoon vanilla extract
2 Tablespoons sugar
48 strawberries
Powdered sugar

Beat cream cheese and cream until thick. Add lemon juice, vanilla, and sugar. Beat well. Right before serving put a teaspoon of the filling in each tart shell. Top with a strawberry and sprinkle with powdered sugar. *Yield:* 48 tarts.

Mrs. Francis DeCoster (Donna)

STRAWBERRY PIE

3 Tablespoons cornstarch
2¼ cups water
2 cups sugar
3 drops red food coloring
1 (3 ounce) package cream
  cheese, softened

2 (9-inch) pie shells, baked
2 quarts strawberries, washed
  and capped
1 pint whipping cream,
  whipped

Cook cornstarch and water until thick. Remove from heat and add sugar. Stir in food coloring until red. Spread softened cream cheese over pie shells. Heap strawberries into pie shells. Cover with sauce and cool. Top with whipped cream when pie is served. *Yield:* 12 servings.

Mrs. E. A. Rowe (Lucille)
Martin, Tennessee

LUSCIOUS PUDDLES

30 vanilla wafers, crushed
2 Tablespoons sugar
3 Tablespoons salted peanuts,
   chopped

3 Tablespoons butter, melted
1 quart vanilla ice cream

Mix crushed wafers, sugar, peanuts, and butter. Pour into a deep 9-inch pie pan. Bake at 325 degrees for 7 minutes. Cool. Scoop ice cream into cooled pie pan and freeze.

Sauce:
1 cup sugar
2 squares unsweetened
   chocolate
¼ cup light corn syrup

¾ cup sweetened condensed
   milk
1 teaspoon vanilla

Mix sugar, chocolate, syrup, condensed milk, and vanilla in a pan. Boil 5 minutes and stir until thick. Serve over frozen pie. *Yield:* 8 to 10 servings.

Mabel Gladieux
Treasure Island, Florida

SOFT DRINK MIX PIE

1 (13 ounce) can of evaporated
   milk
1 (0.25 ounce) package
   strawberry flavored
   unsweetened soft drink mix

1 cup sugar
2 (8-inch) graham cracker
   pie shells

Pour can of evaporated milk into aluminum ice tray and place in freezer. Hint: It helps to place electric mixer beaters in freezer. When ice crystals have formed around edges of ice tray, take evaporated milk out and pour into large deep mixing bowl. Whip evaporated milk until soft peaks form. Fold in soft drink mix and sugar. Pour ½ mixture into each pie shell. Return to freezer. Serve when frozen. *Yield:* 12 to 16 servings.

Mrs. Steven Allbrooks (Pam)

APPLE PIE WITH CHEESE PASTRY

1 cup apples, diced and pared
½ cup sugar
¼ teaspoon cinnamon
¼ teaspoon nutmeg
¾ of one orange
2 teaspoons butter

Spread apples evenly in pastry lined 9-inch pie pan. Sprinkle apples with sugar, cinnamon, and nutmeg. Squeeze juice of orange over the apples and dot with butter. Strip pastry over edges. Bake at 350 degrees for 1 hour.

Pastry:
1½ cups self-rising flour
1 Tablespoon sugar
¼ teaspoon salt
3/8 cup shortening
1 cup shredded Cheddar cheese
¼ cup cold water

Mix and sift flour, sugar, and salt. Cut in shortening, add cheese and mix well. Use just enough water to make dough stick together. Roll thinly onto floured board. Cut 2 inches larger than inverted pie pan. Ease into 9-inch pie pan. *Yield:* 6 to 8 servings.

Mrs. Bobby Stratton (Margie)

FRESH CHERRY PIE

1 (9-inch) pie shell
4 cups (1 quart) fresh cherries
1⅓ cups sugar
4 Tablespoons cornstarch
1 drop almond flavoring
1 Tablespoon butter
Red food coloring (optional)

Fill pastry lined 9-inch pie pan with cherries. Sprinkle with sugar and cornstarch, mixed. Drop in almond flavoring and dot with butter. Cover with lattice pastry top. Bake at 450 degrees for 10 minutes. Reduce heat to 350 degrees and bake for 30 minutes. Serve slightly warm. *Note:* A few drops of red food coloring may be mixed with cherries to enhance red color. *Yield:* 6 servings.

Mrs. James Short (Mary Catherine)

CHERRY CREAM PIE

1 Tablespoon butter
6 egg yolks
¾ cup sugar
6 level Tablespoons flour
Pinch of salt
2½ cups milk

Dash of almond flavoring
1 (10 ounce) jar maraschino
cherries, drained, reserving
juice
1 (9-inch) pie shell, baked

Mix butter, egg yolks, sugar, flour, salt, cherry juice, milk, and almond flavoring. Cook until mixture becomes thick. Cut up cherries and add to mixture. Mix and pour into baked pie shell. Top with meringue and bake at 400 degrees for about 10 minutes or until a delicate brown. *Yield:* 6 to 8 servings.

Betty Gatlin

ORANGE CHIFFON PIE

8 lady fingers
1 envelope unflavored gelatin
¾ cup sugar, divided
⅛ teaspoon salt
2 eggs, separated
½ cup cold water

1 (6 ounce) can frozen orange
juice concentrate
1 cup whipping cream,
whipped
Grated orange peel for garnish

Split lady fingers. Cut ends off enough lady fingers to line sides of a 9-inch pie plate. (They should extend above the rim to hold the filling). Line bottom of pie plate with remaining lady fingers; set aside. Combine gelatin, ½ cup of sugar and salt in medium saucepan. Beat egg yolks and water; stir into gelatin mixture. Cook over low heat; stir constantly until gelatin dissolves and mixture thickens slightly, about 5 minutes. Remove from heat. Add orange juice concentrate, and stir until melted. Mixture should mound slightly when dropped from spoon (if not, chill a few minutes). Beat egg whites until stiff peaks form. Gradually add remaining ¼ cup sugar to egg whites and beat until very stiff. Fold into gelatin mixture. fold in whipped cream. Pour into pie shell and chill until firm, but do not freeze. Garnish with grated orange peel. *Yield:* 6 servings.

Mrs. Floyd Soeder (Suzanne)

MACAROON PIE

3 egg whites, beaten until stiff
1 cup sugar
12 dates, chopped
¾ cup chopped pecans

12 saltine crackers (roll and
  make crumbs)
1 teaspoon almond extract

Beat egg whites until stiff. Fold in sugar. Add dates, pecans, cracker crumbs, and almond flavoring. Spread in a lightly greased 9-inch pie pan or pyrex dish. Bake 20 minutes at 350 degrees. Cut oven off and leave pie in 10 more minutes. Top with ice cream, if desired. *Yield:* 10 servings.

Mrs. Malcolm Beasley (Bonnie)
Nashville, Tennessee

Variation: Omit almond extract.

Mrs. Robert E. Wells (Cooper)

GRASSHOPPER PIE

14 chocolate cookies, crushed
4 Tablespoons margarine,
  melted
24 large marshmallows, melted
⅔ cup milk
1 cup whipping cream,
  whipped

3 Tablespoons green crème
  de menthe
1 ounce white crème de cocoa
Semi sweet chocolate, grated

Crush chocolate cookies. Add melted margarine. Mix with crumbs and press into an 8-inch or 9-inch pie pan. Place in freezer until set. In double boiler, melt marshmallows in milk. Chill. Mix whipping cream, crème de menthe and crème de cocoa. Combine with chilled marshmallow mixture. Pour into pie shell and sprinkle grated chocolate on top. Refrigerate 3 hours before serving. *Yield:* 6 to 8 servings.

Mrs. William Holman (Kate)
Tampa, Florida

COCONUT CREAM PIE

⅔ cup sugar
¼ cup cornstarch
½ teaspoon salt
3 cups milk
4 egg yolks, slightly beaten

2 Tablespoons butter
2 teaspoons vanilla
¾ cup coconut
¼ cup coconut for topping
1 (9-inch) pie shell, baked

Stir sugar, cornstarch, and salt. Blend milk and egg yolks together, stir in sugar mixture. Cook over medium heat, stirring constantly, until it comes to a boil. Boil 1 minute and remove from heat. Add butter, vanilla, and coconut. Pour into pie shell. Top with meringue, sprinkle with coconut and brown. *Yield:* 6 to 8 servings.

Mrs. Nelson Sweeney (Beth)

PEANUT BUTTER PIE

1 (3 ounce) package cream
cheese
¼ cup crunchy peanut butter
1 cup powdered sugar

1 (12 ounce) carton non-dairy
whipped topping
1 (9-inch) graham cracker pie
crust

Blend cream cheese, peanut butter, and powdered sugar in mixer. Fold in whipped topping. Pour into graham cracker crust. Place in refrigerator to set. *Yield:* 6 to 8 servings.

Mrs. Norman W. Griswold (Josephine)
Nashville, Tennessee

LEMONADE PIE

1 (6 ounce) can frozen
lemonade
1 (14 ounce) can sweetened
condensed milk

1 (6 ounce) container non-dairy
whipped topping
1 (9-inch) graham cracker crust

Using a hand mixer, mix lemonade, sweetened condensed milk, and whipped topping. Pour into graham cracker crust and chill 1 hour before serving. *Yield:* 6 to 8 servings.

Mrs. Dale Vincent (Charlotte)
Earlington, Kentucky

MILLION DOLLAR PIE

1 (14 ounce) can sweetened
condensed milk
¼ cup lemon juice
1 (16 ounce) can sliced peaches,
drained
1 (15¼ ounce) can crushed
pineapple, drained

1 (8 ounce) carton non-dairy
whipped topping
2 (9-inch) graham cracker pie
shells

Mix milk and lemon juice. Add peaches and pineapple. Fold in whipped topping. Pour into pie shells. Freeze and serve. *Yield:* 12 to 16 servings.

Mrs. Farris Galbraith (Kitty)

EXQUISITE PIE

6 eggs
2 cups sugar
1 cup butter or margarine
1 cup coconut
1 cup chopped pecans

1 cup raisins
2 Tablespoons vinegar or
lemon juice
2 (9-inch) pie shells

Blend eggs with sugar and butter. Mix well. Fold in coconut, pecans, and raisins. Mix well. Add vinegar or lemon juice. Pour into 2 (9-inch) pie shells. Bake for 45 minutes at 350 degrees. *Yield:* 12 servings.

Mrs. Tom Neal (Betty)
Arrington, Tennessee

PIE CRUST

2½ cups flour
1 cup margarine
1½ teaspoons salt

2 Tablespoons sugar
5 or 6 Tablespoons ice water

Combine flour, margarine, salt, sugar, and ice water. (May be mixed in food processor). Let stand in refrigerator until cold. (Overnight, if desired). Roll out between 2 sheets of waxed paper; this eliminates using more flour. *Yield:* 2 (9-inch) pie shells or 1 double crust.

Mrs. Wilson Herbert (Ann)

HAWAIIAN PIE

2 (9 inch) pie crusts, baked
4 sliced bananas
1 cup chopped pecans, toasted
   in butter
1 (20 ounce) can crushed
   pineapple
1 cup sugar

6 Tablespoons flour
1 egg
2 cups whipping cream,
   whipped
¼ cup toasted coconut
Maraschino cherries

In each baked crust, slice two bananas and add pecans. Cook pineapple with juice, sugar, flour, and egg until thickened. Cool. Pour over bananas and pecans. Cover top with whipped cream. Garnish with coconut and cherries. *Yield:* 12 to 16 servings.

Mrs. Tom Adkisson (Marilyn)

FRESH PEACH PIE

3 Tablespoons cornstarch
3 Tablespoons gelatin
1 cup sugar
1 cup boiling water

4 fresh peaches, sliced
1 (9-inch) pie crust, baked
Whipping cream, whipped
   (optional)

Mix cornstarch, gelatin, and sugar. Add to boiling water. Let this boil a few seconds, then cool. Add peaches. Pour into cooked pie crust and refrigerate. Add a dollop of whipped cream on each serving. *Yield:* 6 to 8 servings.

Mrs. George E. Bivins, Jr. (Maxine)

"OUT OF THIS WORLD" BLACKBERRY COBBLER

¾ quart fresh or frozen
  blackberries
1¼ cups sugar
2 heaping Tablespoons
  cornstarch

½ teaspoon salt
¼ cup sherry
2 (9 inch) pie crusts,
  extra deep

Place berries in saucepan. If using fresh berries, add just enough water to prevent sticking. Heat slowly to boiling. Add 1 cup sugar and continue to heat. Mix ¼ cup sugar, cornstarch, salt, and sherry. If this mixture is thick, use water or liquid from berry mixture to make medium thin consistency. Then add to berry mixture. Heat until it just begins to thicken. Pour into 1 pie crust and cut the other crust into strips to form lattice top. (Put ½ of the strips across the top and repeat crosswise). Bake at 375 degrees 15 to 20 minutes until top is lightly browned. *Yield:* 6 servings.

Mrs. Bobby Stanfield (Mildred)
College Grove, Tennessee

FRUIT PIZZA

1 package sugar cookie mix
  or one roll prepared sugar
  cookie dough
12 ounces cream cheese
2 Tablespoons sugar
1 (8 ounce) can crushed
  pineapple, reserve juice

1 (31 ounce) can cherry pie
  filling
2 large bananas
¼ cup chopped nuts

Have cookie dough and cream cheese at room temperature. Spread cookie dough over large pizza pan. Bake at 375 degrees for 8 minutes or until golden brown. Cool. Mix cream cheese, sugar, and pineapple juice to spreading consistency. Spread over cookie dough, covering completely. Place cherries on outer ring of dough 2 inches deep. Put 2 circles of sliced bananas inside cherry ring. Fill remaining circle with pineapple. Sprinkle nuts over pineapple. Refrigerate 2 hours before serving. *Yield:* 8 to 10 servings.

Mrs. James Jordan (Dianah)

Riverview or Splendored

Desserts

CHOCOLATE CREPES

1 cup flour	2 eggs, beaten
1½ Tablespoons sugar	1⅓ cups milk
Pinch of salt	2 Tablespoons butter, melted
1½ Tablespoons cocoa	Rum Cream Filling
1½ Tablespoons instant coffee	Chocolate Sauce

Sift together flour, sugar, salt, cocoa, and coffee. Stir in eggs, milk, and butter until smooth. Strain and let batter stand for 2 hours. Batter should be as thin as cream. For each crepe, generously butter a small skillet and add 2 to 3 tablespoons of batter. Swirl pan to coat bottom and cook for 1 minute on each side. Cool on wire rack. Fill with Rum Cream Filling; roll and place seam side down on serving plate. May be wrapped with plastic and refrigerated until serving. Top with chocolate sauce before serving.

Rum Cream Filling:

2 cups whipping cream	¼ cup light rum
¼ cup sugar	

Whip cream; gradually add sugar. Fold in rum.

Chocolate Sauce:

3 Tablespoons flour	1 teaspoon vanilla
4 Tablespoons cocoa	Milk to thin
½ teaspoon butter	1 cup sugar

Mix above ingredients and stir over medium heat until thickened.
Yield: 24 crepes.

Mrs. Herbert Patrick (Lyn)
Savannah, Tennessee

ALMOND DESSERT
From the collection of "Miss Mary", noted Franklin cook.

½ cup butter, softened
2 cups powdered sugar
3 eggs, beaten, separately
1½ Tablespoons almond
  flavoring

1 cup vanilla wafer crumbs
Whipping cream, whipped
Slivered almonds

Mix first 4 ingredients together and pour into a 9 inch square pan that has been lined well with vanilla wafer crumbs. Add crumbs on top. Refrigerate overnight or for several hours before serving. Top with whipped cream and toasted slivered almonds, just before serving. *Yield:* 6 servings.

Mrs. Tom Robinson (Mary)

CHOCOLATE MOUSSE

¾ cup butter, softened
1½ cups sugar
3 eggs, separated
1 Tablespoon brandy
½ teaspoon almond extract
8 ounces semi-sweet
  chocolate chips, melted

¼ cup slivered almonds,
  toasted
2 cups whipping cream,
  whipped
Shaved chocolate

Cream butter until fluffy. Add sugar gradually, then egg yolks, brandy, and extract. Add chocolate and almonds. Beat egg whites until stiff and fold into chocolate mixture. Fold in whipped cream. Freeze until firm. Remove from freezer 30 minutes before serving. Garnish with extra whipped cream and shaved chocolate. *Yield:* 10 to 12 servings.

Mrs. Joseph Barker (Sherry)

COFFEE MOUSSE
Especially delicious in hot summer.

16 marshmallows
½ cup very strong coffee
Pinch of salt
1 Tablespoon sugar

½ pint whipping cream,
  whipped
½ teaspoon vanilla

Melt marshmallows in hot coffee, to which a pinch of salt has been added. Mash well with a fork. Beat in sugar. Add whipping cream and vanilla. Put into sherbet glasses and chill. Serve topped with more whipping cream. *Note:* Nice and light after a heavy meal. *Yield:* 6 servings.

Mrs. Cecil Crowson (Evelyn)

CHOCOLATE RUM MOCHA MOUSSE
WITH CAFÉ CREAM

1 (12 ounce) package semi-
  sweet chocolate chips
½ cup sugar
3 eggs

3 Tablespoons instant coffee
  (granulated, not flaked)
¼ cup light rum
1 cup hot milk

Blend all ingredients on high speed for 1½ minutes. This mixture will be very liquid. Pour mixture into individual serving dishes. Chill 1 hour in the refrigerator. Top with a dollop of café cream just before serving.

Café Cream:
1 cup heavy cream
3 Tablespoons powdered sugar

1 Tablespoon instant coffee
  (granulated, not flaked)

In a small mixing bowl, whip cream, sugar, and coffee until they are the consistency of whipped cream. Store in refrigerator until time to serve. *Yield:* 6 to 8 servings.

Mrs. Robert A. Plummer (Mary M.)

JAMOCA MOUSSE

1 (12 ounce) package semi-
  sweet chocolate chips
8 egg yolks
⅓ cup rum
1 Tablespoon instant coffee

8 egg whites
Dash of salt
1 cup sugar
Whipped cream
Chocolate curls

In a 1 quart saucepan melt chocolate chips over low heat. Add egg yolks, one at a time, stirring after each addition. Remove from heat. Blend in rum and coffee. Beat egg whites with salt, until stiff peaks form, add sugar gradually. Stir in small amount of egg white mixture into chocolate. Pour chocolate into egg whites. Fold evenly. Spoon into dessert dishes and chill. Serve with whipped cream and chocolate curls. *Yield:* 6 servings.

Linda P. Tarkington

BREAD PUDDING

1 loaf French bread
1 quart milk
3 eggs
2 cups sugar

2 Tablespoons vanilla
1 cup raisins
3 Tablespoons butter or
  margarine, melted

Soak bread in milk; crush with hands until well mixed. Add eggs, sugar, vanilla, raisins and stir well. Pour melted butter into bottom of 3 quart ovenproof dish. Add mixture and bake at 350 degrees for 30 minutes or until firm. Let cool. Cut pudding into squares and place in individual dessert dishes. When ready to serve, add whiskey sauce and broil until bubbly.

Whiskey Sauce:
½ cup butter
1 cup sugar

1 egg, beaten
Whiskey to taste

Cook butter and sugar in a double boiler until sugar is dissolved. Add beaten egg and beat with a whip very fast. Let cool and add whiskey to taste. *Yield:* 8 to 12 servings.

Mrs. Philip Miller (Nancy)

HOT FUDGE PUDDING
Easy and deliciously rich!

1 cup flour
¾ cup sugar
½ cup milk
2 teaspoons baking powder
½ teaspoon salt

2 Tablespoons cocoa
2 Tablespoons margarine,
melted
½ cup nuts

Mix dry ingredients. Add milk and margarine. Spread in deep 2 quart casserole.

Topping:
1 cup brown sugar
4 Tablespoons cocoa

1½ cups boiling water

Mix sugar and cocoa. Sprinkle on top of pudding mixture. Pour water over this. DO NOT STIR. Bake at 350 degrees for 40 minutes. Top with ice cream. *Note:* This recipe makes its own fudge sauce. *Yield:* 6 to 8 servings.

Mrs. Bill Meek (Frances)
Columbia, Tennessee

ANGEL PUDDING

½ envelope unflavored gelatin
2 Tablespoons cold water
¼ cup plus 2 Tablespoons
boiling water
3 ounces lemonade
concentrate, thawed

¼ cup sugar
1 cup prepared whipped
topping
5 ounces frozen strawberries,
halved

Sprinkle gelatin on cold water. Allow gelatin to absorb the cold water, then add the boiling water and stir until gelatin is dissolved. Add lemonade concentrate and sugar; mix well. Chill mixture until slightly thickened. Whip thickened gelatin mixture until fluffy. Fold in whipped topping. Pour into serving dish. Chill until thick. Top with strawberries. *Yield:* 6 servings.

Mrs. Steve Hester (Chandra)
Henderson, Kentucky

BANANA PUDDING

¾ cup sugar
4 Tablespoons flour
¼ teaspoon salt
4 eggs (3 separated)
3 cups milk
1 teaspoon vanilla

1 (7¼ ounce) box vanilla
   wafers
5 or 6 ripe bananas
¼ teaspoon cream of tartar
¼ cup sugar
1 teaspoon vanilla

Combine sugar, flour, and salt in top of double boiler. Mix in one whole egg and 3 egg yolks; stir in milk. Cook uncovered over boiling water, stirring constantly until thickened. Remove from heat, add vanilla. Spread ¼ of the pudding mixture in bottom of a 3 quart casserole. Cover with layer of vanilla wafers, and then a layer of bananas. Repeat twice and spread remaining pudding mixture on top. Beat remaining 3 egg whites, in which cream of tartar has been added, until stiff but not dry. Gradually add ¼ cup sugar and beat until stiff peaks form. Add 1 teaspoon of vanilla. Spread on top of first mixture and bake at 375 degrees until golden brown. Serve hot or cold. *Yield:* 12 servings.

Mrs. A. C. Frensley (Betty)

PUDDIN 'N PIE

1¾ cups flour
14 Tablespoons margarine
1 cup chopped nuts
2 cups powdered sugar
1 (8 ounce) package cream
   cheese

2 cups whipped topping
1 small package chocolate or
   butterscotch pudding mix,
   prepared according to
   directions

In 9 inch pan blend flour, margarine, and nuts. Bake at 350 degrees for 25 minutes. Cool. Mix powdered sugar, cream cheese, and 1 cup whipped topping. Smooth over first mixture. Then spread prepared pudding over 2nd layer and chill. Add 1 cup whipped topping as desired and sprinkle with nuts. *Yield:* 8 to 10 servings.

Mrs. Rich McDavitt (Linda)
Brentwood, Tennessee

LEMON JELLY ROLL

3 large eggs
1 cup sugar
⅓ cup water
1 teaspoon vanilla

1 cup sifted flour
1 teaspoon baking powder
¼ teaspoon salt

Grease a 15½x10½ inch jelly roll pan and line bottom with greased brown paper or with aluminum foil. Beat eggs in small mixing bowl until very thick and lemon colored. Pour into large bowl and gradually beat in sugar. Mix well. On low speed, blend in water and vanilla. Sift together flour, baking powder, and salt. Slowly add dry ingredients mixing on low speed until batter is smooth. Pour into prepared pan. Bake at 375 degrees for 12 to 15 minutes until top springs back when lightly touched. Turn upside down immediately on a towel sprinkled with powdered sugar. Carefully remove paper. Trim off any stiff edges. While cake is still hot, roll cake and towel from narrow end. Cool. Unroll cake, remove towel. Spread with soft (not syrupy) jelly or filling. Roll again. If desired, sprinkle with powdered sugar. Cut in 1 inch slices. Wrap in heavy foil. This freezes well.

Lemon Filling:

¾ cup sugar
3 Tablespoons cornstarch
¼ teaspoon salt
¾ cup water
2 large egg yolks, slightly
   beaten

2 Tablespoons grated lemon
   rind
⅓ cup lemon juice
1 Tablespoon butter

Mix in saucepan sugar, cornstarch, and salt. Gradually stir in water. Bring to boil over direct heat, stirring constantly and boil 1 minute. Stir half of hot mixture into egg yolks. Blend into remaining mixture and boil 1 minute more. Remove from heat and add lemon rind, juice, and butter. Cool. Spread out on cake, roll and sprinkle with powdered sugar. *Yield:* 8 to 10 servings.

Mrs. Robert K. Hesson (Pat)

APPLE KUCHEN

Crust:
1 (18½ ounce) yellow cake mix   ½ cup margarine

Combine cake mix with margarine. Press into a 13x9x2 inch pan. Bake crust at 350 degrees for 10 minutes.

Filling:

1 can apple pie slices	1 egg
½ cup sugar	1 cup sour cream
1 teaspoon cinnamon	

Arrange apples on crust. Combine sugar and cinnamon. Sprinkle on apples. Combine beaten egg and sour cream. Drizzle over apples and sugar. Bake 20 to 25 minutes at 350 degrees. *Yield:* 12 to 16 servings.

Mrs. David Gaines (Donna)
Brentwood, Tennessee

BLACKBERRY MARBLE FREEZE

1½ cups graham cracker crumbs	¼ cup butter, melted
	¼ cup sugar

Combine graham cracker crumbs, butter, and sugar. Blend well and press on bottom and sides of 9 inch pie plate.

2 cups fresh blackberries, washed and drained	1 Tablespoon white crème de menthe
⅓ cup sugar	⅓ cup light corn syrup
1 cup heavy cream	

Put blackberries through sieve or food mill; add sugar. Whip cream, crème de menthe, and corn syrup until mixture holds its shape. Turn cream into pie crust. Pour blackberry mixture in thin stream over top to create a marbled effect. Freeze. Cut into wedges to serve. *Yield:* 6 to 8 servings.

Mrs. Jimmy Williams (Nancy)

257

APRICOT TORTE

Meringue:
3 egg whites
¾ cup sugar
½ teaspoon vinegar

½ teaspoon vanilla
½ cup graham cracker crumbs
½ cup shredded coconut
1 cup chopped nuts

Beat egg whites until soft peaks form. Gradually add sugar, vinegar, and vanilla, beating until stiff peaks form. Mix crumbs, coconut, and nuts. Fold into egg white mixture. Oil bottom and sides of 9 inch pie pan. Spoon meringue into pie plate shaping to form shell. Bake at 300 degrees for 30 minutes. Turn off oven and leave torte in oven to dry and cool.

Filling:
2 cups drained stewed apricots   1 Tablespoon sugar
Sugar to taste
1 cup whipping cream,
  whipped

Add sugar to drained apricots and whip lightly with a fork. Spread over torte. Whip cream with 1 tablespoon sugar and spread over top. Refrigerate for 2 to 3 hours. *Yield:* 6 to 8 servings.

Mrs. Richard Dodson (Carolyn)

FROZEN FRUIT CUP
Perfect for showers or brunches.

1 (17 ounce) can apricot halves,
  drained and cubed
2 bananas cubed
1 (16 ounce) can peach slices,
  drained and cubed
½ (10 ounce) package frozen
  strawberries, thawed

¾ cup sugar
1 cup pineapple juice
1 (6 ounce) can frozen orange
  juice concentrate, thawed,
  undiluted
¼ cup lemon juice

Combine all ingredients. Spoon into 13x9x2 inch baking pan or into 5 ounce paper cups, filling ⅔ full. Place in freezer until frozen. Remove 15 minutes before serving. *Yield:* 15 servings.

Mrs. Steve Hester (Chandra)
Henderson, Kentucky

258

PINK STRAWBERRY FREEZE

Crust:
1 cup flour
¼ cup brown sugar
½ cup nuts, chopped
½ cup margarine, melted

Mix all ingredients. Press ½ of crust mixture in 9x13 inch pan. Bake at 350 degrees until brown, stirring occasionally.

Filling:
2 egg whites, beaten
1 cup sugar
2 Tablespoons lemon juice
1 cup whipping cream,
  whipped
2 cups strawberries,
  frozen or fresh

Beat egg whites until stiff, adding sugar slowly. Add lemon juice and whipped cream. Fold in strawberries and mix well with electric mixer. Spread this over baked crust, top with remaining crumb mixture and freeze. *Yield:* 12 to 14 servings.

Mrs. Jim Darnell (Sherri)

BROWNIE MINT TORTE

3 egg whites
Dash of salt
¾ cup sugar
½ teaspoon vanilla
¾ cup chocolate wafer crumbs
½ cup pecans, chopped
1 cup whipping cream,
  whipped
Sugar to taste
¼ cup crushed peppermint
  stick candy
1 (1 ounce) square chocolate,
  shaved

Beat egg whites and salt until soft peaks form. Add sugar, 1 tablespoon at a time and beat until glossy. Beat in vanilla. Fold in crumbs and nuts. Spread in buttered 9 inch pie pan, piling high at sides. Bake in slow oven 325 degrees for 35 minutes. Let cool. About 3 hours before serving, whip cream until stiff. Fold in sugar and crushed candy. Pile into chocolate shell. Chill. Trim with curls of shaved chocolate. *Yield:* 6 servings.

Mrs. Thomas P. Anderson, Jr. (Sylvia)

LIGHT AND LOVELY

3 cups crushed crackers
1 cup butter, melted
4 Tablespoons sugar
2 (3 ounce) packages instant
   coconut cream pudding

1½ cups milk
1 quart vanilla ice cream,
   softened
1 (9 ounce) carton non-dairy
   whipped topping

Combine 2¼ cups crackers, butter, and sugar. Reserve ¾ cup and press remainder into 13x9x2 inch pan. Beat pudding and milk until thick. Fold in ice cream. Pour into pan over crumb mixture. Spread whipped topping over pudding and top with reserved crumbs. Refrigerate 24 hours. *Note:* I use Ritz crackers. *Yield:* 10 to 12 servings.

Mabel Gladieux
Treasure Island, Florida

CHEESECAKE DELIGHTS

⅓ cup light brown sugar
1 cup unsifted flour
½ cup chopped walnuts
⅓ cup butter, melted
1 (8 ounce) package cream
   cheese, softened

¼ cup sugar
1 egg
2 Tablespoons milk
1 Tablespoon lemon juice
1 teaspoon vanilla

Preheat oven to 350 degrees. Grease 8 inch square pan. Mix sugar, flour, and nuts. Stir in melted butter until well blended. Reserve ⅓ cup crumbs. Pat remaining crumbs gently into an 8 inch pan and bake at 350 degrees for 12 to 15 minutes. In small bowl, with electric mixer on medium, beat cream cheese and sugar until smooth. Beat in egg, milk, lemon juice, and vanilla. Pour over baked crust and sprinkle remaining crumbs on top. Bake at 350 degrees for 25 minutes more until set. Cool on wire rack. When cooled, cut into 2 inch squares then in triangles.

Mrs. Jed Becker (Kay)
El Paso, Texas

ENGLISH TRIFLE

2 (3 ounce) packages
  ladyfingers
½ cup raspberry or currant
  jam
1½ cups chopped strawberries

½ cup sugar
½ cup dry sherry
3 cups custard, cold
2 cups heavy cream, whipped
Mint leaves (optional)

Place ladyfingers in the bottom of a glass serving bowl or 12 individual parfait glasses. Heat jam until warm and drizzle over ladyfingers. Top with strawberries, sugar, and sherry. Spoon in cold custard. Top with whipping cream. Garnish with mint leaves. Chill before serving.

Custard:
1 quart milk
1 cup sugar

4 eggs, well beaten
1 Tablespoon vanilla

Heat milk in a double boiler until milk steams. Add sugar to eggs and beat until foamy. Gradually pour hot milk into egg mixture then back into double boiler. Cook until the mixture coats a spoon, stirring constantly. Pour through a strainer and cool. Restrain and add vanilla. Refrigerate. *Yield:* 12 servings.

Mrs. Herbert E. Patrick (Lyn)
Savannah, Tennessee

QUICK APPLESAUCE CRISP

2 cups applesauce
½ cup packed brown sugar
¼ cup raisins
½ teaspoon ground cinnamon
1 cup biscuit mix

⅓ cup sugar
3 Tablespoons margarine or
  butter
¼ cup chopped nuts

Heat oven to 375 degrees. Mix applesauce, brown sugar, raisins, and cinnamon in ungreased 9 inch pie pan. Heat in oven 15 minutes. Combine biscuit mix, sugar and margarine until crumbly; stir in nuts. Sprinkle evenly over applesauce mixture. Bake until golden brown, about 25 minutes. *Yield:* 4 to 6 servings.

Joyce Smithson
College Grove, Tennessee

TIPSY SQUIRE

An old North Carolina tidewater tradition. May be a Christmas season tradition for you!

1 round layer of sponge cake about one inch thick	1 quart chilled boiled custard
½ cup blanched almonds, cut in half lengthwise	1 cup sherry or brandy
	1 cup heavy whipping cream, whipped

In a large round bowl, larger than the layer of cake, put 3 cups of custard. Stick nuts on top of cake with points up. Then place cake on top of custard in the bowl. Pour sherry or brandy over cake, covering entire surface. Pour the remaining 1 cup of custard on the cake; then cover top with slightly sweetened whipped cream. Chill. Serve from bowl cutting down through cake, custard and all. This may be made in individual dishes, cutting cake to suit the small dish. *Note:* Sponge cakes as for strawberry shortcake can also be used. *Yield:* 12 to 14 servings.

Mrs. J. R. Smith (Margaret Rawlings)
Wilson, North Carolina

FROZEN STRAWBERRY CAKE

1 quart strawberry ice cream, softened	1 (8 ounce) can crushed pineapple, drained
1 angel food cake, broken into small pieces	1 (8 ounce) carton non-dairy whipped topping
1 (10 ounce) package frozen strawberries, partially thawed	

Combine the first 4 ingredients. Fold in whipped topping. Pour into two 8x8x2 inch pans. Cover with foil and freeze. Remove from freezer about 15 minutes before serving. Cut into squares and serve. *Yield:* 18 to 24 servings.

Mrs. David Gentry (Susan)

FROZEN CHOCOLATE DELIGHT
Excellent to have in freezer for unexpected company.

4 cups heavy cream
1 (16 ounce) can chocolate
  syrup
1 (14 ounce) can sweetened
  condensed milk

1 teaspoon vanilla extract
2 Tablespoons brandy
½ cup slivered almonds,
  toasted

In a large mixing bowl, combine cream, syrup, milk, vanilla, and brandy. Cover and chill in refrigerator for 6 hours. Whip until thick and mounding. Spoon into aluminum foil muffin cups. Sprinkle with almonds. Cover with plastic wrap and freeze. Also may be spooned into parfaits or sherbets and frozen. *Yield:* 16 to 20 servings.

Mrs. Fayette Williams, Jr. (Mary Elizabeth)
Tupelo, Mississippi

LEMON FROZEN DESSERT
Delightfully light after heavy meal.

1¾ cups vanilla wafers,
  crushed fine
9 Tablespoons lemon juice
1½ cups sugar

3 cups whipping cream,
  whipped
6 eggs, separated
¼ teaspoon salt

Line angel food cake pan with 1 cup vanilla wafer crumbs. Dissolve sugar in lemon juice, stir thoroughly. Whip cream; set aside. Beat egg yolks and add salt. Add egg yolks to sugar mixture and stir until smooth and creamy. Fold in whipped cream. Beat egg whites until stiff but not dry. Fold into mixture. Put in cake pan, top with remaining crumbs and freeze. May also use 13x9x2 inch pan.

Mrs. Tom Turbeville (Mary O.)
Nashville, Tennessee

CHOCOLATE ANGEL FOOD CAKE DESSERT

2 (4 ounce) bars German
  chocolate
3 Tablespoons sugar
3 Tablespoons water

1 pint whipping cream,
  whipped
4 eggs, separated
1 angel food cake

In small pan, combine chocolate, sugar, and water; heat until chocolate is melted. Remove from heat and cool. When mixture has cooled, whip cream until thick and beat egg whites until stiff. Add egg yolks, one at a time to chocolate mixture, beating well. Mix in whipped cream, then fold in egg whites until mixture is smooth. Break cake into bite size chunks and make a layer in a 13x9x2 inch pan. Pour ½ of chocolate mixture over cake layer; repeat with another layer of cake chunks; pour remaining chocolate on top. Refrigerate at least 6 hours before serving. *Yield:* 12 or more servings.

Mrs. Arthur Gerecke (Frances)
Pekin, Illinois

ICE BOX CAKE

¼ cup water
½ cup sugar
2½ (1 ounce) squares baking
  chocolate
4 eggs, separated

1 cup butter or margarine,
  softened
1 cup powdered sugar
1 teaspoon vanilla
2 dozen ladyfingers

Put water, sugar, and chocolate in double boiler. Cook until smooth and chocolate melted. Add beaten egg yolks and cook one minute longer. Cool. Cream butter and slowly add powdered sugar and vanilla. Add to cooled chocolate mixture. Fold in stiffly beaten egg whites. Line 12x8x2 inch pan with waxed paper. Arrange split ladyfingers on bottom of pan. Add a layer of cake mixture, another layer of ladyfingers and remainder of cake mixture on top. Place in refrigerator for 24 hours. Serve with whipped cream. *Yield:* 16 servings.

Mrs. John B. Molitor (Ruth)

ALMOND ICE CREAM DELIGHT

1 (7¼ ounce) box vanilla
  wafers
½ gallon vanilla ice cream,
  softened
½ cup margarine, melted

2 cups powdered sugar
1 egg
1½ teaspoons almond extract
½ cup almonds, toasted

Crush vanilla wafers and line bottom of 13x9x2 inch pan. Spread ½ of the ice cream over crumbs. Combine margarine and sugar; then stir in egg and extract. Spread ½ of this mixture over ice cream layer. Repeat layers and sprinkle with almonds. Freeze until ready to serve. *Yield:* 12 servings.

Mrs. Jerry Brinkley (Gayle)

FRUIT BOWL

1 (22 ounce) can peach pie
  filling
1 (16 ounce) can pineapple
  chunks, drained
3 to 4 bananas
½ teaspoon reconstituted
  lemon juice

2 (11 ounce) cans mandarin
  oranges, drained
20 ounces sweetened frozen
  strawberries, thawed

Place pie filling in large 2 or 3 quart bowl. Cut each pineapple chunk in half. Slice bananas and soak in lemon juice 3 minutes. Then add pineapple, oranges, strawberries, and bananas to pie filling. Store covered in refrigerator. Best prepared 8 hours ahead. Keeps several days. *Yield:* 8 servings.

Judy Foy

AUNT MARY'S FRUIT CRUMBLE

DESSERTS

1 (31 ounce) can pie filling, any flavor
1 teaspoon salt
1 cup flour
1 cup sugar
1 teaspoon baking powder
1 egg
4 Tablespoons butter
1 teaspoon vanilla

Pour filling into bottom of greased 8x8 inch pan or similar size. Mix salt, flour, sugar, baking powder, egg, butter, and vanilla. Crumble or spread on top of fruit. Bake at 375 degrees for 45 minutes. *Yield:* 6 to 8 servings.

Mrs. Ira V. Miller (Mary)
Dayton, Ohio

CHOCOLATE SAUCE
Renowned Gray Drug Soda Fountain Recipe. (Circa 1920)

2 Tablespoons flour
1 cup sugar
2 Tablespoons cocoa
2 Tablespoons butter
½ cup boiling water
½ cup milk
1 teaspoon vanilla

Blend flour with sugar. Add cocoa, butter, and boiling water. Cook over medium heat until smooth; add milk. Cook until it thickens. Remove from heat and add vanilla. Serve over pound cake or vanilla ice cream. *Yield:* 1 pint.

Mrs. T. P. Anderson (Adeline)
Nashville, Tennessee

HOT FUDGE SAUCE
Delicious, especially over vanilla ice cream.

1½ (1 ounce) squares
  unsweetened chocolate
½ cup margarine

1 cup sugar
¼ cup milk

In a saucepan melt chocolate and margarine. Gradually stir in sugar; then stir in milk. Cook for 1 minute on high heat, stirring constantly. *Yield: 1½ cups.*

Mrs. Jerry Brinkley (Gayle)

MUD FLAT PIE

1 cup flour
½ cup or 1 (3 ounce) package
  pecan pieces

1 Tablespoon sugar
½ cup butter, softened

Mix together and spread in 13x9x2 inch pan for the crust. Bake at 350 degrees for 10 to 15 minutes and cool.

1 (8 ounce) package cream
  cheese

1 cup powdered sugar
2 to 3 cups whipped topping

Mix the ingredients together in mixer and spread over cooled crust.

1 (6 ounce) package instant
  chocolate pudding
3 cups cold milk

Enough whipped topping to
  spread over top

Mix pudding and milk well with mixer. Spread over other filling. Top with whipped topping. Refrigerate. *Yield: 12 to 16 servings.*

Mrs. Joe Mac Lipscomb, Jr. (Frances)
Springfield, Tennessee

Variation: For Lemon Fluff Dessert! Substitute instant lemon pudding for instant chocolate pudding and sprinkle top with ½ cup pecans.

Mrs. Harv Gerecke (Mary)
Pekin, Illinois

ELEGANT CHEESECAKE

1 cup flour	½ cup butter
¼ cup sugar	1 egg yolk
1 teaspoon grated lemon peel	¼ teaspoon vanilla

Combine flour, sugar, and lemon peel. Cut in butter. Add egg yolk and vanilla. Blend thoroughly. Pat ⅓ of dough on bottom of spring-form pan. Bake at 400 degrees for 6 minutes until golden brown. Cool. Attach sides and spread rest of the dough on the sides up to about 2 inches all around. Pour in filling.

Filling:

5 (8 ounce) packages cream cheese	3 Tablespoons flour
¼ teaspoon vanilla	¼ teaspoon salt
¾ teaspoon grated lemon peel	5 egg yolks
1¾ cups sugar	2 whole eggs
	¼ cup cream

Stir cheese to soften and beat until fluffy. Add vanilla and peeling. Mix in sugar, flour, and salt. Add 5 egg yolks and 2 whole eggs one at a time, beating well after each. Stir in cream. Pour in crust lined pan. Bake at 500 degrees for about 5 minutes until top edge of crust is golden brown. Reduce heat to 200 degrees for 1 hour. Cool in pan 3 hours before removing sides. Keeps well in refrigerator. *Yield:* 12 servings.

Gloria Brinton
Nashville, Tennessee

Variation:
Topping:

1 cup crushed ripe strawberries	6 to 8 drops red food coloring
¼ cup water	3 Tablespoons cornstarch
¾ cup sugar	1 pint whole strawberries

Bring crushed strawberries, water, sugar, food coloring, and cornstarch to boil, cook until thickened. Strain and cool. Dip whole strawberries in glaze and place on chilled cake. Pour remaining glaze over the top of cake.

Mrs. Douglas C. York (Vicki)

CHOCOLATE MINT STICKS

2 eggs, beaten
½ cup margarine, melted
1 cup sugar
2 (1 ounce) squares chocolate, melted

½ teaspoon peppermint extract
½ cup flour
½ cup slivered almonds

Combine eggs, margarine, and sugar. Beat well. Add chocolate and peppermint extract. Stir until thoroughly blended. Add flour and almonds. Mix well. Pour into greased 9 inch square pan. Bake at 350 degrees for 25 minutes.

Frosting:
2 Tablespoons margarine
1 Tablespoon cream or milk

1 cup powdered sugar
1 teaspoon peppermint extract

Thoroughly blend margarine and cream. Add sugar and flavoring. Spread over cooled baked cake.

Topping:
1 (1 ounce) square chocolate

1 Tablespoon margarine

When frosting is firm, spread melted topping over it. Place in refrigerator until cool. Cut into forty eight ¾x2¼ inch strips. *Yield:* 48 servings.

Paula Sevier
Brentwood, Tennessee

CHERRY BERRIES IN THE SNOW

6 egg whites
½ teaspoon cream of tartar

¼ teaspoon salt
1¾ cups sugar

Heat oven to 275 degrees. Grease a 13x9x2 inch pan. Beat egg whites, cream of tartar, and salt until stiff. Gradually add sugar. Beat until very stiff and glossy (about 15 minutes). Spread this mixture into the pan in "pie shell" fashion. Bake 1 hour. Turn the oven off and leave the meringue shell in oven until cool. About 12 hours or overnight.

2 (3 ounce) packages cream
cheese
1 cup sugar
1 teaspoon vanilla

2 cups whipping cream,
whipped
2 cups miniature
marshmallows

Mix cream cheese with sugar and vanilla. Gently fold in whipped cream and marshmallows. Spread in meringue shell.

1 (31 ounce) can cherry pie
filling
1 teaspoon lemon juice

2 cups sliced fresh strawberries
(or frozen)

Mix pie filling with strawberries and lemon juice. Pour over filling. Keep refrigerated. *Yield:* 10 to 16 servings.

Mrs. Robert T. Embry (Bettye)

BLACK WALNUT ICE CREAM

6 eggs, separated
2 cups sugar
Salt to taste
1 (14 ounce) can sweetened
condensed milk

1½ cups walnuts, crushed
1 teaspoon black walnut
extract
1 quart half-and-half
3 quarts milk

Beat egg yolks and add sugar, salt, condensed milk, walnuts, and extract. Beat egg whites until stiff and fold into mixture. Pour into 1½ gallon container and add half-and-half and milk. Freeze (by hand or electric) according to freezer directions. *Yield:* 1 gallon.

Arvemia Wilburn
Brentwood, Tennessee

CHOCOLATE RUM ICE CREAM

¼ cup sugar
⅓ cup water
2 Tablespoons instant coffee
1 (6 ounce) package semi-sweet
  chocolate chips

3 egg yolks
2 ounces dark rum
1½ cups heavy cream, whipped
½ cup slivered almonds,
  toasted

In a small saucepan, place sugar, water, and coffee. Stirring constantly, bring to a boil and cook for 1 minute. Place the chocolate chips in a blender or food processor, and with the motor running pour the hot syrup over and blend until smooth. Beat in egg yolks and rum and cool slightly. Fold chocolate mixture into whipped cream, then pour into individual serving dishes or small mold. Sprinkle with toasted almonds. Freeze. To serve, remove from the freezer at least 5 minutes before serving. *Yield:* 6 servings.

Mrs. Donald N. Edmands (Isabel)

CHOCOLATE ICE CREAM DESSERT

⅓ box graham crackers,
  crushed
½ cup butter, melted
8 chocolate bars with almonds
24 marshmallows

1 cup milk
½ pint whipping cream,
  whipped
½ gallon chocolate whirl
  ice cream

Make a graham cracker crust by mixing graham crackers and butter. Press in the bottom of a 13x9x2 inch pan. Freeze. In the top of a double boiler, melt chocolate bars, marshmallows and milk. When cool, fold in whipped cream. Spread over crust and freeze. When set, spread softened ice cream over chocolate mixture. To serve, top with a spoon of whipping cream and a cherry. *Yield:* 12 servings.

Mrs. Jim Roberts (Margaret)

CHOCOLATE ICE CREAM

Step I:

1 (13 ounce) can evaporated milk

1 (6 ounce) package semi-sweet chocolate chips

2¼ cups powdered sugar

Over low heat, melt milk and chocolate. Add sugar and stir well. Cool.

Step II

1 (14 ounce) can sweetened condensed milk

2 cups whipping cream

1 cup sugar

½ gallon whole milk

Mix all ingredients with mixer. (Add chocolate mixture and mix well). If mixing bowl is too small for all ingredients, add some of the whole milk after you have placed mixture into ice cream freezer. Stir well. Freeze according to manufacturer's instructions. *Note:* For vanilla ice cream delete step I and add 1 teaspoon vanilla. *Yield:* 5 quarts.

Mrs. Joe Mac Lipscomb (Frances)
Springfield, Tennessee

FOREVER AMBERS

1 pound orange slice candy, cut up fine

1 (7 ounce) can coconut

2 cans sweetened condensed milk

1 cup chopped pecans

1 teaspoon vanilla

1 teaspoon orange flavoring

(1 cup or so) powdered sugar

Combine all ingredients except powdered sugar. Spread this mixture in a slightly greased 13x9x2 inch pan. Bake for 45 minutes at 275 degrees. Remove from oven. Immediately pinch off a spoonful at a time. Roll into balls and roll in powdered sugar to coat well. Place on waxed paper to cool. *Yield:* 60 to 80 balls.

Mrs. W. C. Gatlin (Annie Mae)

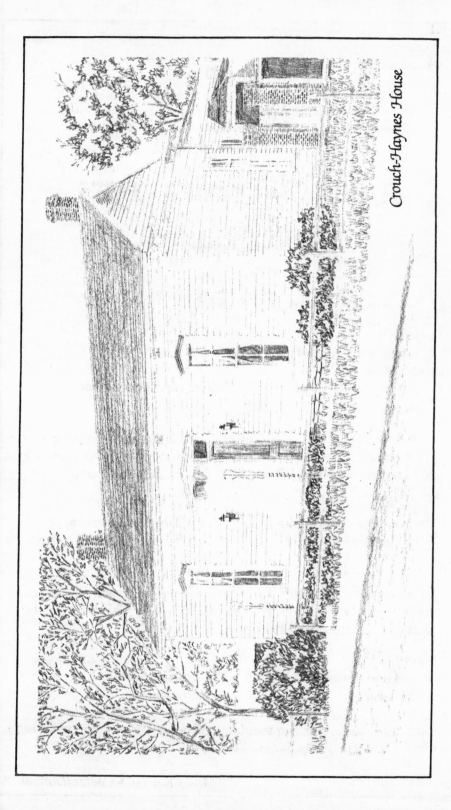

Crouch-Haynes House

CROUCH—HAYNES

This Victorian home was originally owned by William H. Crouch in 1850. Since that time the home has had eight additions with six different roof levels. Today it is owned by Mrs. Willis Haynes.

Cookies, Candy, Bars, and Squares

CHOCOLATE PEPPERMINT BARS

Layer #1:

2 ounces unsweetened chocolate
½ cup butter or margarine
2 eggs
1 cup sugar
½ cup flour
½ cup chopped almonds (optional)

Melt chocolate and butter. Cream eggs and sugar. Add flour and chocolate mixture. Mix well. bake in 8x8 inch pan at 350 degrees for 20 minutes. Turn oven off and bake 5 more minutes. Cool.

Layer #2:

1½ cups powdered sugar
3 Tablespoons butter or margarine
2 to 3 Tablespoons cream
1 teaspoon peppermint extract

Cream sugar and butter. Blend in cream and extract. Spread on cooled first layer. Refrigerate until chilled. *Note:* This layer can be tinted red or green for Christmas.

Layer #3:

3 ounces unsweetened chocolate
3 Tablespoons butter or margarine

Melt chocolate and butter together and pour over peppermint layer. Chill. Cut into small squares. *Yield:* 24 to 30 bars.

Mrs. Francis DeCoster (Donna)

CREAM CHEESE CRESCENTS
Freezes well!

Dough:
3 cups flour
½ pound cream cheese
½ pound margarine
Powdered sugar

Mix flour, cream cheese, and margarine thoroughly by hand. Form balls the size of walnuts, with palms of hands, out of dough. Store in refrigerator overnight. Roll each ball out in powdered sugar until thin. Use generous amounts of sugar for rolling out balls. Fill with nuts, preserves, or date filling below. Use one tablespoon filling per cookie. Put filling at one side of circle and roll loosely or gently into roll and form to make horseshoe. Bake 325 to 350 degrees for 20 to 25 minutes.

Fillings:
Date filling:
1 pound chopped dates
1 cup sugar
½ cup water

Cook dates, sugar, and water until thick; set aside until cool.

Nut filling:
¾ cup chopped nuts
¾ cup sugar
1 to 2 egg whites (enough to
  make consistancy not too
  runny)

Blend nuts, sugar, and egg whites and use.

Apricot filling:

Cook apricots according to directions on box. *Note:* I also use Solo brand filling for baking. *Yield:* 35 to 40 servings.

Mrs. James Danyi (Anna Kelle)
Dayton, Ohio

OLD FASHIONED ICE-BOX COOKIES
This is an old recipe with a unique flavor.

1 cup sugar
1 cup light brown sugar
1 cup shortening
3 eggs
3½ cups flour

2 teaspoons cinnamon
1 teaspoon baking powder
1 teaspoon baking soda
1 cup chopped nuts (optional)

Cream sugars and shortening. Add whole eggs and mix well. Sift the flour and the dry ingredients and add to creamed mixture. Mixture will now be fairly stiff. Divide mixture into 3 parts and form into rolls with floured hands. Wrap the rolls in waxed paper and refrigerate until cold. Slice about ¼ inch thick and place on greased pan. Bake in 350 degree oven until done, about 8 to 10 minutes. These are handy to have on hand to slice and cook when needed. *Yield:* 4 dozen.

Mrs. Joseph L. Willoughby (Betty)

IRVINE PUMPKIN BARS

4 eggs
1 (16 ounce) can pumpkin
2 cups sugar
1 cup oil
2 cups flour

2 teaspoons baking powder
½ teaspoon salt
2 teaspoons cinnamon
1 teaspoon baking soda

Beat eggs, pumpkin, sugar, and oil. Add flour, baking powder, salt, cinnamon, and baking soda. Bake in a jellyroll pan, (10x15 inches). Bake at 350 degrees for 30 minutes. Cool before frosting.

Frosting:
2½ cups powdered sugar, sifted
1 teaspoon milk
1 teaspoon vanilla
3 ounces cream cheese, softened

6 Tablespoons butter or margarine

Blend all ingredients. Frost and cut into bars. *Yield:* 40 bars.

Miss Anne Westfall

UNUSUAL OATMEAL WAFER
"This is thin and crispy"

1 cup sugar
½ cup butter
½ cup pure lard
3 cups sifted flour
1 teaspoon baking soda

1 teaspoon cream of tartar
½ teaspoon salt
½ cup cold water
2 cups rolled oats (not instant)

Cream sugar, butter, and lard until light and fluffy. Combine in a separate bowl; flour, soda, cream of tartar, and salt. Add flour mixture to sugar mixture, a small amount at a time. Add ½ cup of cold water as needed to mix. Fold in oats and knead. This will be a rather stiff dough. Roll out the dough and cut with a 2 inch round cookie cutter. Place on a greased cookie sheet and bake at 375 degrees until edges brown slightly, about 8 to 9 minutes.

Mrs. Gerald P. Sieberling (Bernice)
Director, Carnton Association

SUGAR COOKIES WITH ICING
Kids love to do this at holiday time!

1 cup margarine
1⅓ cups sugar
1 egg, unbeaten

1 Tablespoon milk
2 teaspoons vanilla
3 cups self-rising flour

Cream margarine. Gradually add sugar. Add egg, milk, and vanilla. Blend in flour and mix well. Roll out to ⅛ inch thickness. Cut with cookie cutter. Bake at 400 degrees for 5 to 8 minutes.

Icing:
3 Tablespoons butter
1½ cups powdered sugar
2 Tablespoons milk

1 teaspoon vanilla .
Food coloring

Melt butter in small saucepan. Add sugar, milk, and vanilla. Stir until smooth. Add more milk if needed to make smoother. Color with food coloring for desired color. Spread on cookies when they are cool. *Yield:* 5 to 6 dozen.

Mrs. E. Fred Durham (Paula)

PUMPKIN DESSERT SQUARES

1 (18.5 ounce) box yellow
  cake mix

½ cup butter or margarine
1 egg

Grease bottom only of 13x9x2 inch pan. Reserve 1 cup cake mix. Mix remainder with butter and egg. Press into pan.

Filling:
1 (16 ounce) can pumpkin pie
  mix

2 eggs
⅔ cup milk

Combine all ingredients and mix until smooth. Pour over crust.

Topping:
1 cup reserved cake mix
¼ cup sugar

1 teaspoon cinnamon
¼ cup butter or margarine

Combine all ingredients and sprinkle over filling. Bake at 350 degrees for 45 minutes. Chill. Cut into squares and serve with whipped topping. *Yield:* 2 to 3 dozen.

Mary Robinson

BROWNIES (MICROWAVE)

2 eggs
1 cup sugar
½ teaspoon salt
1 teaspoon vanilla
½ cup (¼ pound) butter or
  margarine, melted

¾ cup sifted flour
½ cup cocoa
1 cup chopped nuts (optional)
1 (6 ounce) package chocolate
  chips (optional-may be
  substituted for nuts)

Cream eggs, sugar, salt, and vanilla until light (about 1 minute). Add melted butter. Beat until thoroughly blended. Mix in flour and cocoa and blend at low speed. Stir in nuts. Spread evenly in 8 inch square dish. Microwave at high (full power) 5 to 7 minutes; rotate dish ¼ turn every 2 minutes. Allow to cool before cutting. *Yield:* 1 dozen.

Mrs. Michael Lynch (Donna)

FUDGE MELTAWAYS

½ cup margarine
1 (1 ounce) square
  unsweetened chocolate
¼ cup sugar
1 teaspoon vanilla
1 egg, beaten
2 cups very fine graham
  cracker crumbs

1 cup coconut
½ cup chopped nuts
¼ cup margarine
1 Tablespoon cream
2 cups sifted powdered sugar
1 teaspoon vanilla
1½ squares (1½ ounces)
  unsweetened chocolate

Melt margarine and 1 square chocolate in saucepan. Blend sugar, 1 teaspoon vanilla, egg, crumbs, coconut, and nuts into margarine-chocolate mixture. Mix well and press into ungreased baking dish, 11½x7½x1½ inch or 9 inch square pan. Refrigerate. Mix ¼ cup margarine, cream, powdered sugar and 1 teaspoon vanilla. Spread over crumb mixture. Chill. Melt 1½ square chocolate and spread evenly over chilled filling. Chill again. Cut into tiny squares before completely firm. *Yield:* 3 to 4 dozen.

Mrs. Loy Hardcastle, Jr. (Rosemary)

APRICOT SQUARES

1½ cups flour
1½ cups quick rolled oats
  (uncooked)
1 teaspoon baking powder
⅓ cup coconut (canned or
  fresh frozen)

1 cup light brown sugar
Grated rind of 1 lemon
¾ cup butter or margarine
1 (12 ounce) jar apricot
  preserves

In mixing bowl, mix flour, oats, baking powder, coconut, brown sugar, and lemon rind. Cut in butter until mixture is crumbly. (A pie crust blender works well) Pat ⅔ of mixture into 9x13 inch pyrex dish, pressing down firmly with palm of hand. Distribute preserves evenly over surface. Crumble remaining ⅓ of flour mixture on top of preserves. Bake at 350 degrees for 35 minutes. Remove from oven and cool. Cut into 2 inch squares. *Yield:* 24 squares.

Mrs. Malcolm Beasley (Bonnie)
Nashville, Tennessee

ALLIE'S BROWNIES

2 (1 ounce) squares bitter
   chocolate, melted
½ cup margarine or butter,
   softened
2 cups sugar

4 eggs
1 teaspoon vanilla
1 cup flour, sifted
½ teaspoon salt
1 cup pecans, chopped

Melt squares of chocolate in microwave or in double boiler over boiling water. Set aside and cool. In mixer, cream butter until light and fluffy. Add sugar to butter and mix thoroughly. Add eggs one at a time and beat well after each addition. Stir in vanilla. Sift flour and salt together. Add gradually to butter mixture. Stir well. Blend in chopped pecans. Pour into a greased and floured 9 inch square pan. Bake for 30 minutes at 275 degrees. Turn oven to 375 degrees and bake for 15 additional minutes. Cool. Cut into squares. *Yield:* 20 squares.

Mrs. William F. Greenwood, Jr. (Sandra)

CHOCOLATE COVERED CHERRY COOKIES

1½ cups flour
½ cup cocoa
¼ teaspoon salt
¼ teaspoon baking powder
¼ teaspoon baking soda
½ cup butter or margarine
1 cup sugar
1 egg

1½ teaspoons vanilla
1 (10 ounce) jar maraschino
   cherries
1 (6 ounce) package semi-
   sweet chocolate morsels
½ cup sweetened condensed
   milk
4 teaspoons cherry juice

In a large bowl, stir together flour, cocoa, salt, baking powder, and baking soda; set aside. In mixing bowl, beat butter and sugar. Add egg and vanilla, mixing well; add dry ingredients. Shape dough into 1 inch balls. Place on ungreased cookie sheet. Press down center of dough with thumb and place a cherry in center. In small pan, combine chocolate chips and condensed milk and heat until chips are melted; stir in cherry juice. Spoon 1 teaspoon frosting over each cherry, spreading to cover cherry. Bake at 350 degrees for 10 minutes. *Yield:* 48 cookies.

Mrs. Orville Haning (Gloria)
Minier, Illinois

CREAM WAFERS

Wafer ingredients:
1 cup butter, melted
⅓ cup whipping cream

2 cups flour
Sugar

Mix melted butter, whipping cream, and flour. Cover and chill in refrigerator for 1 hour. Mixture will be oily at first, but soon will get hard. Roll dough onto floured board to ¼ inch thickness. Works best when working with ⅓ of dough at a time. Cut with small round cookie cutter. Coat each cookie with sugar and prick 4 times with fork. Place on ungreased cookie sheet. Bake at 375 degrees for 7 to 9 minutes. *Do not brown* cookies. Cool completely before filling with cream filling.

Filling ingredients:
¼ cup butter
¾ cup powdered sugar

1 teaspoon vanilla
Food coloring

Mix butter, sugar, and vanilla until smooth. Tint with food coloring. Fill wafers and serve at room temperature. *Yield:* 24 servings.

Mrs. Steve Hester (Chan)
Henderson, Kentucky

SKILLET COOKIES

½ cup butter
1 cup sugar
1 egg, beaten
1 (8 ounce) package chopped
    dates

1 teaspoon vanilla
2 cups crisp rice cereal
1 cup nuts

Mix butter, sugar and egg. Cook for 5 minutes in a skillet on low. (Should become foamy as you stir.) Add dates and cook, stirring often, 5 more minutes. Remove from heat. Add vanilla, rice cereal, and nuts. Mix well in large bowl. Divide onto 4 pieces of waxed paper and form into rolls. Refrigerate and cut each roll into thin slices. *Yield:* 2 dozen.

Mrs. Robert H. Hutcheson, Jr. (Nancy)

LOVE LETTERS

Dough:

1⅓ cups flour (measure, then
  sift)
½ pound butter
1 small egg

1 small egg yolk
3 scant Tablespoons sour
  cream
Powdered sugar

Mix flour and butter well, by hand. Make a well in flour mixture and add egg, egg yolk and sour cream. Mix well. If sticky, add flour gently or refrigerate dough until it becomes firm to make balls. Roll dough into balls, with palms of hands, about the size of a walnut. Refrigerate overnight. In rolling out balls use flour generously. Roll out 3 to 4 at a time until thin. Put 1 tablespoon of filling on dough. Fold top to middle and bottom to middle—not overlapping, then ends to center as top and bottom. (Turn in to make it look like an envelope). Pick up with spatula and place on cookie sheet. Bake at 450 degrees for 8 to 10 minutes. Cool and dust with powdered sugar.

Filling:

3 small egg yolks
3 small whole eggs

1½ cups sugar
2 cups ground nuts

Beat egg yolks and eggs until light and fluffy. Add sugar. Add nuts gradually while beating. Put one tablespoon filling on each cookie. Freezes well in airtight container with waxed paper between layers of cookies. *Yield:* 35 to 40 servings.

Mrs. John Danyi (Katherine)
Dayton, Ohio

TOFFEE BARS

1 cup butter or margarine,
  softened
1 cup brown sugar
1 large egg yolk
1 teaspoon vanilla

1 cup sifted flour
¼ teaspoon salt
½ pound sweet chocolate
  (large candy bar)
1 cup chopped nuts

In a large mixing bowl, cream butter and brown sugar well, add egg yolk and continue beating until light and creamy. Add vanilla. Sift flour and salt; add to batter. Dough will be stiff. Pat out onto a jellyroll pan. Bake approximately 15 minutes in a 350 degree oven. Melt chocolate and chopped nuts in a small pan over low heat. Spread this mixture over warm cookie mixture. Cut into squares and place pan in refrigerator to set-up the chocolate topping. These bars keep well in a tight container in a cool place or in the refrigerator. *Yield:* 24 to 36 squares.

Mrs. Robert Hesson (Pat)

DATE BARS

1 cup sugar
2 Tablespoons melted butter
2 eggs
1 (8 ounce) package pitted
  dates chopped
3 Tablespoons hot water

1 cup flour
1 teaspoon baking powder
1 teaspoon vanilla
1 cup chopped nuts
⅓ cup powdered sugar

In mixer blend sugar and butter. Add eggs and beat well. Put dates in with hot water and mix and add to sugar, butter, and eggs. Add flour, baking powder, and vanilla and mix well. Add nuts and mix well. Pour into greased and floured 8x8 inch pan. Bake at 350 degrees for 40 minutes. Cut into squares while hot. Let cool. Sprinkle with powdered sugar. *Yield:* 36 bars.

Helen Horcsik
Lorain, Ohio

APRICOT BUTTER SQUARES

12 ounces vanilla wafers,
  crushed
½ pound butter, melted
2½ cups powdered sugar
2 eggs

1½ teaspoons vanilla
1 (16 ounce) can apricot halves,
  cut and drained
4 ounces chopped pecans
2 cups heavy cream

In a 13x9x2 inch pan, make a layer of half the crushed vanilla wafers. Mix together the butter, powdered sugar, eggs, and vanilla. Pour this over vanilla wafers. Cover this mixture with the apricot halves, then sprinkle with chopped nuts. Whip cream until stiff and spread over apricots. Cover the top with the remaining half of the vanilla wafers. Refrigerate for at least 24 hours. Cut into squares to serve. *Yield:* 16 squares.

Mrs. Donald N. Edmands (Isabel)

DATE COOKIES

1 cup butter
1 cup sugar
1 cup brown sugar
3 eggs

4 cups flour
1 teaspoon soda
1 teaspoon cinnamon
½ teaspoon salt

Cream butter and sugars until fluffy, add eggs, one at a time, mixing thoroughly after each addition. Sift dry ingredients; add to creamed mixture. If dough seems soft, chill slightly before rolling. Roll on a floured board to ½ inch. Spread with filling and roll like a jellyroll. Store in refrigerator until ready to bake. Slice. Bake at 375 degrees for 10 to 15 minutes.

Filling:
1 pound dates, chopped
½ cup sugar

½ cup water
1 cup chopped nuts

Combine dates, sugar, and water. Cook until thick paste is formed. Add nuts, set aside to cool. Spread on dough. *Note:* Refrigerator cookies. Stores well and can be frozen before or after being baked. *Yield:* 4 dozen, ½ inch cookies.

Mrs. James Danyi (Anna)
Dayton, Ohio

MOLASSES COOKIES

¾ cup shortening
1 cup sugar
¼ cup molasses
1 egg
2 teaspoons baking soda
2 cups sifted flour

½ to ¾ teaspoon cloves
½ to ¾ teaspoon ginger
1 teaspoon cinnamon
½ teaspoon salt
Sugar

Melt shortening in a 3 or 4 quart saucepan on low heat. Remove from heat and let cool. Add to shortening, sugar, molasses, and egg and beat well. Sift dry ingredients and add to first mixture. Mix well and chill. When mixture has chilled, roll into 1 inch balls. Roll balls in sugar. Place 2 inches apart on greased cookie sheet. Bake at 375 degrees for 8 to 10 minutes. Let stand 1 minute before removing. *Yield:* 3 to 4 dozen.

Mrs. Robert Pilling (Nancy)

CRISP AND DELICIOUS SUGAR COOKIES
Delicious!

1 cup margarine or butter
1 cup sugar
1 cup powdered sugar
2 eggs
1 cup oil

2 teaspoons vanilla
1 teaspoon cream of tartar
1 teaspoon baking soda
¼ teaspoon salt
5 to 6 cups flour

Cream margarine, sugars, eggs, and oil. Add all other ingredients. Form into small balls (1 teaspoon dough) and place on ungreased baking sheet. Flatten slightly with hand. Bake at 400 degrees for approximately 10 to 12 minutes. *Note:* These may be topped with pecan halves, cherries, chocolate frosting with almonds, etc. for many different looks. *Yield:* 130 cookies.

Mrs. Earl A. Vinson (Vivian)
Petal, Mississippi

GRANDMA'S SUGAR COOKIES
Great for dunking too!

3 cups sugar
1½ cups shortening
4 medium or 3 large eggs
1 (5 ounce) can of evaporated
   milk

1 teaspoon baking soda
1 teaspoon salt
2 teaspoons baking powder
1 to 2 teaspoons vanilla
6 cups flour

Cream sugar, shortening, and eggs. Add milk and remaining ingredients. Place by teaspoonfuls onto greased cookie sheet. Bake at 350 degrees for 15 to 25 minutes. Makes a large batch of cookies. Store in airtight container with waxed paper between layers. Can be frozen. *Note:* May add chocolate chips or M&M's.

Mrs. D. E. Westfall (Versie)

SUGAR COOKIES

1 cup butter or margarine
1½ cups powdered sugar
1 egg
1 teaspoon vanilla

2½ cups flour
1 teaspoon baking soda
1 teaspoon cream of tartar
¼ teaspoon salt

Cream butter. Add sugar gradually, cream until fluffy. Add unbeaten egg and vanilla. Beat well. Sift together dry ingredients. Blend into creamed mixture. Refrigerate. Roll out onto floured board and cut with cookie cutter. Bake on ungreased cookie sheet for 6 minutes at 400 degrees. *Yield:* 3 to 4 dozen.

Mrs. Aaron Moss, Jr. (Marjorie)
Central City, Kentucky

OAT CRISPS

⅔ cup margarine
½ cup sugar
2 cups old-fashioned oats
1 cup grated coconut
½ teaspoon cinnamon

1 teaspoon vanilla extract
1 teaspoon lemon rind
1 teaspoon orange rind
½ teaspoon salt

Cream margarine and sugar. Add remaining ingredients and mix well. Form into 2 long rolls, each about ¾ inch in diameter. Wrap in waxed paper. Chill until completely firm. Preheat oven to 325 degrees. Cut rolls into ¼ inch slices. Place cookie slices 1 inch apart on an ungreased baking sheet. Bake 15 to 20 minutes or until cookies are lightly browned and slightly firm to the touch. Cool before removing to paper towel lined racks. *Yield:* 3 dozen cookies.

Mrs. Robert H. Wickham (Cindy)

PECAN PIE SURPRISE BARS

1 (18.5 ounce) yellow cake mix
½ cup melted margarine or
    butter
4 eggs
½ cup firmly packed brown
    sugar

1½ cups dark corn syrup (or
    ¾ cup dark corn syrup plus
    ¾ cup light corn syrup)
1 teaspoon vanilla
1 cup chopped pecans

Set aside ⅔ cup cake mix. Combine remaining cake mix, margarine and 1 egg. Mix with fork until crumbly. Press crumbs into 13x9x2 inch pan. Bake at 350 degrees for 15 to 18 minutes or until light golden brown. While crust is baking, combine reserved cake mix, 3 eggs, brown sugar, corn syrup, and vanilla in mixing bowl. Beat at medium speed 1 to 2 minutes. Pour over partially baked crust and sprinkle with pecans. Bake at 350 degrees for 30 to 35 minutes. Cool and cut into bars. *Yield:* 2 to 3 dozen.

Mrs. Charles Camp (Marie)
Dothan, Alabama

CHESS PIE COOKIES

1½ cups flour (unsifted)
¾ cup soft butter
3 Tablespoons sugar
2 cups light brown sugar

3 egg yolks
½ teaspoon vanilla flavoring
3 egg whites (beaten)

Mix flour, butter, and sugar. Spread on bottom of 9x13 inch pan. Bake in 375 degree oven for 15 minutes. Cream together brown sugar, egg yolks, and vanilla. Fold in egg whites. Place on top of first mixture. Bake in 350 degree oven 25 to 30 minutes. *Yield:* approximately 3 dozen squares.

Ann E. Lynch
Nashville, Tennessee

KIFLE
Little horseshoe cakes!

Dough:
5 cups flour
½ pound margarine
½ pound butter

1 package dry yeast
3 egg yolks
1 cup sour cream

Work flour, margarine, butter, and yeast like pie dough by hand. Add egg yolks and sour cream; mix well. Divide dough into 14 to 17 balls and refrigerate. Can be stored this way a couple of days or frozen for use later. When ready to bake, roll out each ball in confectioners sugar or flour in shape of pie crust. Cut in 8 triangle shapes. Fill at wide end and roll to narrow end of triangle. Shape like horse shoe on cookie sheet.

Filling:

Use ½ Tablespoon filling for each cake.
1. Can use Solo filling
2. Can use filling as desired or fillings of Cream Cheese Crescents. Bake 350 degrees 15 to 20 minutes. When cool, sprinkle with powdered sugar. *Note:* I use Solo filling. *Yield:* 130 cakes.

Grace Danyi
Dayton, Ohio

FUDGE CAKE

2 cups sugar
½ cup cocoa
1½ cups flour
1 cup margarine, melted

4 eggs
1 cup nuts, chopped
1½ teaspoons vanilla

Melt margarine in heavy saucepan. In large mixing bowl, combine sugar and cocoa. Add 1½ cups flour. Pour melted margarine into dry mixture and add eggs, one at a time. Mix well. Grease 13x9 inch cake pan and after adding nuts and vanilla to mixture, pour into pan. Bake at 350 degrees for 15 minutes. Open door and shake pan so cake will fall. Bake for 15 more minutes.

Frosting:
½ cup marshmallow creme
½ cup margarine, melted
½ cup cocoa
1 (16 ounce) box powdered
  sugar

½ cup milk
1 teaspoon vanilla flavoring

Remove cake from oven and top with marshmallow creme, spreading thinly with knife. In small saucepan melt margarine, and add cocoa. Let simmer for 1 minute. Remove from heat and add sugar and milk, stirring well. (You may not need the entire ½ cup of milk.) Add vanilla and spread over cake. When cool cut into squares. *Yield:* 36 to 40 squares.

Mrs. Franklin Bracey (Barbara)

LACE COOKIES

½ cup margarine, melted
¾ cup sugar
1 cup quick oats
1 egg, beaten

3 Tablespoons sifted flour
½ teaspoon baking powder
1 teaspoon vanilla
½ teaspoon salt

Melt margarine, and add other ingredients. Cover cookie sheet with foil and grease slightly. Drop by ½ teaspoon far apart. Bake 8 to 10 minutes at 350 degrees. Edges should be brown. Cool slightly and peel off.

Mrs. William Miller (Laura May)

MERINGUE COOKIES

3 egg whites
1 cup sugar
¼ teaspoon salt

1 teaspoon vanilla
¾ cup chopped pecans
¾ cup chopped dates

Heat oven to 300 degrees (slow). Blend egg whites, sugar, salt, and vanilla in top of double boiler. Place over boiling water; beat with a rotary beater until mixture stands in stiff peaks, scraping bottom and sides often with rubber scraper. Stir in pecans and dates immediately. Drop heaping teaspoonfuls of dough on 2 lightly greased baking sheets. (Bake one sheet at a time). Bake 12 to 15 minutes or until lightly browned. Remove from baking sheets immediately. *Yield:* 3 dozen.

Mrs. Loy Hardcastle, Jr. (Rosemary)

SNOW BALLS

2½ cups flour
6 Tablespoons powdered sugar
½ teaspoon salt
1 teaspoon vanilla

1 to 2 cups ground pecans
1 cup margarine, melted
Powdered sugar

Mix all ingredients in large mixing bowl. Shape into teaspoon size balls. Bake at 350 degrees for 20 minutes on cookie sheet. Roll in powdered sugar while hot. *Yield:* 4 dozen.

Mrs. Robert Frazier (Jeanette)
Sikeston, Missouri

SEVEN LAYER COOKIES

½ cup butter (melted)
1 cup graham cracker crumbs
1 cup coconut
6 ounces chocolate chips

6 ounces butterscotch chips
1 (14 ounce) can sweetened,
 condensed milk
1 cup chopped pecans

Melt margarine. Mix with graham cracker crumbs and press into the bottom of a 9x13x2 inch pan. Arrange ingredients in layers as listed. Bake at 325 degrees for 30 minutes. Cut into squares. *Yield:* about 3 dozen squares.

Mrs. Ed Anderson (Mary Jane)

CINNAMON COOKIES

2 cups flour
1 Tablespoon cinnamon
½ pound butter, softened
1 cup sugar

1 egg yolk
1 cup pecans
1 egg white

Mix all ingredients except egg white and spread in a greased and floured jellyroll pan. You will need to pat this out since it is a very thick batter. Brush slightly beaten egg white over top. Bake 30 to 40 minutes at 325 degrees. Cut into squares, remove from pan and cool. *Yield:* Approximately 2 dozen.

Mrs. Bobby Pitts (Florence)

CHOCOLATE COOKIE DELIGHT

12 chocolate cream filled
   cookies
1 (8 ounce) box chopped dates
¾ cup water
2 cups miniature
   marshmallows

1 cup chopped pecans
1 cup whipping cream,
   whipped
2 teaspoons vanilla

Crush 9 cookies. Press into bottom of 9 inch square pan. Place dates and water on stove. Bring to boil, simmer, and stir 3 minutes. Remove from heat and add marshmallows. Stir until melted. Add pecans and stir. Pour over cookies. Whip cream and add vanilla and spread over top. Crush 3 cookies and sprinkle over top. Refrigerate overnight. *Note:* I use Oreo cookies. *Yield:* 9 servings.

Juliet Randolph

LEMON SQUARES

1 cup sifted flour   ¼ cup powdered sugar
½ cup soft butter

Mix sifted flour, butter, and powdered sugar. Press into bottom of an 8x8 inch pan. Bake at 325 degrees for 20 minutes.

2 eggs, beaten   2 Tablespoons lemon juice
1 cup sugar   ½ teaspoon salt
2 Tablespoons flour

Combine eggs, sugar, flour, lemon juice, and salt. Place on top of "crust" layer. Bake again for 30 minutes at 325 degrees. Sprinkle with powdered sugar and cool before cutting. *Yield:* 12 squares.

Mrs. William Milton (Lucy)

PRALINE BARS

⅓ (16 ounce) box Honey   ½ cup sugar
 Graham Crackers   ¾ cup broken pecans
1 cup butter, no substitutes

Break the graham crackers apart into 3 sections and line bottom of 10x15½ inch jellyroll pan. Bring butter and sugar to a boil and boil 3 minutes, stirring constantly. Pour evenly over crackers and add pecans. Bake at 350 degrees for 12 minutes. Let cool a few minutes and lift out with spatula onto waxed paper or foil to cool completely. (For variations, add 1 package of milk chocolate morsels to crackers after baking by sprinkling on top while crackers are hot). *Yield:* 40 bars.

Mrs. Jim Crowell (Mary Ann)

FORGOTTEN COOKIES

2 egg whites
¼ teaspoon cream of tartar
½ cup sugar
½ teaspoon vanilla

Pinch of salt
1 cup broken pecans
1 (8 ounce) package chocolate chips

Beat egg whites until stiff. Add cream of tartar. Add sugar (little at a time). Add vanilla, salt, pecans, and chips. Drop by scant teaspoonfuls onto greased cookie sheet. Preheat oven to 350 degrees and place in oven. Turn off heat and leave overnight. *Do Not Open Door. Yield:* 2 dozen.

Mrs. B. R. Wilkerson (Lu)

CZECHOSLOVAKIAN PASTRY

½ cup butter
1 cup sugar
2 egg yolks
2 cups flour

1 (16 ounce) jar orange marmalade
1 cup chopped pecans

Cream butter with sugar, add egg yolks. Mix in flour (mix will be crumbly). Spread dough on bottom of oblong cake pan, reserve ½ cup for topping. Press dough firmly into pan. Spread marmalade on top of dough. Sprinkle with chopped pecans. Sprinkle reserved crumbs on top. Bake at 325 degrees until light brown. Cool, cut into pieces. *Yield:* 2 dozen.

Mrs. Ronald L. Barrett (Betty)

CHOCOLATE TOFFEE

1 cup butter, softened
2 cups powdered sugar
3 eggs, separated
2 (1 ounce) squares chocolate, melted

1 teaspoon vanilla
1 cup walnuts, chopped fine
½ pound vanilla wafers
Whipped cream

In a mixing bowl cream butter and sugar. Add the egg yolks and melted chocolate, which has been cooled, and mix well. Add vanilla and nuts. Beat egg whites separately until stiff peaks form; fold into mixture. Roll vanilla wafers fine and place ½ of the mixture in a 7x11 inch pan. Pour the chocolate mixture over and spread out. Sprinkle the remaining crumbs on the top. Refrigerate until very cold. Top each serving with whipped cream. *Yield:* 8 to 10 servings.

Mrs. Paul F. Hayes, Jr. (Dee)
Nashville, Tennessee

HEAVENLY PRALINES
Very rich and creamy!

1 cup light brown sugar
   (firmly packed)
½ cup white sugar
½ cup milk

¼ cup white corn syrup
1 teaspoon vanilla
¼ cup margarine
1 cup broken pecans

Mix first 4 ingredients. Cook slowly and stir only until sugar dissolves. Boil to a good soft ball stage, on candy thermometer 238 degrees. Remove from heat and add vanilla and margarine. Beat until it thickens. Add pecans. Continue beating. Drop with a teaspoon onto waxed paper. *Yield:* 20 servings.

Mrs. B. R. Wilkerson (Lu)

BUCKEYES

1 (16 ounce) box powdered
  sugar
½ cup margarine, softened
2 cups crunchy peanut butter
6 Tablespoons milk (more
  or less)

¼ bar paraffin, melted
1 (6 ounce) package chocolate
  chips
Toothpicks

In a large mixing bowl, mix powdered sugar and margarine. Add peanut butter, mixing well. Add milk, 1 tablespoon at a time, until mixture will form balls about the size of a walnut. Melt paraffin and chocolate chips in a double boiler, then insert a toothpick into the balls and dip in the chocolate paraffin mixture. Set aside on waxed paper for about 1 hour. Can be made ahead and frozen. *Note:* The candy should resemble buckeyes. *Yield:* 3 to 4 dozen.

Mrs. Dean Campbell (Anna Marie)
Columbia, Tennessee

BOSTON CREAM CANDY
Especially good during the holidays.

6 cups sugar
3 cups rich cream (½ pint
  whipping and 1 pint of
  half-and-half)
2 cups white corn syrup
2 teaspoons vanilla

1 pound walnuts-coarsely
  chopped
1 pound Brazil nuts-coarsely
  chopped
1 (6 ounce) jar maraschino
  cherries (drained)

In a large kettle, boil the first three ingredients over medium heat until it forms a firm ball (240 degrees). Stir frequently while cooking. When done (about 1 hour), remove from heat and beat until it begins to harden, then add the last four ingredients. Blend thoroughly and pour into lightly buttered pans. *Yield:* 3 to 4 pounds.

Mrs. Walter Stewart (Dorothy)
Betty Washington

PEGGY'S CHOCOLATE BAR CANDY
This resembles a Heath Bar

1 pound butter
1 (16 ounce) box light brown
  sugar

½ pound chocolate bar
1 cup chopped pecans

In heavy saucepan, cook butter and brown sugar slowly to hard crack (300 degrees on candy thermometer). Stir occasionally. While cooking, melt chocolate bar in double boiler. Grease 15x10x1 inch jellyroll pan and sprinkle with pecans. Pour sugar mixture over chopped pecans. Spread melted chocolate over the pecans. Allow to cool and break into pieces.

Mrs. Robert Morris (Peggy)
Paducah, Kentucky

NEW ORLEANS PECAN PRALINES

¼ cup margarine
2 cups white sugar
1 (16 ounce) box light brown
  sugar

1 (5 ounce) can evaporated
  milk
Pecan halves

Mix all ingredients in a heavy pot. Cook slowly, stirring continually. When mixture starts to thread or when a small amount added to cold water forms a soft ball, turn off heat. Stir in as many pecans as desired. Cool for 5 minutes. Beat to make creamy and pour onto a buttered aluminum foil strip.

Mrs. Arthur Defratis
New Orleans, Louisiana

ENGLISH TOFFEE

1 cup sugar
1 cup butter
1 cup toasted, blanched
almonds, chopped

⅓ cup semi-sweet
chocolate bits

Boil sugar and butter to 300 degrees or hard crack in water, about 12 minutes. Pour carefully over ½ cup almonds in a buttered 9x12 inch pan. Let cool 10 minutes, then sprinkle with chocolate bits and spread as they melt. Next sprinkle the other ½ cup of almonds over top of chocolate. Let cool. Turn out and break into pieces. (Hint: use a wooden spoon to stir.)

Mrs. Bobby Pitts (Florence)

MICROWAVE MILK CHOCOLATE FUDGE

6 ounces semi-sweet
chocolate morsels
½ (14 ounce) can sweetened,
condensed milk

½ teaspoon vanilla
Pinch of salt
¼ cup chopped pecans

Cook chocolate morsels on high for 1 minute. Turn dish ½ turn and cook another 1 minute on high. Add other ingredients and mix well. Turn into a buttered 8x8x2 inch dish. Refrigerate until hard; then cut into squares. *Yield:* 2½ dozen.

Mrs. Hugh Sloan (Pam)

PAT'S PARTY MINTS

¾ cup margarine
15 to 20 drops oil of peppermint
1 (16 ounce) box powdered
sugar, sifted

⅛ teaspoon salt
¼ cup cream or evaporated
milk
Few drops of food coloring

Melt margarine, add oil of peppermint. Add sugar to margarine mixture; add salt and cream. Mix well; add coloring. Press through cake decorator onto waxed paper. Let dry overnight. Store in airtight container.

Mrs. Jake Russell (Pat)
Beaver Dam, Kentucky

MARTHA WASHINGTON CANDY

1 (14 ounce) can sweetened
condensed milk
2 (16 ounce) boxes powdered
sugar
1 Tablespoon vanilla
2 cups coconut

1 cup margarine, softened
2 cups chopped pecans
¼ pound paraffin
1 (12 ounce) package semi-
sweet chocolate chips

In a large bowl mix condensed milk, powdered sugar, vanilla,
coconut, margarine, and chopped pecans. Mix thoroughly. Roll into
1 inch balls. Refrigerate about 2 hours. In double boiler, melt paraffin and chocolate chips. Dip balls into chocolate with toothpick.

Mrs. Spaulding Bell (Bertha)
Betty Washington

SCRUMPTIOUS CHOCOLATE CANDY

1½ (6 ounce) packages semi-
sweet chocolate morsels
1 (14 ounce) can sweetened
condensed milk

1 teaspoon vanilla
1½ to 2 cups pecans
Pinch of butter

Melt chocolate morsels with condensed milk in double boiler.
Remove from heat and set in pan of cold water. Add vanilla and
pecans. Add butter. Beat a short time and drop by teaspoonful onto
waxed paper. Refrigerate 24 hours. Remove from refrigerator and
store in container. *Yield:* 16 to 24 pieces.

Mrs. Walter Berg (Ruth)
Nashville, Tennessee

BOURBON BALLS

1 pound butter
2 (16 ounce) boxes powdered
   sugar
1 Tablespoon bourbon or
   rum

Chopped nuts (optional)
1 (8 ounce) package bitter
   sweet chocolate
1 Tablespoon paraffin

Cream butter; add sugar slowly. Add bourbon to taste (also may add chopped nuts if desired). Chill mixture for 30 minutes to 1 hour. Roll into balls to size desired. Chill balls thoroughly. Melt chocolate and add paraffin. Dip creamed balls into chocolate and drain on waxed paper.

Mrs. James Culberson (Frances)

PATRICIA'S PEANUT BRITTLE

3 cups sugar
1 cup white corn syrup
1 cup water
1 pound shelled raw peanuts

¼ teaspoon salt
1 teaspoon vanilla
2 Tablespoons butter
1 Tablespoon baking soda

Cook sugar, syrup, and water to hard ball stage (250 degrees). Add peanuts and continue the warming until slightly caramelized (300 degrees). Remove from heat, and add salt, vanilla, butter, and soda. Stir until frothy and pour onto a warm, buttered cookie sheet. Spread quickly. When cool, break into pieces.

Mrs. Jimmy Williams (Nancy)

DATE BALLS

1 (8 ounce) package dates
1 (7 ounce) package flaked
  coconut
1 Tablespoon rum
1 (14 ounce) can sweetened
  condensed milk

1 cup of pecans, chopped
½ cup or more powdered
  sugar

Mix all ingredients well in a large bowl. Press into a well greased 9x13 inch pan. Bake for 15 minutes at 300 degrees. Sprinkle powdered sugar on waxed paper. Turn mixture out onto powdered sugar. Pinch off a spoonful at a time and roll into balls. Roll each ball in powdered sugar to coat well. *Yield:* about 5 dozen.

Mrs. W. C. Gatlin (Annie Mae)

DATE NUT ROLL

3 cups sugar
½ cup milk
½ cup whipping cream
¼ cup butter

1 (7½ ounce) package dates,
  chopped
1 cup chopped pecans

Combine sugar, milk, and cream in extra heavy saucepan and cook without stirring to soft ball stage. Add butter, dates, and nuts. Let candy come to a rolling boil again. Remove from heat and beat until thick. Dip a cloth into cold water and wring water out. Spoon candy onto cloth and form a roll as you wrap in damp cloth. When cold, slice into ½ inch pieces.

Mrs. Tom Turbeville (Mary O.)
Nashville, Tennessee

Ewin House

EWIN HOUSE

This quaint log home was built in 1932 by William Winstead
Ewin, Sr. Today it is occupied by William Winstead Ewin, Jr.

Preserves and Relishes

SPRING MINT JELLY

1½ cups packed fresh mint
½ cup cider vinegar
1 cup water

3½ cups sugar
Green food coloring
½ bottle liquid pectin

Wash and dry mint by rolling it lightly in a terry cloth towel.
Refrigerate for 1 to 2 hours. Set aside enough 2 inch sprigs from the
mint tops to place in glass jars. When NO water remains on the
mint, measure, and crush to bruise the leaves and release the oil that
carries the flavor. Place crushed mint, vinegar, water, and sugar in a
deep saucepan and bring quickly to boil. While mixture is heating,
add food coloring to desired shade. When mixture boils, add pectin,
stirring constantly, and bring to full, rolling boil that cannot be
stirred down. Boil 30 seconds and remove immediately. Place a
sprig of mint in each hot half-pint jar. Strain jelly into them. Seal. Do
not disturb until jelly sets. Store for 1 to 2 weeks for best flavor.
Yield: 3½ cups. *Note:* The mint sprigs will rise to top of jars.

Mrs. Walter Berg (Ruth)
Nashville, Tennessee

APRICOT-PINEAPPLE PRESERVES

1 pound dried apricots
6 cups sugar

2 (No. 2) cans crushed
pineapple in heavy syrup

Wash and soak apricots overnight in 1 quart of water. Cook in same
water until soft. Mash apricots fine. Add sugar and pineapple, using
syrup in pineapple. Cook until thick, stirring constantly. Pour into
sterile jars. *Yield:* 4 pints.

Mrs. Clifton York (Frances)
Nashville, Tennessee

STRAWBERRY FREEZER JAM
Can be frozen for sweeter days.

1¾ cups crushed strawberries
   (about 1 quart)
4 cups sugar

2 Tablespoons lemon juice
½ bottle fruit pectin

Thoroughly mix fresh, crushed strawberries with sugar and let stand 10 minutes. Combine lemon juice with fruit pectin and add to fruit mixture. Stir for 3 minutes. Ladle into any 5 scalded jars (8 ounces or smaller) with screw tops or plastic containers with snap lids. Cover immediately and let stand at room temperature for 24 hours to set. Keep what you can eat in the refrigerator and freeze the rest.

Mrs. Larry Bollweg (Mary Ann)
Wapakoneta, Ohio

BREAD AND BUTTER PICKLES

1 gallon cucumbers, sliced
8 small onions, sliced
2 green peppers, chopped

½ cup salt
1 quart cracked ice

Wash cucumbers. Slice crosswise, not too thin. Combine cucumbers, onions, and peppers and mix with salt and bury pieces of ice (1 quart) in mixture. Cover with a weighted lid and leave for 3 hours. Drain thoroughly.

Pickle syrup:
5 cups sugar
1½ teaspoons tumeric
½ teaspoon ground cloves

2 Tablespoons mustard seed
1 teaspoon celery seed
5 cups mild vinegar

Mix sugar, tumeric, and cloves. Add mustard seed, celery seed, and vinegar. Pour over drained vegetables. Place over low heat and paddle occasionally with a wooden spoon. Heat to boiling point, but DO NOT BOIL! Pour into sterilized jars and seal.

Mrs. K. C. Shaver (Bertie)-Deceased
Central City, Kentucky

MARYLAND STYLE WATERMELON PICKLE

3 pounds watermelon rind
3 pounds sugar
1 pint vinegar

Whole cloves (small handful)
3 to 4 sticks cinnamon
1 Tablespoon whole allspice

Peel off green rind. Some, but very little, pink can be left on rind. Cover rind with cold water, bring to boil, and simmer until a fork will stick through rind easily. While rind is cooking, put remaining ingredients in another pot and cook until rind is done. Drain rind, soak in cold water several times. When cool, drain, and cover with ice cubes. (I do all this in the sink.) After rind is thoroughly chilled, add above syrup and rind in pot and let come to boil. Reduce heat and simmer for ¾ hour. Put in jars while hot. *Yield:* 6 to 8 pints. *Note:* Some put spices in a cloth bag and remove but we put ours loose in the jars.

Mrs. G. H. Hoddinott (Betty)

GREEN TOMATO RELISH

2 quarts of chopped green
  tomatoes
10 small onions
12 red sweet peppers
12 green sweet peppers

5 Tablespoons salt
2½ cups sugar
2 Tablespoons mustard seed
1 quart vinegar

Grind green tomatoes, onions, and peppers in food grinder. In large dishpan or soup tureen, add all ground ingredients plus the rest of ingredients as listed. Heat to the boiling point, let simmer for 30 minutes. While this is simmering, heat lids and sealing rings to 12 pint jars. When relish has completed 30 minute simmer, spoon into jars. Place lids and covers on jars tightly. (Lids and rings are heated in boiling water.) *Yield:* 12 pints.

Mrs. Larry Nichols (Ellen)

PICKLED VEGIES

5½ quarts of mixed vegetables
  (green beans, squash, okra,
  green peppers, broccoli,
  asparagus, onions, or
  whatever you have)

Salt
2 quarts strong vinegar
1 pound sugar
2 Tablespoons each pickling
  spice, cloves, and cinnamon

Sprinkle the vegetables with salt, mix well, and let stand overnight. The next day, pour boiling water over the mixture, drain, and squeeze dry. Then mix the vinegar with all the remaining ingredients. Bring to a boil, and boil 10 minutes. Put vegetables into sterilized jars. Pour pickling liquid into jars, filling jars up to the top. Cover tightly and store. *Yield:* 5½ quarts.

Mrs. Ed Steiner (Bettie)

KRAUT RELISH
Delicious with white beans and pinto beans!

1 (16 ounce) can shredded
  kraut
¼ cup salad oil
½ cup sugar

½ cup vinegar
½ cup onion, chopped
½ cup green pepper, chopped
½ cup celery, chopped

Drain kraut. Boil salad oil, sugar, and vinegar until sugar dissolves well. Pour this over kraut and add remaining ingredients. Marinate in refrigerator overnite. Lasts a long time. *Yield:* 10 to 12 servings.

Mrs. Brad Reed (Jeraldyne)
New Castle, Alabama

PICKLED CRAB APPLES

5 pounds crab apples
1 quart vinegar
1 (2 inch) cinnamon stick

7 cups sugar
1 Tablespoon whole cloves

Wash crab apples, leaving skin and stem, and prick several holes in each. Bring the remaining ingredients to a boil. Add crab apples. Cook slowly until tender. Pack apples in sterilized jars and fill jars with the hot syrup. Seal and store. *Yield:* 4 to 6 pints.

Mrs. Ed Steiner (Bettie)

SWEET PICKLE STICKS

3 quarts cucumbers
3¾ cups vinegar
3 Tablespoons salt
4½ teaspoons pickling spice

3 cups sugar
2½ teaspoons celery seed
¾ teaspoon mustard seed

Use fresh, firm, medium cucumbers. Wash, peel and cut into quarters. Pour boiling water over them and let stand overnight. Next morning, pack solidly into clean jars. Make pickling solution, boil 5 minutes. Pour hot solution over cucumbers. Put on lids and seal. *Yield:* 6 pints.

Karen Steiner

PICKLED OKRA

Garlic cloves (1 clove per pint jar)
Hot peppers (1 pod per pint jar)
Okra (small pods)
Dillseed (1 teaspoon per pint jar)

1 quart vinegar
1 cup water
½ cup salt

Place garlic, cloves, and hot peppers in bottom of jars. Pack firmly with okra. Add dillseeds. Bring vinegar, water, and salt to boil. Let simmer for 5 minutes. Pour over okra. Seal jars. *Yield:* 6 pints.

Mrs. James B. White (Virginia)

PICCALILLI

2 quarts chopped green tomatoes
1 green pepper, chopped
1 sweet red pepper, chopped
2 cups chopped onion

1 pint vinegar
¼ cup salt
3 cups sugar
½ cup pickling spices (in bag)

In a large container, mix all ingredients. Bring to a boiling point. Turn heat down and cook slowly for 30 minutes, stirring occasionally. Remove spice bag. Pour into clean, hot jars and seal. *Yield:* 4 pints.

Mrs. Leon Stone (Joyce)

DILL CUCUMBER PICKLES

4 quarts cucumbers
1 gallon cold water
Fresh dill sprigs
Garlic cloves

Hot red peppers
1 quart vinegar
3 quarts water
1 cup salt

Clean and soak cucumbers in the cold water for 24 hours. Put into each sterilized jar 2 sprigs of dill, a peeled garlic clove, and a pepper. Then pack the cucumbers whole, into the jars. If your cucumbers are large, you can slice them first. Now make a brine of the vinegar, water, and salt, boil it a minute or two, and add it to the jars. Seal tightly and store.

Mrs. Ed Steiner (Bettie)

CHRISTMAS RELISH

1 large mango pepper
1 cup celery
1 medium onion
1 small can pimento
1 large can sauerkraut, drained

¼ cup vegetable oil
½ cup vinegar
⅛ cup water
1½ cups sugar

In large bowl chop pepper, celery, onion, and pimento. Add kraut. Mix oil, vinegar, water, and sugar. Pour over first mixture and refrigerate for several hours before serving.

Mrs. Spalding Bell (Bertha)

CUCUMBERS TO FREEZE

7 cups thinly sliced or
  grated cucumbers
1 cup grated onion
1 cup diced green peppers

2 cups sugar
1 cup vinegar
1 teaspoon salt
1 teaspoon celery seed

Measure cucumbers, onions, and green peppers after thinly slicing or grating. Mix sugar, vinegar, salt, and celery seed. Stir until sugar dissolves. Pour over cucumbers, onions, and green peppers. Refrigerate overnight. Pour into containers and freeze next day. *Yield:* 6 pints.

Julie Westfall

RED PEPPER RELISH

8 to 10 large onions	2 cups sugar
4 red hot peppers	1 teaspoon salt
15 large ripe red peppers	Vinegar

Grind onions and hot peppers, reserving juice. Grind red peppers. Drain well. Combine onions, hot peppers, juice, red peppers, sugar, and salt. Mix well. Add vinegar to cover ½ inch above the mixture. Let come to a boil and continue cooking on medium heat for 20 minutes. Seal while hot in sterile jars. *Yield:* 5 pints.

Mrs. Roy J. Dennis (Mary Tom)
Nashville, Tennessee

Long-Babbit House

LONG-BABBIT HOUSE

The original home was built by Mrs. Judith Long after 1832. The unusual Y-shaped design was added before 1890. Today this home is owned by Mary Frances Ligon.

Men's

PRALINE CHEESECAKE

Crust:

1¼ cups crushed graham crackers

½ cup sugar

¼ cup chopped pecans, toasted

¼ cup butter, melted

In small mixing bowl, combine cracker crumbs, sugar and chopped pecans. Stir in melted butter. Press crumb mixture over bottom and 1½ inches up the sides of a 9 inch springform pan. Bake at 350 degrees for 10 minutes.

Filling:

3 (8 ounce) packages cream cheese, softened

1 cup brown sugar

1 (5⅓ ounce) can evaporated milk (⅔ cup)

2 Tablespoons flour

1½ teaspoons vanilla

3 eggs

1 cup pecan halves, toasted

Beat together cream cheese, brown sugar, evaporated milk, flour, and vanilla. Add eggs; beat just until blended. Pour into baked crust. Bake at 350 degrees 50 to 55 minutes. Cool and remove from pan.

Sauce:

1 cup dark corn syrup

¼ cup cornstarch

2 Tablespoons brown sugar

1 teaspoon vanilla

Combine corn syrup, cornstarch, and brown sugar in small saucepan. Cook and stir until thickened and bubbly. Remove from heat. Stir in vanilla. Cool slightly. Arrange 1 cup toasted pecan halves on top of cheesecake. To serve, spoon warm sauce over nuts on cheesecake. Pass remaining sauce. *Yield:* 12 to 16 servings.

Dr. Tom Covington

CHRISTMAS STOLLEN

1 cup milk
½ cup sugar
½ teaspoon salt
1 package active dry yeast
¼ cup warm water
5 cups sifted flour
½ cup cut-up citron
½ cup cut-up candied
 cherries

1 cup slivered almonds
1 grated lemon rind
1 cup seedless raisins
2 eggs, well beaten
¾ cup butter or margarine,
 softened
¼ teaspoon nutmeg
½ teaspoon cinnamon
2 Tablespoons sugar

In large saucepan, scald milk; add ½ cup sugar and salt; cool until lukewarm. Dissolve yeast in lukewarm water. Add to lukewarm milk with 1 cup flour; beat to remove lumps. Cover and let rise in warm place until doubled in bulk (2 hours). Now stir in citron, cherries, almonds, lemon rind, raisins, eggs, butter, nutmeg, then 3 cups flour. On floured surface, knead 1 cup flour into dough until dough is smooth and elastic. Roll into large 18x12 inch oval, about ½ inch thick. Brush with melted butter, sprinkle with cinnamon and 2 tablespoons sugar. Make lengthwise crease down center of dough, fold over on large greased cookie sheet and push dough into crescent shape; then, with palm of hand, press down along crease to shape. Brush with melted butter. Cover with waxed paper, then a towel. Let rise until double in size. Bake at 350 degrees for 45 to 50 minutes. Cool and sprinkle with powdered sugar. *Yield:* 1 large, or 2 small loaves.

James Rhea Kelso

BRAUNSCHWEIGER SPREAD

½ pound (1 cup)
 braunschweiger
1 cup sour cream
½ envelope dry onion soup mix

1 teaspoon Worcestershire
 sauce
Few drops hot pepper sauce

Combine all ingredients in order given and chill. Serve with crackers. *Yield:* 2 cups.

Ira V. Miller
Dayton, Ohio

T. J'S CHEESY POTATO SKINS

Vegetable oil
3 medium baking potatoes
Seasoned salt
1 cup Cheddar cheese,
  shredded

6 slices bacon, cooked and
  crumbled
Sour cream

Scrub potatoes thoroughly and rub skins with oil. Bake at 400 degrees for 1 hour or until done. Allow potatoes to cool to touch. Cut in half lengthwise. Carefully scoop out pulp, leaving ¼ inch to ⅛ inch shell. (Pulp may be used for mashed potatoes or reserved for another recipe.) Deep fry in hot (375 degree) oil for 2 minutes or until lightly browned. Drain on paper towels. Place skins on a baking sheet; sprinkle with seasoned salt, cheese, and bacon. Place under broiler until cheese melts. Serve with sour cream. *Note:* I use Crisco oil. *Yield:* ½ dozen appetizer servings.

Tom Wilz, Sr.
Dayton, Ohio

SENATOR BROCK'S MEAT LOAF SUPREME

4 pounds ground beef
2 eggs, slightly beaten
⅛ teaspoon curry powder
1 Tablespoon salt
1 teaspoon pepper
½ cup bread crumbs
1 (10½ ounce) can vegetable
  soup

⅛ teaspoon garlic salt
1 teaspoon parsley flakes
¼ cup red wine
½ cup chili sauce
¾ cup water

Combine all ingredients except wine, chili sauce, and water. Form into 2 loaves and place in 9x5x3 inch loaf pan. Put loaf pan into a roaster with the water in the roaster. Mix wine and chili sauce together and pour over the loaves. Bake at 350 degrees for 2 hours. *Yield:* 2 loaves.

Ed Steiner

312

BARBARA'S FAMOUS CRAB DISH

1 (8 ounce) package cream
  cheese, softened
6 scallions, chopped
1 Tablespoon Worcestershire
  sauce
1 cup catsup
3 teaspoons horseradish

4 drops hot sauce
1 (6 ounce) package frozen
  crabmeat, thawed or (6½
  ounce) can crabmeat
2 Tablespoons lemon juice
1 cup parsley, chopped
Crackers

Spread softened cream cheese in layer on bottom of dish; cover with chopped scallions. Sprinkle with Worcestershire. Mix catsup, horseradish, and hot sauce. Spread on top of scallions. Cover with crabmeat. Top with lemon juice and parsley. Serve with crackers. Cream cheese may be unwrapped and microwaved at low for 1 minute to soften. *Yield:* 4 servings.

Dr. Jim Manson

SHISH KEBAB

2 pounds beef tenderloin,
  cubed
¼ cup dry white wine
½ teaspoon oregano
2 Tablespoons lemon juice
½ cup olive oil
1 bay leaf
¼ cup onion, finely chopped

1 small carrot, grated
1 stalk celery, minced
Salt and pepper to taste
24 large mushrooms
24 small onions or wedges
24 cherry tomatoes
2 large bell peppers, cut into
  wedges

Combine the wine, oregano, lemon juice, oil, bay leaf, onion, carrot, celery, salt, and pepper in a large plastic container with tight fitting lid. Marinate the beef in this mixture overnight in refrigerator. Remove 1 hour before grilling to allow to come to room temperature. On skewers, alternate marinated meat with mushrooms, onions, tomatoes, and bell peppers. Baste with marinade and grill over hot fire to desired doneness. *Yield:* 6 servings.

Dr. Douglas C. York

CHOCOLATE BAR CHILI
If you don't think it's good, try it!

4 pounds ground beef
4 (17 ounce) cans pinto beans
4 (17 ounce) cans kidney beans
2 (28 ounce) cans whole
tomatoes
2 large onions, chopped

1 pound milk chocolate candy
bar
1 Tablespoon salt
1 Tablespoon pepper
1 Tablespoon chili powder
Jalapeno peppers (optional)

Sauté ground beef until brown; remove excess grease from skillet. Pour ground beef, pinto beans, kidney beans, tomatoes, onions, salt, pepper, and chili powder into a 16 quart pot and mix well. Simmer for 30 minutes, then add chocolate candy. Simmer for 1 hour on low heat, stirring often. *Note:* May be frozen easily. *Yield:* 25 servings.

Paul Nelson Sweeney

ED'S GOULASH

1½ pounds ground beef
1 (7 ounce) box Spanish rice or
pre-cooked rice

1 (15 ounce) can tomato sauce
1 (8 ounce) can tomato sauce
8 to 10 slices cheese

Brown ground beef in large skillet; drain fat. Cook rice according to directions. Add rice and tomato sauce to beef. Cover and cook on low heat for 5 minutes. Add cheese and simmer until cheese melts. Serve with tossed salad. *Yield:* 6 to 8 servings.

Ed Anderson

TOM'S BAKED CORN AND CHIVE SAUCE

2 (12 ounce) cans whole kernel
corn, drained
1 (4 ounce) container whipped
cream cheese with chives

¼ teaspoon salt
Dash of pepper

In a 1 quart casserole, put all ingredients in given order. Cover and bake at 325 degrees for 45 minutes. *Yield:* 6 servings.

Tom Wilz
Dayton, Ohio

GRILLED BARBECUED CHUCK ROAST

3 to 4 pound chuck roast or
   sirloin tip roast
1½ cups salad oil
¾ cup soy sauce
2 Tablespoons Worcestershire
   sauce
2 Tablespoons dry mustard

2 Tablespoons salt
1 Tablespoon pepper
1 cup dry, red wine
⅓ cup lemon juice
2 Tablespoons finely chopped
   parsley

Place roast in a shallow pan and pour all ingredients over it. Let roast marinate about 4 hours, turning meat frequently. Remove roast from marinade and place on grill. Cook over hot coals about 30 to 50 minutes basting often with marinade. *Yield:* 6 to 8 servings.

Mickey Curry
Petal, Mississippi

GLAZED BACON STRIPS
You'll get raves!

1 pound bacon, (slices cut in
   half)

1 (16 ounce) box brown sugar
   (enough to coat bacon well)

Roll each slice of bacon in brown sugar covering both sides. Place on broiler pan or rack. Bake at 325 degrees for 15 to 30 minutes. Keep checking until bacon is browned and fat cooked fro n it. Place cook-ed bacon on *foil* to cool. It will crisp as it cools. Serve at room temperature. This can be made early in the day or the day before and stored covered in refrigerator until ready to use. Serve on a silver tray. *Note:* I use Oscar Mayer bacon. *Yield:* 30 or more pieces.

Don Westfall
Brentwood, Tennessee

ORIENTAL MEATBALLS

Meatballs:

1 pound ground round
1 Tablespoon horseradish
¼ teaspoon salt

1 (8 ounce) can water
  chestnuts, minced

Mix ingredients and make small meatballs (bite sized). Place in a 2 quart baking dish and bake until brown at 350 degrees.

Sauce:

½ cup orange marmalade
2 Tablespoons soy sauce
¼ teaspoon garlic powder

1 Tablespoon lemon juice
2 Tablespoons flour

Mix the above ingredients, and pour over browned meatballs. Bake at 350 degrees until meatballs are done (approximately 15 to 20 minutes). Serve hot with toothpicks. *Yield:* 36 meatballs.

Dr. James Rogers

RICE CONSOMMÉ (DAD'S FAVORITE)
Tastes like you fussed when you didn't!

½ cup butter or margarine
1 onion, chopped
1 cup uncooked rice

2 (10½ ounce) cans beef
  consommé

In 2 quart casserole add butter, onion, rice, and beef consommé, mixing well. Cook for 1 hour uncovered at 350 degrees. Stir once or twice after 30 minutes in oven. *Yield:* 6 to 8 servings.

David S. Myers

CHICKEN SALAD

4 cups chicken breasts, cooked
  and diced
1 cup celery, diced
3 hard boiled eggs, chopped
1 cup white seedless grapes,
  halved

¾ cup slivered almonds
1 teaspoon salt
⅛ teaspoon pepper
2 Tablespoons vinegar
¾ cup mayonnaise
½ cup milk

Combine chicken, celery, eggs, grapes, and almonds. Mix salt, pepper, vinegar, mayonnaise, and milk. Mix with chicken mixture. Refrigerate until served. *Yield:* 16 servings.

William Milton

FLORIDA COOKIES
Excellent for amusing children on rainy days!

¼ cup butter or margarine
½ cup milk
⅓ cup cocoa
2 cups sugar

⅓ cup peanut butter
1 teaspoon vanilla
3 cups quick oats
1 cup chopped nuts (optional)

Mix butter, milk, cocoa, and sugar together and boil hard for 1 minute. Remove from heat and add peanut butter, vanilla, oats, and nuts (if desired). Drop by tablespoons onto waxed paper and let cool.

Eddie Steiner (Age: 15 yrs.)

BROWNIES

2 squares unsweetened
  chocolate
½ cup butter
1 cup sugar
2 eggs

1 teaspoon vanilla
½ cup flour
1 cup frosted flakes cereal,
  crushed
½ cup chopped nuts

Melt chocolate and butter together in a saucepan. In bowl combine chocolate mixture with sugar, eggs, and vanilla. Stir in flour. Add frosted flakes and nuts. Mix well. Bake in greased 11x7 inch pan at 325 degrees for 30 minutes. *Yield:* 2 dozen.

Sam Coleman

OCEAN ISLE CRAB CAKES
A must for seafood lovers!

2 eggs
¼ cup chopped onion
¼ cup chopped green pepper
1 teaspoon prepared mustard
1 Tablespoon Worcestershire
  sauce

¼ teaspoon hot sauce
3 slices white bread, crumbled
4 teaspoons mayonnaise
Salt and pepper to taste
1 pound regular crabmeat

Mix all ingredients well, except crabmeat. Gently stir in crabmeat and drop by tablespoonful onto buttered grill or frying pan. Brown on both sides. *Note:* I use Tabasco. *Yield:* 12 cakes.

Lenox D. Rawlings, Jr.

CHRISTMAS MORNING POPOVERS

1 cup milk
1 cup unsifted flour

2 eggs
½ teaspoon salt

Combine ingredients and stir until moist, but still lumpy. Pour into a greased popover pan, muffin tin, or custard cups, filling half full. Place in a cold oven; set temperature at 450 degrees, and bake for 30 minutes. Do not open oven door while baking! Remove from oven, cut slit in top of each popover and serve hot with lots of butter, preserves, and hot tea. *Yield:* 12.

Herbert E. Patrick, Jr.
Savannah, Tennessee

MILKMAN'S CHOCOLATE CARAMEL CANDY BAR
ICE CREAM

12 chocolate caramel candy
  bars
1 quart whipping cream
2 quarts half-and-half

½ to 1 cup sugar
20 pounds cracked ice
2 to 3 pounds ice cream salt

Melt candy bars in a little cream in double boiler. When melted, mix with cream, half-and-half, and sugar. Put into ice-cream freezer can. After freezing, add more ice and salt, and pack down for 2 or 3 hours. *Note:* I use Milky Way candy bars. *Yield:* 1 gallon.

Phil Green
Donelson, Tennessee

Courtney House

COURTNEY HOUSE

Robert Courtney built this house in 1838. It consisted of a foyer, right hand parlor, and a half-story above until 1889 when a front porch was added. This home today is owned by Patti Roberts.

Potpourri

COTTAGE GARDEN SCENT
For those who like the unusual.

1 quart rose petals
1 Tablespoon whole cloves
1 Tablespoon ground nutmeg
1 Tablespoon ground cinnamon
1 Tablespoon crushed benzoin

5 drops patchouli
5 drops rose geranium
5 drops jasmine
Orange peel
Lemon toilet water

Crush dried rose petals between waxed paper with rolling pin. Add cloves, nutmeg, cinnamon, benzoin, patchouli, rose geranium, jasmine, orange peel, and lemon toilet water. Benzoin may be purchased from druggist. Patchouli, rose geranium, jasmine, and lemon toilet water are available from cosmetic counter. Orange peel should be chopped as fine as possible. Place in covered jar for 1 week. It may then be divided into sachets or just in an open bowl to impart a delicate aroma to the air. From time to time, it may be strengthened by adding a few more drops of one or more of the scents called for in the original recipe. *Note:* Not edible.

Mrs. William W. Wells (Joan)

CHRISTMAS POTPOURRI
For delightful fragrance, not consumption.

1 quart pineapple juice
1 quart water
1 quart apple cider
4 pieces ginger
3 (3 inch) sticks cinnamon

1 teaspoon ground allspice
16 whole cloves
1 or 2 teaspoons pickling
  spice

Place all ingredients in large cooking kettle and allow to come to a boil for several minutes. Turn heat down and simmer ingredients, allowing room to fill with a wonderful Christmas-time fragrance. Add water and stir as needed.

Mrs. Jerry Holcomb (Tinker)

FLOWER IN GELEE
Table or platter centerpiece.

⅔ cup sugar
2 envelopes unflavored gelatin

2 cups boiling water
1 cup cold water

Use a rose or any medium-size flower. A small bunch of violets, pansies, or a sprig of holly with berries may also be used. Mix sugar and gelatin. Add boiling water to dissolve sugar mixture; then cold water to cool. Pour mixture over inverted flower that has been placed in a bowl slightly larger than the flower. Refrigerate. Use tape from one side of bowl to the other to hold stem in place. Unmold by dipping in warm water a few seconds. *Note:* Not edible.

Mrs. Richard Lane (Susan)

ICE SCULPTURE BOWL

Fill a metal bowl with water and set in freezer. After a while, since water starts freezing from the outside inwards, a piece of ice will have formed that is hollow and full of water in the center. Make a hole in the top, pour off the water, and return to freezer. When ready to use your "ice bowl", briefly run hot water over bottom of metal container, and it will slip out. Fill the "bowl" with fresh seafood, vegetables, or dip.

Mrs. Ronald Jones (Jane)
Memphis, Tennessee

PINEAPPLE THING
This is a delicious side dish for ham!

1 cup sugar
6 Tablespoons flour
1 (16 ounce) can pineapple
   chunks, drained

2 cups shredded cheese

Mix sugar and flour. Add to the pineapple; then add cheese. Pour this into a baking dish.

Topping:
½ cup butter, melted
1 individually wrapped roll
   of crackers, crushed

Combine butter and crackers and sprinkle over pineapple mixture. Bake at 350 degrees for 30 minutes. *Note:* I use Ritz crackers.

Mrs. Allan W. Castle (Evelyn)
Nashville, Tennessee

GRAPE CATSUP
Great with game and meats!

5 pints grapes, washed
   and stemmed
4 cups brown sugar,
   packed
1 pint cider vinegar
2 Tablespoons ground
   allspice

2 Tablespoons ground
   cinnamon
2 Tablespoons ground
   cloves
1 teaspoon mace
1 teaspoon cayenne
1 teaspoon salt

Cook grapes slowly in enamel kettle until soft (about 25 minutes). Put through colander. Combine with remaining ingredients. Boil until thick (about 45 minutes). Stir frequently with wooden spoon. Pour into hot sterile glass jars. *Note:* I use Concord grapes.

Mell Isaacs

"SPIN-A-PEACH"

Peel 1 small ripe peach for each person. Prick the peach several times with a fork on all sides. Place each peach in a large stemmed glass and fill with sparkling wine. As soon as sufficient carbonic acid bubbles have collected underneath the peach, it will turn over and begin to "spin". After a while, when the peach has imparted some of its aroma to the wine, remove it from the liquid and enjoy its enhanced taste, using the wine as a chaser.

Mrs. Ronald Jones (Jane)
Memphis, Tennessee

GALA FROSTED FRUITS

Frost dates, apples, oranges, grapes, kumquats, plums, pears, or any whole fruits to garnish or for centerpiece. Dip fruits into egg whites beaten until frothy. Dip into sugar to cover and place on rack to dry. For more sparkle dip into sugar again just before drying is completed. Arrange in crystal bowl.

Mell Isaacs

MARINADE FOR BEEF

½ cup soy sauce
½ cup vegetable oil
2 Tablespoons sugar
½ cup orange juice

1 Tablespoon powdered ginger
Button of garlic (optional)

Mix all of the above for marinade.

Mrs. Jesse Short, Jr. (Alma)

323

GLAZED PECANS

1 cup sugar
1 teaspoon ground cinnamon
⅛ teaspoon ground nutmeg
½ cup orange juice

1 teaspoon butter
1 teaspoon vanilla
2 cups pecan halves

In medium saucepan cook sugar, cinnamon, nutmeg, and orange juice until soft ball forms. Stir occasionally. Remove from heat. Stir in butter and let stand 5 minutes. Stir in vanilla and pecans until thick. Place on waxed paper. Separate nuts, cool, and store in air tight container. Will stay fresh 1 to 2 months.

Mrs. Tom Van Olst (Vonnie)
Hendersonville, Tennessee

PORCUPINE PECANS

½ cup butter or margarine
1 pound pecans

Salt to taste

Melt butter, stir in pecans, and coat well with butter. Put on flat pan in a single layer. Sprinkle with salt and bake at 300 degrees for 45 minutes to 1 hour. Place in jars for your teacher, if you don't eat them all.

Edward Patrick (Age 7)
Savannah, Tennessee

CHRISTMAS ORNAMENT DOUGH

1 cup sugar
4 eggs

4 cups flour

Cream sugar and eggs until light colored. Add flour and mix well. Roll out on floured board and cut into different Christmas shapes. Brush with beaten egg and bake at 400 degrees until golden. Glaze with colored icing. Tie onto Christmas tree with ribbon.

Ashley Sweeney (age 4)

Trabue-Brown House

TRABUE—BROWN HOUSE

Mr. Sims, a merchant, had this home built for his daughter and her husband in 1818. Located just outside Franklin's city limits, the original house had two rooms upstairs and two downstairs, with a central hall. This home is owned by Mr. and Mrs. Larry Brown.

Index

INDEX

331

Flaunting Our Finest
P.O. Box 541
Franklin, Tennessee 37064

Please send me _____ copies of *Flaunting Our Finest* at $16.95, plus $5.00 each for postage and handling.

Name: _____

Address: _____

City: _____ State _____ Zip _____

MAKE CHECKS PAYABLE TO JUNIOR AUXILIARY OF FRANKLIN. All profits realized from the sale of this cookbook will be returned to the community through the service of the Junior Auxiliary of Franklin.

- -

Flaunting Our Finest
P.O. Box 541
Franklin, Tennessee 37064

Please send me _____ copies of *Flaunting Our Finest* at $16.95, plus $5.00 each for postage and handling.

Name: _____

Address: _____

City: _____ State _____ Zip _____

MAKE CHECKS PAYABLE TO JUNIOR AUXILIARY OF FRANKLIN. All profits realized from the sale of this cookbook will be returned to the community through the service of the Junior Auxiliary of Franklin.

- -

Flaunting Our Finest
P.O. Box 541
Franklin, Tennessee 37064

Please send me _____ copies of *Flaunting Our Finest* at $16.95, plus $5.00 each for postage and handling.

Name: _____

Address: _____

City: _____ State _____ Zip _____

MAKE CHECKS PAYABLE TO JUNIOR AUXILIARY OF FRANKLIN. All profits realized from the sale of this cookbook will be returned to the community through the service of the Junior Auxiliary of Franklin.

Reorder Additional Copies